CHILDREN'S SPORTS INJURIES

A GUIDE FOR PARENTS AND TEACHERS

DAVID HOWELL, F.R.C.S.

William Heinemann Australia

First published 1989 by
William Heinemann Australia
85 Abinger Street, Richmond, Victoria 3121

Copyright © David Howell 1989

All rights reserved. Without limiting the rights under copyright above, no part of this publication may be reproduced, stored in or introduced into a retrieval system, or transmitted in any form or by any means (electronic, mechanical, photocopying, recording or otherwise), without the prior written permission of both the copyright owner and the above publisher of this book.

Edited by Sarah Overton
Designed by Sandra Nobes
Illustrated by Rebecca Pannell
Typeset in 10/11 pt Century Schoolbook
by Solo Typesetting, South Australia
Printed in Hong Kong
by Sheck Wah Tong Printing Press Ltd

National Library of Australia
 cataloguing-in-publication data:

Howell, David, 1928–
 Children's sports injuries: a guide for parents and teachers.
 Includes index.
 ISBN 0 85561 295 9.

 1. Sports—Accidents and injuries—Prevention. 2. Sports—Accidents and injuries—Treatment. 3. Sports medicine. I. Title.

617'.1027

To my parents
who gave me a wonderful start to life
and
To my wife
without whom nothing would be possible

Acknowledgements

My thanks as an author (and those of the parents who read this book) should go to the thousands of specialists and sports medicine experts all over the world who have contributed to the explosive growth in medical knowledge now available to doctors and allied professionals. My special thanks go to the staff of the library of the Prince of Wales Hospital, the Biological Library of the University of New South Wales and the Lewisham Hospital Sports Medecine Clinic, for their unfailing help and courtesy. I would also like to acknowledge the assistance of Geoff Currey, Editorial Manager of William Heinemann Australia, and that of Nick Williams of Methuen Australia. I must thank my editor, Sarah Overton, who has striven mightily to keep the language as simple and understandable as possible and the medical jaw-breakers to a minimum, and finally Dawn Fraser Australia's own athlete without peer who has so kindly written a foreword.

Foreword

David Howell has produced a very timely book, incorporating the results of the most recent research in Australia and overseas. Directed especially at parents and teachers, this comprehensive manual describes the effects of sport on the body; it provides essential facts about the different physical development of boys and girls, and discusses the special difficulties encountered by young women, including natural aches and pains caused by over-exercise which can easily be confused with surgical or menstrual problems.

The book covers over forty sporting activities including ballet, break dancing, cheerleading and gridiron. There is a section on the effects of the food we eat and some interesting revelations about what Eskimo children eat as sweets! A special chapter is provided for parents keen on aerobics and jogging and there is a discussion of the importance of hereditary factors in choosing a suitable sport. If your child is a budding gymnast but has a family history of bad backs and other problems such as flat feet, perhaps he or she should try something else.

For those like me with aquatic interests, there is some alarming information about swimming pools. These can cause skin rashes, infected cuts, conjunctivitis, earache, sore throats and fever. Organisms which flourish in a watery environment include the viruses causing gastro-enteritis, poliomyelitis and hepatitis. Freshwater lakes and rivers have their hazards too.

As a child, I always wanted to excel at sports and to keep up with my seven older brothers and sisters. To my delight, I succeeded to the point where the boys actually wanted me to join their team when they chose sides. My brother Don taught me to swim and but for his encouragement and that of my family and my coach, Harry Gallagher, I doubt that I would have gone on to become a champion.

Doctor Howell writes that encouraging a child to learn to swim is perhaps the most important potentially life-saving present that a parent can give. Swimming was a wonderful thing for me and it remains an important part of my adult life. However, he also warns against pushing children to attempt too much too soon or to train too hard in any sport. In these often overly-competitive times, it is a lucky child who has many interests, he says.

People today are increasingly interested in ways to stay fit and healthy, from childhood onwards. *Children's Sport Injuries* will, I believe, help provide this knowledge.

Dawn Fraser
January 1989

Contents

Introduction xiii

PART A Sports Medicine— the Basic Facts 1
1 Sudden Death 3
2 Beware, Take Care 7
3 Diagnostic Signs 14
4 Bone Growth 16
5 Head, Neck and Spine 22
6 Resuscitation 31
7 Thorax, Abdomen and Pelvis 37
8 Eyes 40
9 Teeth 44
10 Skin 46
11 Problems Pertaining Especially to Girls 52
12 Joint by Joint 59
13 Food 74

PART B A to Z Guide to Sports 83
Archery 85
Athletics 85
Australian Rules 95
Badminton 97
Ballet 97
Baseball 101
Basketball 104
Boxing 109
Break Dancing 112
Cheerleading 113
Cricket 115
Cycling 120

Fencing   124
Golf   125
Gridiron   127
Gymnastics   136
Handball   141
Hockey (Field)   142
Horseriding   143
Ice Hockey   146
Ice Skating   148
Lacrosse   151
Martial Arts and Self-defence   151
Netball   155
Racquetball   156
Roller Skating   156
Rowing   157
Rugby   159
Scuba Diving   165
Skateboarding   169
Skiing   171
Soccer   181
Softball   184
Squash   186
Swimming   187
Tennis   194
Touch Football   196
Trampoline   197
Volleyball   200
Water Sports   201
Weight Lifting   206
Wrestling   211

PART C   Something for Parents   219
Jogging   221
Aerobics   229

To Sum Up   233

Preface

I first became interested in sports medicine at the age of seven or eight, watching my father deal with the host of problems experienced by my friends, ranging from fractures and sprains, minor concussions and bloody noses, to sprig marks, gravel rash, and even ringworm. Faced with problems, quick thinking was his greatest resource and indeed a way of life for a whole generation of doctors. Father started life as a country practitioner. What he learned by close experience from ghastly train smashes, isolated farm dramas, and even the odd murder, was supplemented by consultations with my uncles in neighbouring towns, who had learned their craft in the fields of Flanders and Damascus.

Sports medicine in that era did not exist. Injuries in sport were a natural extension of general practice, with warm-hearted specialists, often old university champions themselves, taking over the problems he decided to pass on.

If you have such expert spectators on hand you may feel you do not need this book. Nothing in clinical medicine has really changed; only the scope and organisation of treatment. Injuries are mostly referred to busy impersonal casualty departments or accident centres, but the problem for parents and teachers remains, 'which injuries'? Everything? Headmasters today, on advice from School Councils (themselves advised by lawyers), will probably answer: 'yes, everything'. This is simply not practicable, yet apparently trivial incidents may have long-term consequences which can go unnoticed unless parents are aware of what to look for. And there is more to it than just injury. When the five eight of my own under-age rugby team died two days after a match, my father's response was: 'I thought he wasn't well when he dropped all those passes. He said he had a bit of a headache at half time. Meningococcal meningitis! There's an epidemic. He might have been right. But he knew it was not a head injury. He had seen the match. The overworked casualty officer has not and therefore the teacher's or the parent's observations are vital. To know how an injury occurred, or what the athlete was doing at the critical moment, coupled with a knowledge of what is possible, is often the best guide as to the likely damage.

As a nostalgic opus, this book is dedicated to the memory of much loved sports teachers and team managers who coped; to kindly doctors of rich experience who served; and to parents who worried. But it is really a book designed for their successors, who have inherited much more difficult roles. In youthful sport today there is a flavour virtually unknown in my time, the taste of a professional career with hints of financial rewards to come. Striving after and training for maximum performance is seeping into the ethos of younger and younger athletes and leading them towards physical stresses and damage unknown to earlier generations. For many parents there is no escape. They have to immerse themselves in medical logic and detail so that they can guide their children with wisdom and be able to question more closely the advisers, be they coaches or doctors, on whom they rely for the wellbeing of their brood.

However, it would be a disservice to all to imply that the injuries and complications listed here are inevitable, or indeed common. Look on it thus: this knowledge will be a powerful aid to those responsible for the welfare of young hopefuls, some of whom will strive to be the Olympic stars of tomorrow.

Introduction

This book sets out to ensure that if sports-mad children and keen adolescents have accidents, they will be *almost* injured rather than actually hurt. I really should not let you into a trade secret, but the best way for a surgeon to gain experience and be expert at his job is to get into difficulties; to see complications looming and to avoid them. Parents are in the same boat. If you can imagine what injuries could happen you can try to see that they do not. How? By knowledge and luck of course, but to quote an old saw, 'It is amazing how much luck knowledgeable people have'. With knowledge of the risks attaching to each sport parents are in a better position to watch, to spot dangerous habits, and by discussion with other informed parents, to keep individual and team behaviour within bounds. As athletes grow into adults and become more expert they must perforce become their own masters, but at least the parent's role will have been fulfilled and a safe beginning achieved.

It is not easy to convey technical information to the non-specialist reader, but I hope this has been achieved within these covers.

Part A covers basic anatomy and function; it describes medical terms and commonly recurring conditions. It also discusses injuries to organs such as the eye, which can occur in any sport. It really is worthwhile going back over these early chapters carefully. Master them and you will be amazed at your growing interest in sport. You will find your own doctor happy to elaborate on items you cannot grasp because a well-informed patient is easier to cure, and what is a parent but a proxy patient who feels every cut and bruise of their offspring? Believe me, the only minor injury is the one which happens to someone else's child!

Part B deals with the specific problems of each sport, and especially with protection and prevention measures that a parent must be aware of. I urge you to read about every sport. It will build up your general knowledge in an interesting way because many conditions are touched on here and there, but are more logically described in detail under the sport where they would be most likely to occur. Also, this will enable you to become familiar with the contents of the book, making for easy reference in an emergency.

There is a logical progression: for example, you must understand about broken necks before learning how to resuscitate someone, and an overall grasp of the basic medical facts is essential if one is to understand the body and the whys and wherefores of its injuries. After reading this book there may still be points you cannot quite follow but at least you will be alerted as to what you will want your doctor to explain in more detail.

Taken in total the list of possible sport injuries is appalling. Many, indeed most, of the injuries listed are statistically rare, but to the athlete who suffers the injury, the incidence for him or her is one hundred per cent. Someday, somewhere, somehow, everything that possibly can happen, will happen to someone.

If parents are aware of early warning signs, or the range of injuries possible in a particular sport, they can seek treatment for the young athlete in time. The real problem for parents is not the obviously broken bone, but their own feelings of inadequacy as they try to guide their youngsters through all sorts of subtle injuries that could have a significant effect on their future health or continued participation in sport. Virtually every sport is covered in Part B, so that if young Fred or Beatrice rushes home with the news that their heart is set on playing football or learning ballet, then parents can reach for this book, read the facts, and keep a watchful eye on developments.

I hope I can encourage you to keep a record of the family's injuries and illnesses. A doctor's diagnosis can often be more accurate if precise details of previous injuries are available: memory is capricious.

Sports such as gridiron that do not yet have a wide vogue in Australia have also been included. It is only a matter of time before they become established.

Some key references are given, not so much for parents, but for family physicians who may wish to delve more deeply into their young patients' specific sport. The Bibliography will be a good starting point.

The enormous amount of statistical information published by my American colleagues is acknowledged. They have led the world towards a burgeoning interest in 'profiling', best described as an attempt to measure the physical attributes of successful athletes, with the eventual aim of predicting which sport or group of sports will most suit a person's body build, muscle strength, joint flexibility and heart-lung capacity. Of even more impact will be the ability to predict body features that would make an athlete vulnerable to specific injuries in a given sport, or body weaknesses that need improvement by special training.

Parents and coaches have long had that ability, in a very broad sense, developed by observing children at play, and children themselves if left alone will decide by trial and error what sports they will be good at and which to avoid. Our society may have to insist that administrators give young school children the opportunity to try out many sports and to ensure that they have fun in identifying their skills and aptitudes before *profiling* is applied to them. The future will undoubtedly see greater use made of detailed medical measurements to choose elite squads for further training, as a means of rationing scarce economic and human resources. Politics in Eastern-bloc countries already dictate this in what must be a reincarnation of the spirit of Sparta.

There is no chapter on drugs, by which we do not mean medications prescribed by doctors to treat recognised ailments or diseases, but those substances used to enhance performance (stimulants), calm nervous contestants (tranquilisers), or stimulate growth (steroids). Everybody knows these should never, never be used. Nature gives growing children an abundance of the hormones they need and an efficient mechanism for brisk production. Steroids are natural hormones from the adrenal gland; to give more is both unnecessary and dangerous. At abnormal levels nature exacts a penalty. The forced development of muscle groups in training may seem harmless, but the effects of the overdose are positively harmful; high blood pressure, interference with the pituitary gland, damage to sex organs and distorted bone growth, to name but four. No parent should allow this or condone this dangerous interference with growing bodies.

Finally, to a topic that may soon go away: the attempt to make all children equal and the same. *Profiling* will eventually accumulate sufficient statistics to prove convincingly what every parent already knows: boys are boys and girls are girls, and while ever the twain shall meet, this should preferably not be on the sportsfield. State Departments of Education in recent years have tended to lump everyone together as just 'players' and to insist on open competitions. The situation is indeed complex. Ninety per cent of primary school teachers are female and the New South Wales Rugby League, for example, holds special coaching classes for them to Grade 1 level to enable them to coach all pupils up to the age of twelve years. It may well be that at a junior level boys and girls can compete on equal terms in any sport, but in my opinion, a line has to be drawn. This was done in August 1988 when the Federal Attorney

General directed that the organisers of the Sydney Pacific School Games for primary schools students from twenty-three nations should revert to separate events for boys and girls, and indicated that the various anti-discrimination laws which administrators were applying were drafted to correct social ills in adult life and that it was a misconception to apply them to school sport. Most children will no doubt draw a sigh of relief!

PART A

SPORTS MEDICINE—THE BASIC FACTS

1. Sudden Death

What a way to begin a book of help, explanation, reassurance, and guidance for young parents as they watch the apple of their eye fall over! However, sudden death is a problem which needs to be addressed before we even get to the sportsfield. To face the facts (lesson 1 in sports medicine), and calmly to study the facts (lesson 2 in sports medicine), is to appreciate how significant the problem really is (probably infinitesimal), but more importantly to draw conclusions about the need for detection, precaution, and protection (lesson 3 in sports medicine).

The implicit fear is death from heart disease. It would have to be pre-existing, but obviously not diagnosed up to that point in a child's life. In every reported case (and the number is incredibly small), almost without exception death is instantaneous and post mortem examination always reveals one of a small group of heart or coronary artery abnormalities. Whilst an electrocardiogram (measurement of heart action) or echocardiogram (measurement of heart size) would diagnose these well-documented conditions, such tests cannot be done as a routine on vast numbers of athletes.

Pre-participation screening of young athletes, a vital topic in general, presents problems as regards heart disease because a school physician is working in a mass situation and on children at rest, not after exertion. Parents themselves may hold a key to early detection by having noticed whether the youngster has complained after running about of giddiness, breathlessness, thumping in the chest (irregular heart beat), or of feeling faint; or they may have noticed pallor or a 'cold sweat'. If there is a close relative who has had coronary heart disease, a stroke, or very high blood pressure, at an early age such as forty-five years or less, then very careful specialist evaluation of the child is mandatory before strenuous sports begin. The classic example, from medical literature, is an eight-year-old basketball player who fainted during a game; he had had a heart attack, like his father who had died of one at the age of forty. It is worth reemphasising that the child is free of symptoms at rest.

Chest pain can easily be passed off as 'an injury', but when it occurs in response to exercise, it may be a warning. Heart murmurs are tricky. Many turn out to be of no functional significance but all have to be investigated. Specialist diagnostic methods are now sophisticated and precise, as is corrective surgery. If heart disease is diagnosed parents have to plot a course between overcaution, and overenthusiastic encouragement. To choose activities carefully and to proceed slowly on regular medical advice is the only solution.

In the pre-sport examination then, the full history is very important and indeed the only guide the doctor may have to the need for an examination more detailed than routine observations would indicate. Therefore *please* keep your own accurate record of all illnesses and injuries and pass them on to the next school or doctor. Girls at puberty having early heavy periods probably should have a full blood count to detect and correct anaemia, not that it is really common. The growth spurt can be another reason for anaemia, especially if adolescent gourmets fill up on junk food instead of wholesome protein and vitamin-fresh foods. It has been noted that even boys can then have low iron reserves that should be boosted. Be warned too that it is dangerous for the child to 'forget' to mention previous injury, especially to the head or neck. They may get into, say, the football squad that way but reinjury is a common finding in all sports statistics, and it may, in the case of neck injury, be more serious a second time.

Preliminary examinations mainly focus on general body form and symmetry and obvious limb or joint variations that impede efficiency in the sport at hand. If an athlete later decides to take up intensive training that will risk stress injuries it would be good insurance to ask for a much finer anatomical scrutiny by an orthopaedic specialist. To be forewarned is to be forearmed.

There are other causes of death from sport, all quite, quite rare, but the situations in which they may arise cannot be ignored:

Collisions

In football players, even as young as thirteen years, it was noted at autopsy that coronary arteries could be arteriosclerotic (blocked by patches of fat) and lacking flexibility, so that they were further damaged by contact with the chest wall during bumps. Running into fences, goalposts etc. can obviously fracture skulls.

Hits by Ball

In cricket a hit on the temple can fracture the thinner skull bone, and in baseball a blow on the chest has killed, probably by cardiac arrest (sudden failure of the heart beat).

Heat Stroke

Children are more vulnerable to this than adults because they sweat more and have a less efficient and less trained circulation, but it is absolutely preventable (p. 34).

Congenital Syndromes

Parents whose child has been diagnosed as a case of Marfan's, Down's or Turner's syndrome probably know that they are prone to sudden death from cardiac dysrhythmia (irregular pulse) and if it happens on a sports oval, well, they will have died happy.

Botulism

This term for lethal food poisoning is derived from a Latin word for sausage, which is an important clue. The well-known habit of kids to eat all the food they see exposes them to botulism if meats are improperly cooked, left unrefrigerated, and served twenty-four hours later. After-game parties are the classic situation.

Bulbar Poliomyelitis

This rare fatal form of polio which affects the brain is thought to develop if children incubating the virus take heavy exercise. In areas where polio is still epidemic and children have not been immunised, the risk remains.

Anaphylactic Shock

This is a gross reaction to allergy and it is a life-threatening emergency because it results in difficult breathing and low blood pressure. Allergy to bee sting is a perfect example but there are food causes of allergy, and a rare form brought on solely by exercise, and another due to cold immersion. People recognised to have these allergies can only exercise in the company of friends who know how to give injections of adrenalin.

Lightning

pp. 34, 142.

Drowning

This is obvious. However, one wonders how many swimming pools have full resuscitation gear available and, even more importantly, an adult on duty trained to use the mechanical devices. One lethal recreation is for children to try and swim long distances underwater by overbreathing before plunging in. This is a killing trick and they must be specifically warned against it, in case they pick up the idea. Rapid overbreathing washes carbon dioxide out of the lungs and delays the next breath right enough (try it on dry land!), but in the meantime the child becomes unconscious from lack of oxygen and drowns.

(Now would parents please confess: how often did you try that trick? My personal best was 14 metres until a demonstration by a professional swimming coach at a school carnival ended by him being fished out of the pool at the 50 metre end when he stopped moving. Fortunately it was a frightening sight.)

Also to be banned is sitting on the bottom of a swimming pool and attempting to breathe through a length of hosepipe. It won't work and could be dangerous if the keen experimenter panics and inhales water. (The dangers of water pressure are explained under Scuba, p. 165.)

Timely and proper first-aid may turn the tide in all these situations, and also in any of the incredibly rare freak accidents one reads about. To further build up your data base, paste any relevant newspaper items in the back of this book.

REFERENCE:

Goldberg B. et al. Pre-participation sports assessment. *Paediatrics*, 1980; 66: 736.

2. Beware, Take Care

Some children should not play certain sports, or at least not seriously, but for all those little souls eager to participate in something, in anything, heaven forbid that some activity cannot be found suitable to their capacity. Calm consideration of the medical facts imposing limitations designed to prevent present injury or future complications is all that is required. Be alert to the following mixed bag of situations that could be met.

Infections

Measles and mumps etc. mean isolation to prevent further spread of the viruses, everyone knows that. Chronic or mild chest infections are more of a worry and all children seem to know by heart the words 'bud I habbad godda code'. It depends on what they are trying to do. Any infection removes part of their physical fitness and lets viruses and bacteria loose in the bloodstream. The former leads to more fatigue, the latter risks complications from possible lodgement of the infection in active organs elsewhere in the body and more work for the body defences, more demands on the heart and circulation, and so it goes on.

The simple answer is that when one has an infection one should rest the body muscles so that the heart, circulation of blood, and antibodies, can give undivided attention to quelling the invasion. Young children's defence systems have to learn their job, so there is no doubt that the first time they meet an infection, rest is important. Older children will have got used to the common cold and it becomes just a discomfort but sharp influenza with fever, limb pains, and a rapid pulse, is a definite case for rest; the influenza virus has a habit of mutating (changing its nature) so that each epidemic is slightly different. Very occasionally myocarditis (heart inflammation) ensues, and it also might not be influenza but something else developing. Sore throats may be from a virus (new mutants crop up every year), from bacteria lodged in the tonsils, or from a form of glandular fever (due to another virus). Time reveals all. In the early stage of an infection, therefore, insist on body rest for the young. Even the humble measles virus can kill by encephalitis (brain inflammation). If the sore throat is, for example, really glandular fever and the spleen is enlarged, a hit on the left side would rupture it. We sincerely hope that the lethal scourge, diptheria, is not to be considered. Any parents who do not see to it that their infant is vaccinated against diptheria may not enjoy his or her company for long.

When should sport start again after infection? Obviously with measles and the like, not until the doctor ends the quarantine. For bacterial infections of the throat etc., not until the temperature stays down on normal. Parents will probably know first when it is safe; junior is hungry and right back on his or her appetite. Glandular fever is a special case. If the liver or spleen is enlarged it is essential to wait until it is back to normal size.

Short Sight

Youngsters playing are usually jumping, tumbling and throwing in all directions, but sometimes one may be seen who is not participating. Often cranky or angry with frustration, this child may be standing on the sidelines because he cannot compete for moving objects or adjust for close body contact. Such children often turn to reading and are labelled 'bookish', yet in reality suffer from undetected defective sight, a condition easily corrected.

Double Joints

If excessively lax, such joints are prone to dislocations, certainly in gymnastics, football, or indeed in any body contact sport. The shoulder is notorious for redislocating because of its inherent high mobility. Recurrent dislocations as a general rule mean that the offending sport must cease. There is no sense in risking adult arthritis, and in any case there is probably an underlying structural defect needing surgery. In Down's syndrome (mongolism) it is muscle weakness rather than joint laxity that explains the joint dislocations such children are prone to suffer.

Limb Form

Parents can recall the momentary panic at birth when they checked for two arms, two legs, and ten little fingers and toes. Now you have to do it all again in more enlightened detail because many simple variations of form occur which, although of no consequence in occasional school sport, are worthy of expert opinion before serious sport, or certain sports, are encouraged.

The hollow hyperextended knee (genu recurvatum) is prone to patellar (knee cap) dislocation. Knock knee (genu valgum) risks chondromalacia patellae (p. 19). Bow knees (genu varum), because of the knee twist and compensating ankle angle, are likely to cause chronic leg muscle and tendon strain. Similar effects result from so-called pigeon toes that really indicate internal torsion (twisting) of the leg bones. The wide-angled elbow (cubitus valgus) makes success in throwing or gymnastics less easy and more stressful to the joint. Flat feet (pedis planus) or clawed high arch feet (pedis cavus) impose special muscle or tendon strains, perennial blister and corn problems, and, much, much later, arthritic feet or lower back strain. Morton's toe, where the second toe is longer than the big toe, has been implicated in stress fractures of the foot.

Many of these medical expressions will of course mean nothing to the average parent but the point is that anything seeming not right by the age of three or an odd gait must be checked by an orthopaedic specialist. Do not rely on the advice of a shoe salesperson. Note that normal infants are often slightly bow-legged or knock-kneed.

Organ Injury

Previous organ injury cancels any contact or dangerous sport. A ruptured liver for instance is fortunately rare, but it is so serious an injury it must never be risked again. A ruptured spleen has to be removed and obviously cannot recur although the child may be left with a blood disorder and a weakened resistance to infection. Previous simple surgery such as appendicectomy, tonsillectomy, sinus proof puncture, greenstick fracture (p. 20), and other one-off situations pose no permanent restrictions but any significant surgery must be carefully reviewed. The opinions of orthopaedic surgeons after bone and joint surgery must be followed to the letter.

An undescended testis is vulnerable to injury, and *must* be surgically corrected; if there is an associated inguinal (groin) hernia it will be made worse by exertion sports. A related problem is the boy with only one testis. In some sports there is risk of injury to it. The trend today is not to be too restrictive but it remains a worry and only the parents can decide whether the boy should get involved with, say, martial arts, or be a baseball catcher.

A congenital horseshoe kidney is one that lies unprotected across the lower abdomen in the path of blows and it may be the child's only kidney. The American Academy of Paediatrics advises against contact sports for a child with only one kidney. Linking these last two items is the fact that congenital abnormalities of the genitals and urinary organs, in both male and female, are often multiple, so if one is found check for others.

Head or Neck Fractures

Head or neck fractures or x-ray evidence of abnormalities absolutely preclude any return to collision sports (football), falling over sports (hockey), or high risk sports (trampoline). Who needs to be reminded of paraplegia?

Chronic Back Pain

Congenital bone formations, such as spondylolysis (p. 28) or minor spina bifida, show up as weak points because of their inability smoothly to absorb strain. New diagnostic tools such as the radioactive bone scan and CAT scan (computerised axial tomography) have shown that pain can be from areas of the vertebra under stress but not yet damaged or deformed to the point of visibility under x-ray. If the existence of stress can be proved at this pre x-ray stage, the management of an athlete's career by modifications to activity is simplified. Scoliosis (spinal curvature) needs attention but many children are still able to play in a spinal brace.

Recurrent Puzzles

Recurrent anything is a warning to look and then think carefully. Even if it is only a consequence of clumsiness or repetitive movement, is one going to reap reward or trouble? If it is bruising, it may indicate an underlying blood disorder. If it is boils, juvenile diabetes may be awaiting diagnosis. Well controlled diabetics are learning to participate in many sports but the experience needed to achieve this can only be gathered slowly.

Asthma

This is no longer a deterrent or a danger. It was until the severe form, status asthmaticus, could be adequately treated, but modern drugs have allowed some sufferers even to become Olympic champions. There are some general limitations; for instance, swimming is an excellent sport for asthmatics because it builds up the lung capacity, but scuba diving is too risky. Sprinting may be possible but not long distance running. Preventative pre-sport measures, especially in spring or in the cold, are important. Even so attacks can still be unexpectedly triggered by air pollution, humidity, nervous tension, and fatigue. There is a difference between known asthmatic children exercising and asthma that comes on with exercise. It may not show up as a definite wheeze but is to be suspected if a child coughs for a while after playing, gets short of breath with stomach cramps and stops playing, or has other allergies. (There is an exercise-induced allergy called urticaria, which leads to giant skin weals.) Medications must be closely supervised because all drugs have side effects which could complicate their use by athletes.

Cystic Fibrosis

Lung function tests will be a guide to what these children can attempt. Such children benefit handsomely from exercise in muscle fitness and general wellbeing, but their aerobic capabilities may not improve. Also they lose more salt in sweat and in hot areas may need weak salt drinks instead of just water.

High Blood Pressure

This is a definite indication against weight training or any other form of breath-holding activity, but otherwise there is clear evidence that exercise lowers the blood pressure. Unfortunately psychological studies have indicated that overweight students, the ones most likely to have a higher blood pressure, are not enthusiastic about exercise.

Epilepsy

Modern drugs for this condition are a boon, but fatigue or exuberant overactivity might call for a modification of dosages. Such diverse activities as swimming, horseriding and gymnastics are dangerous if there is any lapse of concentration or even momentary loss of consciousness. Sports ought to be chosen carefully and embarked upon cautiously in the early stages so that responses can be tested.

Osteogenesis Imperfecta

This very, very, very rare inherited bone fragility is usually known to families from birth, but occasionally it appears for the first time in adolescence, with multiple fractures occurring after trivial injury. Just living safely, let alone playing sport, is the problem here. In the classic syndrome the white of the eye are an indigo blue colour. Another rare bone disorder can be mentioned, fibrous dysplasia, usually diagnosed in adolescence from X-rays taken after a fracture.

Angio-neurotic Oedema

This hereditary condition of dramatic swelling of the neck, with difficulty in breathing as the fluid gathers around the larynx, is an emergency. It can be brought on by injury, and contact sports such as wrestling and football are out of the question. For sufferers adrenalin injections must be readily available.

In all the above situations when discussions are held with schoolteachers, coaches, trainers and medical experts to assess the dangers for a child in this or that sport, remember that the person taking the risk is not the doctor, the parent, the coach, or the trainer, but the athlete. It is worth repetition that the most important and most common situation parents will meet is still that of the athlete who has already had an injury and needs direction as to the future. Statistics constantly show that where previous injury has occurred, that athlete is much more likely to suffer a repetition of the same injury or one to the same body part than would an athlete with a clean record. Parents' most important duty is to make sure the injury or disability record is disclosed to those responsible for supervising sport, and to doctors carrying out pre-sport examinations.

3. Diagnostic Signs

Fractured limbs, dislocated joints, continuing unconsciousness, and bleeding, are examples of visible injury which obviously must be sent to hospital, but the following is a list of mixed symptoms and signs, worthy of being checked by a doctor before the next match or training session, even if the brave one says: 'it disappeared'.

- Lack of symmetry when comparing one limb or side with its fellow, or, in the case of the spine, when comparing one child's back with another.
- Lumps, hollows or gaps, the natural consequences of asymmetry; they are always due to something.
- Sharp sudden pain during competition. This is most likely due to tearing of muscle fibres and the athlete must stop immediately. A stitch in the side or under the ribs of young runners is thought to be due to lack of circulation in underdeveloped muscles, but deeper organ problems, for example chronic appendicitis, may be responsible.
- Chronic pain during exercise or coming on when at rest or overnight. Ligament tears, slipped epiphyses (p. 17), stress fractures (without displacement; p. 20), neuritis (nerve irritation or inflammation), deep infections, and tenosynovitis (inflammation around tendons), are just some of the possible causes.
- Lack of free movement, limited extension, or locking in any of the joints.
- Excessive movement of the knee or of a finger joint.
- A sense of weakness in a joint, fear of moving it, or loss of power in an accustomed movement.
- Muscle spasm with distortion of the neck or lumbar (lower back) region.
- Specific persistent bone tenderness or overlying bruising.
- Painless lumps or swelling around the knee. There should not be any.
- Knee pain when going up or down stairs or if sitting with the knees bent.
- Growing pains. They aren't!

- Clicks and clunks. Tendons or ligaments are slipping over bony bosses and should not be.
- Tender, swollen, or painful tendons around the ankle or wrist.
- Ankle sprains that are not steadily improving. Sprains are at their worst immediately but bone chips or fractures get worse.
- Blood in the urine. Treat this as urgent. It could be from a ruptured kidney.
- Concussion with momentary unconsciousness. Experts state that to be 'out cold' for less than 10 seconds is probably not harmful, but 'momentary' is an easier time span to assess.
- Double vision or blurred vision or spots in the vision.
- Pain on breathing in.
- Hearing loss. Whilst it might be harmless wax in swimmers, it may be more serious in the body contact sports.
- A frightened child. He or she may not be able adequately to explain what hurts or where exactly the pain is, and in the excitement of a game may not have noticed or remembered anything. However children are honest patients, the first time. Only later may they learn to malinger to avoid stress or through fear of failure or disappointing parents.

Injuries to the head or neck can be so serious that they are given their own chapter, with emphasis on safe handling for transport to hospital (Chapter 5, p. 22). Diagnostic signs in this part of the body are difficult enough for the emergency doctors to elicit, and downright dangerous for anyone else to attempt.

4. Bone Growth

Epiphysis

Epiphysis, epiphyseal plates, epiphyseal growth centres, epiphysitis, are words that echo around every chapter in every book to do with adolescent bones. Epiphyses are part of nature's elegant design for growth, and as they are most active during the growth spurt, which occurs at puberty, that is the time when they are most vulnerable to injury. Epiphyses are what can make adolescent injuries more serious. Epiphyses, in all their considerable anatomical detail, are a topic for doctors. But an effort on the part of parents to understand the principles of epiphyses is worthwhile, because when an epiphysis is damaged bone growth may be altered in length or direction. Pronounce it ep-PIFF-issis!

The whole skeleton begins in the developing baby as tiny rods of cartilage (gristle). Where the ends of two bones meet, and hence where joints must form, their opposed ends forever remain as cartilage, and this cartilage is then shaped into 'articular (joint) cartilage'. All the remaining cartilage is converted into bone and the process of bone resorption, re-creation, and remoulding, that ebbs and flows all through life, is set in motion, beginning with the initial design, through growth, repair, and disease. But bone growth cannot be rounded and symmetrical like Lord Emsworth's prize marrow. Bone must be shaped according to its final role as either a long bone like the femur (thigh bone), a 'small' long bone like each of the five metacarpals in the palm, or a cuboid shaped bone like most of those in the wrist or foot. A bone must also develop projections—bosses, ridges, processes, condyles, epicondyles, tubercles and tuberosities—to give muscles or their tendons special and larger areas for attachment.

For basic development each bone has a central growth site, either in the main shaft of a long bone, or in the middle of a cube, which is continually forming cartilage for conversion to bone. In the long limb bones each end later develops its own centre or even several centres; for example the lower end of the humerus (upper arm bone) has five. Those centres are the ones known as epiphyses, with bone forming in the middle as the proliferating cartilage layers expand outwards. The line along which these springy epiphyseal cartilage layers meet the bone of the shaft is called the epiphyseal plate (diagram 4−1). This plate area does not fuse with the shaft, that is, it is not completely converted to bone until all growth ceases. Thus whilst a child is still growing, there are epiphyseal plates somewhere in all bones that could be affected by sprains, dislocations, and fractures. They can be crushed, sheared off or pulled off, the latter happening because joint ligaments and muscle tendons are stronger than the epiphyseal plate. Where the ligament would tear in an adult, the plate may separate in an adolescent. To repeat, when the epiphyseal plate is damaged bone growth may be altered in length or direction.

It is the same with the projections, each of which has been thoughtfully provided by nature with its own small growth centre to sculpture it for the needs of muscle attachment. These epiphyses are confusingly known sometimes as apophyses, but they are one and the same, attached to the main bone by cartilage plates until the final fusion. Therefore, instead of pulling a hamstring muscle, the adolescent hurdler may pull off the whole attachment along the cartilage plate (diagram 4−2), and this is called 'avulsion of the epiphysis (or apophysis)'. This outcome is better actually for the muscle, and hence for the athlete, provided the avulsed epiphysis is correctly repositioned.

All these epiphyses appear, and later fuse, at widely varying times, and all vary in their growth potential, thus making each area different. For example, the lower end of the femur and the upper end of the tibiz (shinbone) are the main growing ends in the leg, that is the epiphyses there show stronger growth and are more important to height than those in the upper end of the femur and the lower end of the tibia. In practical terms damage around the knee could thus have more effect on leg growth than damage to the hip or ankle. In the arm it is the opposite. The top of the humerus bone, that is the shoulder, and the bottom of the radius (outer forearm bone), that is the wrist, are the main growing sites.

The knee has the longest growth span. The lower femoral epiphysis is present at birth and fuses at seventeen or eighteen years in the female and at nineteen or twenty in the male. The tibial epiphysis is also present at birth and unites a year or so earlier than the femoral one. By comparison, the lower end of the humerus has five epiphyseal centres, appearing at intervals

18 CHILDREN'S SPORTS INJURIES

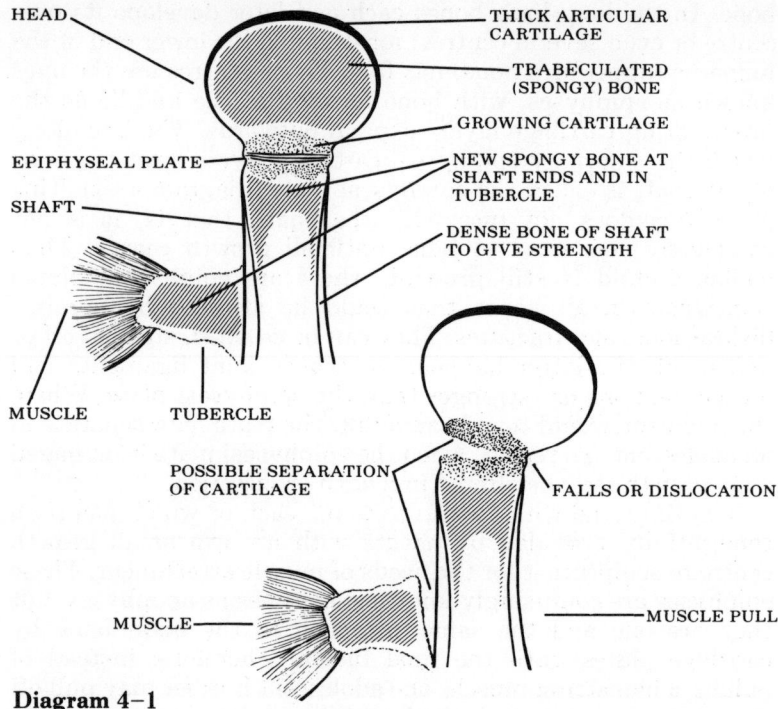

Diagram 4-1
Normal bone development. Note bone being formed on either side of epiphyseal plate.
Diagram 4-2
Damage to epiphyses.

from three to eleven years, and uniting between fifteen and twenty years. The upper humeral epiphysis, the growing one, is partly inside and partly outside the shoulder joint capsule. The medial (inner) ligament of the knee joint is attached above to the femoral epiphysis, and below to the tibial shaft. Therefore, in adolescent knee strain, the femoral epiphyseal plate may separate before the ligament tears. These examples show that *any* injury around *any* joint may involve an epiphysis in some way, up to about twenty years of age in theory, but in practice between eight and eighteen years. The peak danger time is approximately ten to thirteen in girls and twelve to fifteen in boys. No part of the limbs or spine can be considered safe. The possibility of epiphyseal plate damage must be considered every time.

Several other bone conditions will keep cropping up throughout the book:

Osteochondritis

This is a bad term but is now too established to change. The -itis suffix implies infection but it is not. It is a death or degeneration of the epiphysis, probably due to obscure interference with its blood supply, and it occurs in only a few bones. It is possibly a stress injury. Recovery is the rule, possibly with some deformity. When it occurs in the hip it is known as Perthes' disease.

Osteochondritis Dissecans

This is a smaller version of the above, which occurs almost exclusively in the knee and elbow; a small area of bone and articular cartilage dies, separates, and drops into the joint cavity to become a 'loose body'.

Apophysitis or Epiphysitis

Again, this is not an infection but a partial and gradual separation, perhaps with fragmentation, of the apophysis (or epiphysis) by pulling of the muscle or tendon attached to it. The classic example occurs at the tubercle (projection) on the front of the tibia (shinbone) by pull of the ligamentum patellae (knee cap tendon) attached to it. The condition is known as Osgood-Schlatter disease.

Chondromalacia

Almost exclusively a disease of the patella (knee cap), it is a softening of the articular (joint) cartilage. Repeated friction fragments then frets the cartilage, which flakes off into the joint. The irritation causes a reactionary effusion (swelling). It is more likely to occur when the knee mechanics are less than perfect and allow erratic patella movements under stress. Young girls are prone to it.

Greenstick Fracture

Young bone is softish, so that it does not snap like an adult bone but bends without actually breaking. It has to be treated as a fracture but mends rapidly, which is a plus for the under ten brigade.

Stress Fracture

This term constantly appears and it is synonymous with fatigue fracture. It has been recognised for many years in adults, occurring in specific bones as a result of excessive repetitive strain. The 'March' fracture in the foot of soldiers is the most popularly known and credit for the first recognition of it goes to a Prussian military surgeon in 1855. It is only in the last twenty years that stress fractures have become a feature in sport, but they are now appearing in younger and younger age groups. However, it must be said that it is not the average athlete who is affected but the achiever with good anatomy and good movements. In my youth 'pain' was a muscle or tendon problem and many coaches insisted that such pains should be 'run out' or 'trained out'. Not today. Pain must be viewed always with the suspicion that it is due to a stress fracture. The cause is still as it was with the soldiers: excessive and repetitive muscle pull that eventually breaks the bone, although it is a more subtle process than that simple explanation implies. No bone can now be considered immune. No sport really is free of it although naturally some sports afford more opportunity for it to occur. Sometimes it is something other than extra hours of training that gives the added strain, such as change of surface, change of shoes, or a new technique. Military training statistics show that female recruits are six times more vulnerable than males; this indicates, possibly, that as girls train harder and compete more, sports clinics will see more of them with stress fractures.

Why it occurs is unknown but it is probably related to the fact that bone strengthens itself where needed by first absorbing and then laying down new bone in altered form and line. Where there is constant, constant strain, luck alone could dictate that the bone be caught out of balance in the reorganisation and in that case small cracks would occur. Such is the pace of bone activity that these could heal in a short time, only to recur.

This is what the athlete notices: mild pain after exercise that goes with rest, but reappears when training resumes. If training continues the pain appears earlier, gets gradually more noticeable, and takes longer to subside. There is quite specific localised bone tenderness. It is not diffuse. In diagnosis it was once difficult to differentiate this condition from tendinitis (tendon inflammation) because plain X-rays were unable to pick out the very fine fracture line, but newer methods of radioactive bone scan and CAT scan (computerised axial tomography) are very precise.

Treatment is simple. Rest cures it and the moment the point of tenderness goes and there is no pain the fracture has healed. Repeated expensive testing is not needed. To prevent recurrence training methods must be reviewed and modified so that the constant strain is avoided.

REFERENCE:

Benton J. W. Epiphyseal fractures in sports. *Physician and Sportsmed.* 1982; 10: November 63.

5. Head, Neck and Spine

The central bony axis of head, neck, and spine protects our most vital structures and was therefore most cunningly devised by nature. Mind you so was the woodpecker's: clocked at eighteen pecks per second with deceleration force of 60G, its brain is tightly enclosed in spongy bone. Ours floats gently in fluid encased by a hard bone helmet, designed to resist blows, not to give them. The spinal column likewise was designed to absorb everyday shocks, and will absorb higher energy sport bumps *in its natural state of curvature*.

The curvatures plus the fibroelastic discs between the vertebrae absorb vertical force well (diagram 5–1), but the absolutely classic abnormal situation is butting with a flexed neck; the vertebrae break, move, and crush the spinal cord (diagram 5–2). And the classic sport is gridiron. The helmet is no protection although the player may think it is. Any youngster seen doing it must be *severely* reprimanded. The danger in rugby is a collapsed scrum; a player's head can be held down and fixed, his body swung in the melee, and, snap! Young teams deliberately manipulating a scrum must also be reprimanded.

In such situations there are several possibilities. The spinal cord may only have suffered 'shock' or mild bruising, and may not actually be damaged. On the other hand, the victim may be unconscious, or conscious and aware that he cannot move the arms and legs; in that state he is quadriplegic (tetraplegic); when only the legs are paralysed the condition is called paraplegia. Whatever, there can be no certainty at that moment as to the state of the spinal cord. One thing only is certain: *bad first-aid may be what damages the spinal cord, or completes the severance, thus making the paralysis permanent*. This fact is so important that the following rule must be invariable whenever there has been neck injury and a possibility of fracture-dislocation with quadriplegia or paraplegia: *Do not move the unconscious or paralysed player until everything is ready for it to be done properly*.

The principle is that the head must not wobble, flex, or extend. It must be held neutral relative to the shoulders, to

HEAD, NECK AND SPINE

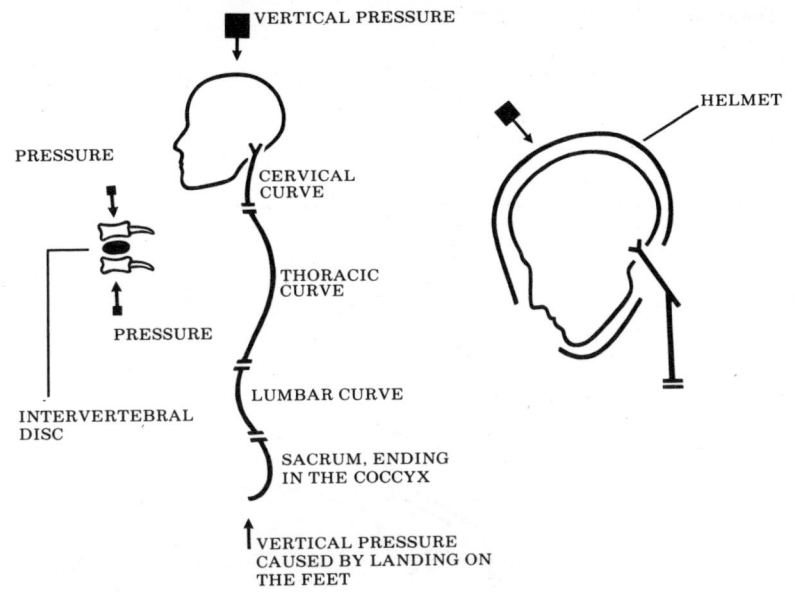

Diagram 5-1
The curvature and discs of the spine absorbing vertical pressure. Note the change of direction of curvature between the four parts of the spine.

Diagram 5-2
Butting with a flexed neck: the vertebrae break, move and crush the spinal cord.

prevent any further movement of the bones which will surely slice the soft spinal cord. So:

- Have four people available to turn the player *slowly* onto the back. One for the legs, one for the pelvis, one for the chest (although for a small child one person can cope with the whole body), and with the most important assistant holding the head steady and in line with the trunk as it is turned.
- Ideally this turn should be onto a flat board or tight stretcher (not a sagging one). Otherwise at least four people must later lift the victim onto such a rigid support for transport to a spinal unit.
- Do not try to remove any head gear or helmet, although the wire face mask may have to be removed to attend to the airway.
- Fix the head position before further movement of the stretcher (diagram 5-3).
- Clear the airway by pulling the tongue forwards or by holding the angle of the jaw up. *Never turn the head sideways.*

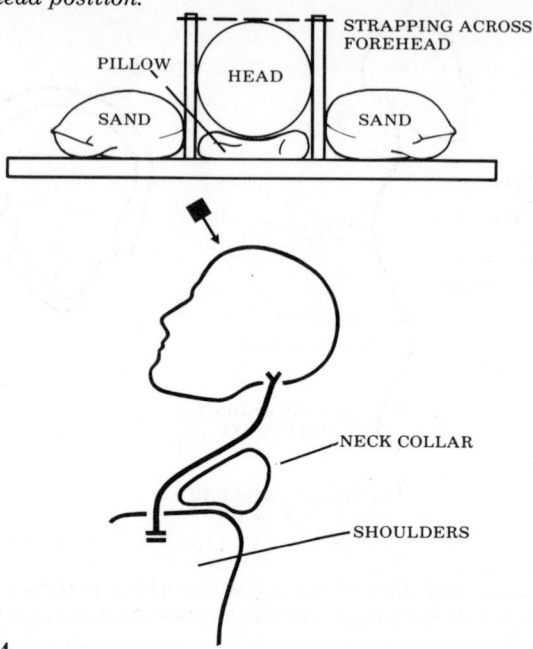

Diagram 5-3
Fixing the head position.

Diagram 5-4
A blow on the forehead causes overextension of the neck. It can be limited by a neck roll or collar, as used in gridiron.

An alternative and better method of transport is the Jordan multilift frame. If this is placed around the patient, adjustable plastic slats can be passed gently under the body for fixation to the frame, the body can be padded, and the whole lifted so that the victim's attitude is unchanged. Inflatable collars are also a major advance and should be part of every first-aid kit.

Compared with the tragedy of paraplegia or quadriplegia, to 'get away' with lesser injuries is definite good fortune. It must be emphasised again and again that damage to the neck (cervical) vertebrae can occur without any external sign or suggestion (symptom) of paralysis or loss of feeling. X-rays, often using special views, are needed to reveal a fracture, and should be done where there is persistent neck pain, unusual stiffness, restriction of free movement, or any odd sensations of taste or swallowing. The latter two symptoms occur because a very important artery, the vertebral artery, can be torn in dislocation of the cervical vertebrae thus stopping the blood supply to vital parts of the brain controlling the nerves of the tongue and throat.

All of the above relates to a flexion injury. Overextension of the neck curve by a blow on the forehead (diagram 5–4) can also lead to pressure on the spinal cord with temporary paralysis and sensory loss, but in this event there is progressive daily recovery. It is presumed that buckling of the various ligaments between the vertebrae, or bulging of the discs, sets up temporary pressure points. Fracture dislocation very rarely results and complete recovery is the rule in the young. (Older people are occasionally left with a burning sensation in the hands.)

Concussion

This is a short period of unconsciousness with a subsequent period of amnesia (loss of memory for recent events). No doubt there is an electrical effect on the brain's memory circuits similar to the result of switching off a computer. Even if on recovery the player seems normal, skull x-rays should still be taken because a hairline fracture of the skull may have occurred, with slow bleeding over the next twelve to twenty-four hours from damaged blood vessels. Young children fortunately are saved by their flexible skull bones which can deform and spring back. However, once the head size is more or less fixed and the multiple skull bones have fused, as they do in the late teens, the cranium (bony brain box) is more rigid and more likely to fracture. Brain damage can then occur by the 'contre coup' effect; that is, if there is a blow to the forehead the brain floats back in its cerebrospinal fluid compartment and bounces off the occiput (back wall of the skull), thus damaging the brain tissue at that end, opposite to the blow. Vice versa of course for blows on the occiput. In these cases, over the next week there may be irrational behaviour or emotional outbursts, impaired vision or lethargy and headache, and in the very rare case focal epilepsy (limb twitching) may be noted. A study of 200 freshmen footballers with concussion at Purdue in the United States showed that 37% had abnormal encephalograms (electrical measurement of brain waves), and intellectual function was still diminished in some up to fifteen days later. Also, tests at the Middlemore Hospital, Auckland, New Zealand, showed that 80% of head injury victims unconscious for any length of time had inner ear hearing defects.

It is now accepted that the effects of repeated concussion are cumulative and place the athlete in danger. Therefore, a concussed player must, repeat must, not return to the game. A period of rest, observation, questioning for relevant symptoms, and medical examination are essential. The reason is that death has followed even quite light second knocks on the head too soon after the initial concussion. The mechanism is not absolutely clear but probably in some there has been undetected, slight damage to the brain tissue or its coverings, causing residual brain swelling and reduced adaptability to any further assault. Viral infections, glandular fever, measles, chicken pox, and the like have also been implicated, probably again because they can cause slight, undetected encephalitis (brain inflammation) with brain swelling and sensitivity to otherwise insignificant head blows. There can be no hard and fast rule as to when a concussed player should return to contact or exertion sports, since medical examination cannot really tell when the brain has recovered from the assault. However, there is no call for a youngster to be a hero to his teammates, and in view of the research quoted above, weeks rather than days of rest would be prudent.

Minor head injury in fact should be taken more seriously than it is, even where there has not been a skull fracture or loss of consciousness. Follow-up analyses of patients admitted to hospital with head injuries, from both sports collisions and traffic accidents alike, are showing a higher than expected number with persistent headache, poor memory and concentration, abnormal psychological test results, and general psychosocial problems. The recovery in the traffic accident group may of course be complicated by legal and compensation factors; a gifted high school athlete injured in representative sport, with thwarted ambitions of a professional career, just might seek inclusion in the same group.

However, the most dangerous and fatal complication of a head injury is the slow bleed from a broken blood vessel. The build-up of intracranial pressure due to a subdural haematoma (blood clot inside the brain) or an extradural haematoma (blood clot outside the dura mater or covering membrane of the brain) leads to a progressive loss of consciousness that calls for urgent neurosurgery. Unfortunately, after a daytime sports injury this will happen silently during sleep, and therefore the injured person *must be observed at night* by a guardian angel. Laboured, noisy breathing or widely dilated pupils are the two danger signs. A disturbing report in the *Journal of Neurosurgery* by Pang states: 'With the advent of CAT scans an increasing number of patients with head injury were scanned because of minor neurological deficits, mild disturbances in the level of consciousness, behavioural abnormalities, or headaches lasting more than a few days. Some of these patients were found to harbour an extradural haemorrhage of considerable size.' It deserves reemphasis that there does not have to be a skull fracture (and greater flexibility of a child's skull makes this less likely) for these dangerous blood clots to form.

Headache after concussion must therefore always follow a diminishing path. If it persists, and particularly if it increases in any way or is replaced by a migraine-like headache with visual disturbances and vomiting, swift medical examination is vital. Headache, other than following head injury, is a medical problem and can have many causes, for example, neck muscle tension, sinusitis, ear disease, impacted teeth, virus infection, or (and this is very rare) meningitis or encephalitis may be developing. Note that headache in children is rare and must *never* be taken lightly.

A broken nose has to be reset under an anaesthetic, but a young nose is mostly cartilage and squashy. Bleeding into the cartilage septum (the division between the two nostrils) of the nose may not be immediately obvious until the swelling silently reaches a size that blocks breathing. This also needs expert surgical care otherwise the clot can become infected and form an abscess. It is sometimes not possible to determine whether the nasal bone has been fractured without an X-ray. Check with the surgeon whether a nose guard should be worn in future.

A sudden nose bleed other than that caused by direct injury usually comes from fragile small blood vessels in the septum below the bone. Only pressure will stop it. Squeeze the soft part of the nose by the clock for well past the normal clotting time of four minutes. If facilities are at hand gently pack the nostrils with gauze soaked in adrenalin or hydrogen peroxide solution. Persistent bleeders may need to have the area cauterised.

A trickle of blood from the ear may be the first warning of a fracture of the base of the skull or a ruptured eardrum. There is no way of being sure without careful examination, and the need is urgent. Funny noises in the ear, a sense of bubbling, lack of balance, dizziness, or deafness, are also evidence that damage has resulted from a blow to the ear.

Vertebrae

All twenty-four vertebrae, except the sacrum (the lower part), sit on top of one another to make a column. In the sacrum, the five original bodies are fused into a solid chunk that wedges itself between the two pelvic bones like the keystone of an arch. Piled on the sacrum are five lumbar vertebrae, twelve thoracic, and seven neck or cervical vertebrae. Viewed from behind the column is straight, but seen from the side it curves gently fore and aft changing direction at the junction between each group. Thus the sacrum and thoracic group are concave forwards, and the lumbar and cervical groups concave backwards. The points where the curve changes direction are the most vulnerable to strain (diagram 5–1).

In basic plan each vertebra has a circular thick body, with a hollow posterior arch attached to it to enclose the spinal cord. Poking out from the arch are one spine pointing backwards in the midline, a transverse process (protuberance) on each side where the body and arch meet, and four articular processes which poke out like the ears of a dog, two on top and two below, each process having a smooth surface and so aligned as to allow of joints between adjoining vertebrae (diagram 5–5). The whole is linked in every conceivable direction by ligaments and enveloped by muscles to give every possible movement. Between each body is a firmly attached fibroelastic disc thus making the whole column into a tough spring, capable of full movement including torsion.

The joints of the vertebrae differ in shape in the three areas, for different needs of strength and mobility. In the cervical (neck) area, movement is all important, so the joints are on flat surfaces, the upper-side ones facing directly backwards and the lower ones facing forwards. Too much direct sideways push and they will slip, that is dislocate (diagram 5–5). The lumbar vertebrae are locked for greater strength by having the lower convex joint surfaces facing outwards, and the upper concave ones of the body below facing inwards and wrapping around them. This still allows the lumbar bodies to slip forwards, and they do if the posterior arch breaks. This slippage is known as spondylolysis or spondylolisthesis, depending on degree, and follows a fracture in the 'pars interarticularis' area (diagram 5–6). The pars interarticularis is the area of the posterior arch between the articular process and the spine. The lumbar curve, the 'hollow of the back', alters in these conditions.

In development each vertebral body has a main growth centre, and at puberty secondary ones develop to form thin plates on

HEAD, NECK AND SPINE 29

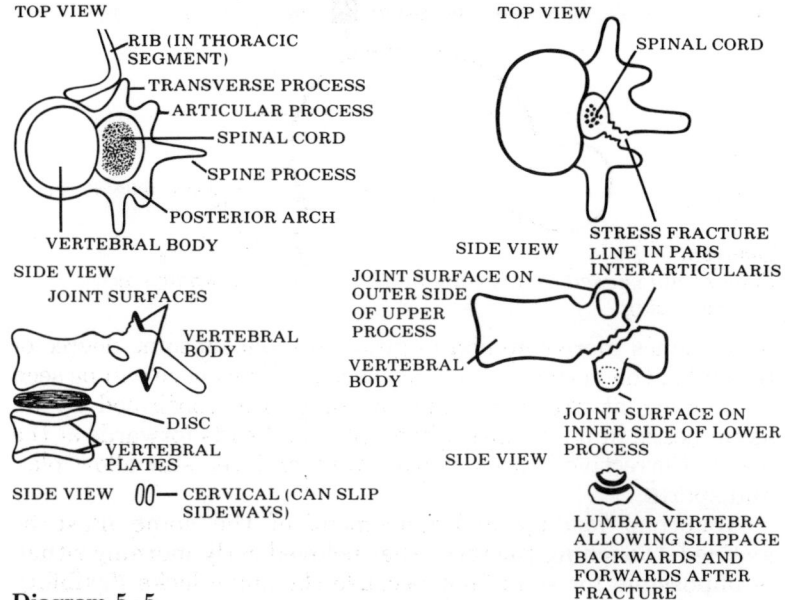

Diagram 5-5
Basic shape of cervical (neck) and thoracic (chest) vertebrae. Note the large spinal cord, the intervertebral disc, and the plane of the joint surfaces.

Diagram 5-6
The lumbar (lower back) vertebrae. Note the smaller canal for the spinal cord, now just a bundle of nerves, the altered plane of the intervertebral joints, and the stress fracture line where movement occurs.

the upper and lower surfaces, called epiphyseal plates. The vertebral body at this stage thus looks like a slice of icecream between wafers. Until these plates fuse firmly with the main body at about twenty years they can be damaged, in which case growth is then lopsided and shows up as a curvature. A special variety common in swimmers is called Scheuermann's kyphosis, caused by fragmentation of the plates to allow front wedging of the thoracic vertebrae making a bigger thoracic curve, or hump, in the upper back. Another rare condition, which is caused by excessive training involving flexion, extension and torsion (for example, endlessly kicking a soccer ball), is damage and fragmentation of the epiphyseal plate so that it presses on the spinal cord to cause lower back ache and sciatica. The same two symptoms will be caused by rupture of the intervertebral disc, also rare in adolescents but it does happen.

Scoliosis (lateral curvature) may also be due to damage of the vertebral plates but, in the young, it is more likely to be a matter of unbalanced muscle pull and is probably hereditary. It

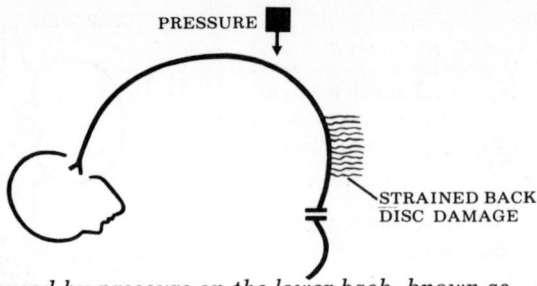

Diagram 5–7
Back strain caused by pressure on the lower back, known as 'piggybacking'.

is ten times more common in girls. In scoliosis some degree of torsion of the vertebral body also occurs. The curve will be seen by looking at the back, and the diagnosis confirmed by an asymmetric hump formed when the child bends forwards at the waist. Corrective braces can be worn and yet still allow play and sports.

Abnormal loading and movement of the spine must be avoided. 'Touching the toes', that beloved early morning ritual, is impossible for some, not because the spine lacks flexibility but because the hamstring muscles of a lanky growing adolescent are too tight. In this state it is a heinous crime to damage the back by pushing down or by 'piggybacking' (diagram 5–7). The correct exercise in this situation is to lie on the back, take the strain off it, flex the thighs onto the trunk, and then work to extend the legs. Hyperextension exercises (backbending) must also not be exaggerated in the lanky. Backache is too large a subject to be dismissed with crisp advice; however, it can be said that a vast number of sore backs (at any age) are due to overworked muscles or muscles suddenly asked to exceed their strength so that strain has to be taken by the binding ligaments. It is often forgotten that strong abdominal muscles are just as important as the back ones in stabilising the vertebrae and many an abdominal pain in athletes is due to weak muscles strained in support of back movements. Bad posture in children does not cause a bad back but is probably due to weak muscles that need to be exercised. Finally, a quick switch of sports can catch back muscles unprepared for different strains and lead to a 'bad back'. The classic example is a boy who moves straight from rowing into the rugby season without time for rest of overworked areas and conditioning of muscles that will be needed for new movements.

REFERENCE:
Pang D. et al. Non-surgical management of extradural haematomas in children. *J. Neurosurgery* 1983; 59: 958–971.

6. Resuscitation

This is as easy as A. B. C.
A = airway, clear it.
B = breathing, help it.
C = colour, observe it.
 To bring the old mnemonic right up to date, it's as easy as A. B. C. C.
C = clock, have someone watch it and note progress.

Airway

The special circumstance of possible fracture of cervical (neck) vertebrae must be emphasised over and over again, so that nobody thoughtlessly turns a victim onto the side, or worse, just turns the head to one side to clear the airway, in any situation where a neck fracture could have happened. Certainly the airway must be clear but in an unconscious person, in ninety-nine times out of a hundred, it is just that slack muscles have let the tongue or jaw fall back to block the throat. Therefore, in whatever position the head is lying, just pull the tongue forward by grasping its slippery tip with a cloth (handkerchief) or pull the angle of the jaw forwards by getting your fingers around it just below the ear. An impacted mouth-guard naturally has to be removed but it is useless at that stage to look for a missing tooth. A known epileptic, blue in the face from muscle spasm during a fit, is a special case. Doctors deal with this by slipping a mouth gag behind the last molar tooth and then a padded prop between the teeth as they are forced open, but don't you put your fingers near or between those grinding teeth! Another special case is drowning. Fluid in the throat and lungs, swallowed fluid being regurgitated, and froth, is best drained with the head and chest down (lift the end of the stretcher) until a mechanical sucker is available. If the victim is left prone (face down), it is not possible to work on the chest or heart and he must be turned over to lie on a flat firm surface. Again, before turning remember the possibility of a broken neck. This is unlikely in someone who simply fell into water, but possible if the victim jumped off a fence and hit the side of the pool, and very likely if a child is found unconscious at the foot of a tree. Semi-conscious patients are protected from further inhalation or aspiration by the cough reflex.

Breathing

Breathing can first be assisted by rhythmic compression of the lungs to expel stale air and allow elastic recoil to suck new air back in; the rhythm should approximate normal breathing, that is fifteen to twenty times per minute. Slowly and steadily, timed by the clock watcher, compress the lower rib cage from the sides, or press the upper abdomen in, to cause up and down diaphragmatic movement. Slow and steady is quite enough. The odd child has actually been killed by vigorous frantic squeezing by a strong man (a parent in a panic). This can, and does, fracture ribs (which then perforate the lung), or rupture the liver and spleen with lethal intraperitoneal (abdominal) bleeding. It cannot be emphasised enough: slow, controlled action, fifteen to twenty times per minute. Shallow spontaneous breathing need only be gently helped, if at all, by an oxygen cylinder and face mask. The same principles then apply but the force here is positive pressure distending the lungs for a few seconds. Apply the face mask when the victim starts to breathe in, thus amplifying the breath, with elastic recoil expelling the air when the mask is removed. The danger with a mask and positive pressure is overdistension and rupture of the lungs, and as a guide in an unconscious patient one can put the mask on and take it off in rhythm with one's own breathing, so that the chest is seen to rise and fall.

Mouth to Mouth

Mouth to mouth techniques are equivalent to using a face mask and oxygen cylinder, in that positive pressure is exerted if the victim's nose is also squeezed shut.

Mouth to mouth revival of unknown victims could pose a danger of infection to the rescuer, and large plastic masks capable of covering both mouth and nose, and with a top blowing nozzle, with non return valves, are now available for first-aid kits. All public authorities and professional paramedic teams carry such or similar gadgets so that mouth to mouth contact is avoided with anonymous people. Hepatitis B is the worry. Both blood and saliva of a sufferer are highly infective and if the jaundice is very slight or it is night the condition may not be suspected. Young active sports-loving children almost certainly would not have the disease but the older teenager just might have embarked on an unfortunate lifestyle which risks contagion, perhaps even of AIDS. Thus, parents in first-aid teams cannot afford to be careless with the blood and body secretions of the general public.

Colour and Cardiac Arrest

Colour is the real guide to progress. Pink is optimum. Blue indicates a good circulation but inadequate oxygen. Pallor or a delicate lilac is bad; check the pulse. If it is absent heart arrest is present, and cardiac stimulation is urgent. The reason for the clock is now seen. It is the only way to know for certain how long the cardiac arrest lasts. The correct technique in big children (and adults) is to place the butt of the hand over the lower part of the sternum (breast bone), the other hand on top of that, then press and relax smoothly and rhythmically every second. With small children place only the butt of the hand along the breast bone; exert no more pressure than will depress the bone for 3 to 5 cms and use the other hand to get the jaw forward. If someone else, and this is the ideal situation, is using a face mask properly, then the proper rate, five compressions to one lung expansion, that is eighty to a hundred per minute, is easy to maintain. An electric defibrillator as carried by resuscitation teams can get the heart going by administering shocks to it, but you must keep efforts going until one arrives, or until the pulse returns. Children have remarkable powers of recovery and have been successfully revived after being pulseless for twenty minutes. It is not easy to detect shallow spontaneous breathing but do the best you can by listening with the ear over the mouth.

Blocked Airway

If it seems that something in the throat is blocking the airway (or the child is found choking on an inhaled toy) try the Heimlich trick which has superseded the good old thump on the back. Essentially this means pressing firmly in the midline, and it must be right in the middle below the breast bone, so that the diaphragm is forced up and the suddenly expelled air dislodges the obstruction. The way to do it is to stand behind the victim and wrap the arms around the victim's midriff. Make a fist of one hand, thumb in the midline, fit it below the ribs, cover it with the other hand and squeeze swiftly backwards several times.

Heat Stroke

Heat stroke should not happen in children's sport. The danger is, or should be, well understood and provided for. Even so the occasional children's surf carnival has had to be called off because of wide distress in the competitors; very hot humid conditions are aggravated if there are delays and the contestants are left to stand around on blinding sand without cold drinks. Indeed the young are unlikely to drive themselves in unfavourable weather, but the older and tougher teenager can show tenacity and be at risk; they should be advised of the need for water during long distance running etc. Children have an inadequate sweating response and an untrained cardio-vascular system (circulation) so that their body temperature can rise quite quickly. Cooling has first priority in resuscitation; hose them or put them in a cold bath, and then use cold drinks. Salt drinks are not vital; they will not have sweated out the sodium ion like an adult.

Lightning

Lightning discharge, although Benjamin Franklin may not have realised it in 1752, is lethal. Because of rain moisture the skin has reduced resistance, not that that is very relevant with a direct current of one million volts, releasing anything up to 200,000 amperes in 100 milliseconds. Wet tree leaves also offer a path of lowered resistance through to the ground, so that anyone standing underneath is surrounded by the flash which sets clothing alight, burns the skin, crushes vertebrae from the jolt, and, in particular, causes cardiac arrest and stops respiration. Those two are the problems. If there are several victims concentrate on those who seem dead and not the ones making feeble movement. The reason is that the electrical surge stops the heart at once and it is more likely to restart spontaneously with quick resuscitation. If a child has climbed into an electricity sub-station to recover a ball, *be careful for your own safety*. To touch him might make you a victim too, and the recommendation is to roll him or drag him away from equipment to a safe spot with a piece of wood etc. If at all possible, particularly in domestic situations, turn off the source of the electricity first.

Drowning

Drowning is death by lack of oxygen, not choking by water in the throat. Certainly water and debris, and vomitus perhaps, can be aspirated into the lungs and cause severe problems for hospital staff later, but the immediate problem is to get oxygen into the system by a mask and artificial respirator. If there is a portable or battery suction apparatus available, well and good, use it to clear the throat. But to repeat, the big need is oxygen. Research has shown that most victims lose consciousness in the water from lack of oxygen, and that the accompanying immersion in very cold water can cause cardiac arrest. (Those two problems again!)

Jaw Fracture

A fractured lower jaw presents a special problem in airway control; the tongue will fall back because the tongue muscles have lost their firm base. Whatever is tried may be resisted by muscle spasm as consciousness and muscle tone return and the only thing left is to turn the victim onto his stomach so that the tongue and jaw fall forward again. This tip has been left to the last so that it does not conflict with the warning given at the beginning about turning unconscious patients. That advice is so important it takes precedence over all else, and before turning the victim over one must be 100% certain that a neck fracture is not possible.

Practice Makes Perfect

In the heat of the moment little or none of the above advice will come to mind unless it has been practised and practised and practised. The best thing to do would be to attend a class, such as those run by the Red Cross, and learn it. Tests of trained hospital personnel have demonstrated that even they often perform lung ventilation poorly, especially when trying to use an anaesthetic bag and mask or mechanical devices. The problem is that it is not easy to effect a mask-mouth seal and extend the head with only one hand. Time is also wasted in setting up complicated equipment. In other words, by far the best and quickest method is the mouth, using one of the large plastic masks described to prevent infection; if it also has an oxygen inlet so much the better. It has been observed in classes for young students (for example lifesavers) that chest compression for cardiac arrest is difficult for them to learn, thus emphasising the importance of attending a class. Individuals who fall off horses in remote areas are far from expert help, but in group and team activities where injury is possible, first-aid resuscitation must be thought of and planned for. If someone in the group is completely competent with the equipment, especially positive pressure oxygen machines, and can be responsible for its upkeep, then that is a plus factor. Resuscitation is rarely needed, but when it is it is decisive. This is one time when it is not good to learn on the job.

7. Thorax, Abdomen and Pelvis

Perforating injuries to the thorax, abdomen and pelvis are serious and obviously a job for hospitals, but blunt trauma sets up shock waves that can literally reverberate through the area and quietly damage vital organs. The only protection for the abdomen is a tensed muscle, so the athlete is in particular danger if caught 'off guard'. The very fragile spleen on the left side and the liver on the right are partially protected by the lower ribs. The kidneys are cunningly hidden on the back wall against the spine and its heavy muscles, but can still be damaged by an unexpected frontal blow, and are also vulnerable to a side-on hit striking between the last rib and the crest of the hip bone. Heart and lungs are well caged-in but so-called closed injuries, that is where the body has been hit but there is no open breach of tissue, have been known to split the lining of the aorta, bruise the heart muscle, or rupture the diaphragm. The ribs themselves are tightly wrapped in muscles, a fact well known to cannibals, so that a fracture is thereby partially splinted and may not be suspected until a persistently sore side is X-rayed some days·later. However a spicule (splinter) of bone can perforate the pleura (membrane encasing the lung), collapse the lung, and hence cause a breathing problem or breathlessness. Fortunately the flexibility of the whole rib cage in the growing child usually prevents fracture except in a crushing situation.

On the spot the question should be 'Is he (or she) just winded or is there a serious organ injury?' The former is far, far more likely but there is no way of being immediately 100% certain because a small rent in the liver, spleen, or kidney, can seal over only to rerupture days later. Therefore these athletes, no matter what is thought at the time, must be observed over the next week and must report any unusual pain or feeling of weakness. They must also be told to report any discoloration in the urine such as fresh red blood or old black blood. One is referring of course to situations where heavy body blows have occured. In such cases the normal cardio-vascular syncope (shallow breathing, fainting, dizziness, wobbly legs, brief loss of consciousness even) will occur as a reflex reaction to the shock blow to the nervous system components of the so-called solar plexus in the pit of the stomach. In this case the victim has been 'winded', the blood pressure drops, and the pulse falters. There is no pain and recovery is quick; if it is not, or if there is more definite shock with cold clammy skin, pallor, and a rapid pulse, the quite rare serious injuries may have happened after all. Fortunately, the modern ultrasound and CAT scans allow of swift diagnosis, or exclude danger.

Remember always to feel the pulse. A blow or kick to the solar plexus very occasionally will stop the heart because it too is controlled by a higher segment of nerves connected to the solar plexus; this is more likely with an adult heart than a young one. Whilst checking for the return of pulse pressure think of what to do for cardiac arrest (p. 33), even though you will probably not have to do it.

The pancreas lies against the spine and very rarely it can be crushed by an elbow dug forcibly and deep into the epigastrium (pit of the stomach) just below the breast bone. A knee or shoulder or the butt end of a stick will do the trick just as well. The victim may collapse at once from severe shock or gradually, over the next few hours, develop increasing pain with tenderness. In the latter event it is still a surgical emergency although it may be neglected or misdiagnosed in the early stages.

Another rarity is escape of air from the lung, not into the pleural cavity, but into the tissues of the chest and neck with the athlete slowly becoming aware of pain behind the breast bone and spreading to the neck or shoulder; there is usually some breathlessness but nowhere as dramatic as that seen in a chest perforation with air in the pleural cavity and a collapsed lung. It has been reported following blows received in gridiron and soccer, and in cricket from fast bowling exertions. The probable cause is a tightly closed mouth and throat associated with grim determination so that rise in gas pressure ruptures one of the delicate surface air sacs of the lung. There can be a crackling in the skin due to escaped air but an X-ray allows speedy diagnosis.

Another oddity is to have what is known as a cervical rib; this is an extra rib, a rudimentary one, lying above the first rib and the collar bone. This will probably be diagnosed only when an X-ray has been taken for a suspected fracture or sore neck. Since it is congenital, it may be found in both brother and sister.

Injury to the testis, if it leads to a swelling or skin bruising, must be observed in hospital in case surgical intervention is needed to preserve the organ from permanent damage by torsion, haemorrhage, or pressure from the swelling.

Athletes normally do not have to be told to empty the

bladder before events but the adrenalin released by competition and the rapid heart beat will temporarily increase the flow of urine. It takes a very bad blow to rupture the bladder and usually it only happens in association with a fractured pelvis.

There have been reports of gymnasts bruising the large intestine in the right lower quadrant of the belly by constantly hitting the parallel bar, causing bleeding into the bowel and black bowel motions. This would need to be checked by a physician.

There is always fear of young girls falling astride, say, a vaulting horse, and doing great damage. The vulval area can certainly bruise badly and look terrible, but permanent harm is almost impossible, and cuts etc. are easily repaired and heal quickly.

8. Eyes

These are at risk in every sport but especially where there are moving objects, sticks, or collisions. This topic is so important that the following rule must apply invariably: *Every blunt eye injury should be examined by a specialist.* Dislocation of the lens, tears or detachment of the retina, bleeding into the chambers in front of or behind the lens, or ulcers of the cornea, are serious possibilities. The player must not return to the game. Warn him or her not to rub the eyes, cover the eye with a plastic shield or piece of cardboard, and hurry to the casualty department. Atropine drops used to dilate the pupil prior to examination are reversed by adrenalin drops; even so the vision will still be impaired for some time, and this alone will prevent further play even if no damage was seen.

Regular annual examination is advisable thereafter because chronic glaucoma has been known in some cases to follow years later. In fact eye tests should be done for any child who seems to have difficulty with games or has slow reflexes, because a surprising number are found to have defective sight and proper glasses or contact lenses make an enormous difference to their participation. Also, undetected poor vision leaves a child vulnerable to serious injury in ball games (especially indoors under variable light) when he has goodnaturedly joined in to make up the numbers. Colour blindness is said to affect one male in every eight but it never has any effect on skill, and therefore does not need correction by exotic contact lenses.

Apart from something rather obviously horrendous such as the tip of a javelin, the most serious objects for the eye to meet are golf balls, squash balls, shuttlecocks, or the point of the elbow, because their small diameter fits all too neatly into the eye socket. So does the edge of an ice hockey puck. A cricket ball or baseball is too large in diameter to fit exactly in and will, instead, fracture the bone ridges above or below the eye. This, in turn, may affect the sinuses or base of the skull, hence altering the eye compartment, although usually not directly harming the eyeball (but see p. 118). A tennis ball, although also of large diameter, is not so safe for the eye because at speed it can deform on the ridges and so squeeze into the socket. Note that the Asiatic eye, not being as recessed as the Caucasian, is not as well protected against even the baseball or softball. With lacerations around the eye, even if the doctor says: 'This will only need a small stitch', ask him to check the eye. The eyeball may have been hit and the patient may not be aware of it.

If a player thinks there is a piece of grit under the eyelid, and this would be the commonest first-aid problem, remember that foreign bodies embedded in the cornea produce the same sensation. Anything seen on the eyeball must therefore *never* be wiped or picked at. This is a certain way to cause corneal ulceration and scarring. The eye should be washed with an eye undine and if the object does not move then it is a task for hospital equipment.

In contact sports such as football and wrestling it is possible for some infections, for example the virus of herpes or the staphylococcus bacterium from a boil, to be passed from one person to another; so where there is a red or watery eye which may be due to infection specialist examination is needed to prevent any possibility of corneal scarring.

After concussion, children are notoriously prone to transient blindness, lasting even a few hours, caused either by shock to the brain centre or by blood vessel spasm. Unfortunately a detached retina will also cause sudden blindness in one eye, or slow onset of poor sight, and detachment can follow any head injury. Football knocks are a trap in that they can so easily be forgotten as the match rolls on. Boxing is another problem sport where this can happen. These cases serve to emphasise how important it is to have even minor eye irregularities properly examined.

Swimmers training endlessly in chlorinated pools should wear protective goggles to prevent irritation. A pterygium (skin-like plaque) can form in the conjunctiva at the inner angle of the eye in many dedicated surfboard riders. It is caused by constant exposure to sun and spray. Whilst board riders can hardly wear glasses or contacts, tinted goggles to screen out the damaging ultraviolet rays would seem indicated for those who clock up long hours. Skiers need quality anti-ultraviolet lenses *all* the time, not just on sunny days.

Contact Lenses

In principle, what contact lens wearers can and cannot do is a matter for individual advice. Contact lens technology is constantly improving. One current oddity concerns the new photosensitive lenses; there are reports of them suddenly turning black, which would cause no little astonishment to an alpine skier! Contact lenses are of course no protection at all for the eye and are not a substitute for proper protective glasses.

Black Eye

The oldfashioned 'black eye' is just blood oozing into the loose tissue of the eyelid from a broken blood vessel; multi-hued iron pigments form and are slowly absorbed. As the tissue tension builds up, back pressure stops the ooze but cold compresses will do it more quickly by causing blood vessels to spasm. The lump of steak which is meant to reduce swelling by osmotic pressure, won't, and if it is produced it would probably be better eaten to restore the victim's spirits.

Single Eye

Children with only the one eye should be very circumspect in their choice of sports. Parents of such children must really ask themselves, is it sensible to risk such a vital organ, now that there is such a wide range of activities and hobbies available to stimulate young brains? Children should be warned time and again about the danger to the eye from sharp things and thrown things, and must be specifically warned about skylarking with dangerous objects and the playing of practical jokes; every fireworks night produces a crop of eye injuries, all avoidable.

Eye Protection

The use of eye protectors is increasing, and some sporting bodies, for example ice hockey associations, insist on their use. Design is improving but players still complain of discomfort, fogging, and restricted lateral vision. At the moment the best protection is provided by plain polycarbonate, or industrial 3mm-centre-thickness CR39 plastic lenses mounted in rigid rims with a posterior retaining lip and no lateral hinge. Fogging remains a problem despite venting and sprays; perhaps one day a wire mesh design may replace the solid lens. Those who need to wear prescription glasses or contact lenses should consult their optometrist about modification of the protective lens.

Open eye guards or frames may seem adequate but fast squash balls, for example, have squeezed through them or displaced them, and the gaps must be checked against the edge of racquets and the tips of hockey sticks etc. to make sure that they really will protect, otherwise you have merely exchanged money for a dangerous false security. If an eye protector is damaged during play, it has been weakened and hard though it is to do so the player *must* stop. Otherwise there again exists a state of false security. Needless to say ordinary reading glasses are *no* protection at all. So-called hardened glass lenses may be shatterproof from light blows, but set in domestic frames they are useless. Concave prescription lenses with thin centres leave short-sighted athletes especially vulnerable.

In 1985 the American National Society to Prevent Blindness found racquetball, squash and tennis responsible for 3500 eye injuries. The 'it won't happen to me' attitude must be condemned.

To repeat: *Every blunt eye injury should be examined by an eye specialist*, remember that after head injuries silent retinal detachment can occur, and wear eye protectors in every sport where eye injury is a possibility.

9. Teeth

First teeth are not reimplanted when knocked out. Nevertheless the victims must not be dismissed with just sympathy or the usual reminder to be brave, because damage to even one first tooth can result in injury to the permanent teeth developing in close proximity. A dentist should be consulted since most sport injuries will be to the aesthetically important front teeth. The greatest risk to the permanent teeth is said to be when injury occurs at about nine years of age.

For permanent teeth there is one absolute rule: *Even a mild blow must not be ignored*. The damage may be invisible—it does not need much force to fracture the root of a tooth and sever the vascular line, thus leading to pulp damage, a dying tooth, possible abscess formation, and either loss of the tooth or permanent discoloration. The tooth cannot heal itself in this situation. Root canal therapy alone can save it. Also, under the age of say, twelve years, the roots are not completely formed and injury at this stage may prevent normal root formation.

If a tooth is completely dislodged it is possible to prevent root resorption if the tooth can be reimplanted within ninety minutes of the injury. Despite the wonders of modern dentistry the effort may fail for technical reasons but it is certainly worth trying, so, clean mud and grass etc. from the tooth with *cold* water. *Do not scrape it*. That only removes living cells. Then either force the tooth back into position, where it can be held by the fingers, or wrap it in wet gauze for transport straight to the dentist. If the tooth cannot be found, then in the heat of the moment it may have been swallowed, which does not matter, or it may have been forced into the antrum (cavity in cheek bone) or aspirated into the lung, both of which matter very much. Later X-rays can check for it in those spots. Note that loosened teeth must be splinted back by the dentist, a simple matter but also not to be delayed.

If the incisor tooth has been chipped or broken off, again remember the danger of so-called minor injury and insist on seeing a dentist. The size of the pulp in a young incisor tooth is large relative to the size of the whole tooth so that even a small chip may expose the sensitive pulp. Speedy treatment is essential.

Finally, a blow severe enough to knock out a tooth might also fracture the jaw or cut the tongue, so the first-aid may initially need to concentrate on a blocked airway. This is the one time in head and neck injury when the patient may be best in a face-down position so that the loose broken jaw can fall forwards, but, as always, make absolutely sure that there is no question of a broken neck.

Mouthguards

Mouthguards should really be used in all contact sports. Their function is not to put a wall around the teeth but to spread the force of a blow evenly to the whole ring of supporting bone. When properly fitted they will protect the soft tissues against laceration by the teeth, and diminish the risk of jaw and neck damage. They can be cheaply homemade from resilient commercial materials, but if they are not a perfect fit they will be more of a danger than not wearing one at all, and many a child has received bad unexpected damage from wearing such a one. A professionally made guard is always preferable. After each use it should be cleaned and put immediately back on its mould to keep its shape through the season. There is the expensive problem that the guard will not be good for ever. It must be checked the following season because by then, the way kids grow, it may be resting on teeth, ready to transmit force directly to them, instead of dissipating the energy evenly. The jaws are not stable until about eighteen years of age.

Bridgework

Bridgework can be a big problem, especially with the all-important and vulnerable front teeth. Modern high temperature metals and porcelain are strong, so much so that the bridge may hold but the supporting teeth crumple. A partial denture, however, can be removed and the gap then incorporated in the mouthguard. Theoretically guards can be carefully fitted around fixed orthodontic appliances but that is surely stretching safe school sport to the limit.

REFERENCES:
Murdoch R. A. F., FRCS Edinburgh, Personal communication, 1987.
Peet B. E., MDS Sydney, Personal communication, 1987.

10. Skin

The skin is in an unlucky position. It is the first part of the body to be attacked, damaged, bitten, infected, burned and frozen. It invariably needs some first-aid, which is essentially what this chapter is about.

Abrasions

With an abrasion the skin is not broken but burned or gouged to a variable depth by friction from grass, gravel, or synthetic surfaces. The affected area is best cleaned with soap and water and then covered with a non-adherent dressing and a firm bandage to stop further friction. Over bone, abrasions can really sting! Antiseptic solutions are not needed as an intact skin is not vulnerable to infection. For large areas a smooth synthetic skin film is best. Sometimes particles are embedded in the area during a slide and if left may become fixed to give a tattoo-like discoloration; it is painful but the particles or granules can be removed with a soft nail brush.

Lacerations

The skin is split and the fatty layer is exposed. If the scalp is split it should be stitched, because here the skin is stretched across the skull under some tension and the edges pout; significant arteries and veins may also have been torn across and if they bleed briskly apply pressure on each side of the wound by pressing the fingertips parallel to the edges for five minutes by the clock. The blood clotting time is four minutes and you will be surprised how long that is when you are timing it. Face wounds heal quickly and plastic surgeons have long said that the fewer the stitches used the neater the scar. In a few months it may be almost invisible. A split lip in which only the mucous membrane has been cut on the teeth does not need stitches, but a torn lip must be properly stitched and the vermilion line of skin–mucous membrane junction carefully realigned.

If the cut runs across the direction of underlying limb muscle fibres, the edges will gape and must be stitched; where the cut is parallel to the muscles, for example down the leg, butterfly skin plasters will keep the edges easily together. Around the wrist or ankle shallow-running flat tendons may have been cut as well, so proper medical examination is needed. The same applies to deep cuts of the hand or foot. Jagged or deeply penetrating wounds, or wounds with foreign material, dirt etc., may have to be cleaned, drained, and carefully stitched under anaesthesia, so resist the temptation to give the victim even a warm drink on the way to hospital.

Much sport is played on grass areas and soil over which animals have long wandered, shedding the tetanus spores that can so easily infect wounds. Tetanus, though now rare, is a horrible disease and all children should be routinely immunised against it (along with their whooping cough and diptheria shots) early in life. If they do suffer wounds later they will be protected although it is usual then to boost their resistance with a quick injection of human tetanus immunoglobulin.

Blisters

They can be drained of fluid by pricking the edge with a cleaned needle, and then covered with a non-adhesive dressing. Leave the deflated top skin on as a protective layer until the red base has dried. This usually takes a few days. If the cause has not been from friction, contact chemical dermatitis must be suspected and all new equipment checked. Synthetic materials are often impregnated with organic dyes. Fibreglass is a tricky cause of dermatitis. Like Marco Polo it travels and has been traced from hockey stick filings into clothes, thence to washing machines, and then to other clothes.

Calluses

These thickened skin layers build up over bone pressure points. Essentially harmless they develop to protect deeper layers from chronic injury so look carefully to see what is causing them. They can be pared back with a sharp thin razor blade. Alternatively a paint of 5% salicylic acid in flexible collodion, obtained at the chemist, can be left on overnight to soften them.

Corns

These rounded calluses have a thick central core which forms a reversed apex as it gets pushed back down through the centre. This apex finally impinges on a deep nerve receptor and causes pain. Watch how an expert podiatrist deals with corns before trying anything yourself. Don't dig at them! For both corns and calluses the cause of the chronic friction must be removed.

Infections

Pimples are simple, but boils are painful tense collections of staphylococcal pus. Sport is impossible with a boil. Infected toenails or so-called ingrown nails are best dealt with by minor surgery. Nearly always it is a puncture of the skin by scissor points or the sharp edges of badly cut nails that lets the infection in.

Acne cannot be eliminated entirely in pubertal males and advice is needed before using sun blockout creams. It is very easy for the infection to spread or be made worse by careless hygiene or stained clothes. It must be minimised by following the doctor's orders in a disciplined way and ask especially whether the blackheads should be squeezed out or not.

Tinea pedis (athlete's foot), and tinea cruris (athlete's groin), are fungal infections that are easily cured, but they can be respread by swapping socks or towels. Plantar (sole) warts also result from a virus picked up from socks and floors. The latter should be sterilised, and in fact someone must swab out both the floors and the showers with dilute formalin solution.

Simple warts are due to a virus and hence are 'caught' by contact. Tom Sawyer had his 'ole Mississippi magic cure but actually they can disappear spontaneously. If big or if picked at so that they bleed they need proper medical removal.

Herpes simplex or cold sores are contagious and a recurrent pest; the vesicles (sores) contain the virus. Body contact sports must not be allowed when vesicles are present. The risk is that fluid may squirt into someone's eye and cause scars on the cornea, and from there it can be massaged into the general circulation, thence to lodge in joints; viral arthritis is not friendly.

Head and body lice and scabies are small living parasites causing an itchy distinctive skin rash; again, swapped clothes, towels and head gear are the spreading agents. The original source must be found and treatment supervised to make sure that proper hygiene is thereafter maintained.

Bites and Stings

Younger and smaller children have to be watched in areas where danger is known to lurk. They are prone to pick up ants and spiders and they must not be allowed to stray into thickets or tall grass in snake country; because of their small size venom doses have more chance of being lethal.

Bee and wasp stings are actually ingenious narrow tubes stuck into the skin; the 'venom' is in a muscular sac on top, which contracts to squirt the stuff in. So don't squeeze that sac between finger and thumb to pull the sting out. Topple it out by running the finger nail along the skin in the sting-skin acute angle. If you have fine tweezers grasp the sting at skin level. Ask youngsters whether they have been stung before, because in the odd case a second sting causes an allergic reaction with giant urticaria (large fluid-filled weals) on the skin, and in the very rare person, fluid secretion into the lung as well. In that event breathing is frothy and there is a real emergency. Full anaphylactic shock with itchy eyes, flushing, and fainting, can develop within fifteen minutes and will need a subcutaneous injection of adrenalin 1 in 1000 strength. First-aid kits should contain ephedrine or adrenalin type drugs for temporary treatment on the way to hospital.

Snakes? The rest of the world may not be aware of it but Australian snakes are the most poisonous in the world. The taipan, the mulga (formerly called the king brown), the eastern brown, the eastern tiger, the black, the copperhead, the death adder, and a few others, are more lethal to adults than the Indian cobra and the American rattlesnake, and even more so to small children. They haunt coastal recreational areas where their natural prey abounds, rats, frogs, cane toads, lizards, rabbits and bandicoots, and can invade houses or sheds in search of rats or water. Where you see prey, think of snakes and do not let children roam in the bush without socks and shoes. If you see a snake it is more likely to be venomous than not. Colourful sea snakes in tropical water are even more nasty as they are positively attracted to another swimming creature.

The Commonwealth Serum Laboratories in Melbourne now make anti-venom against nearly all snakes and the funnel web spider. Supplies are also kept at Sydney's Taronga Park Zoo (telephone 02-969-8949) and the Royal Melbourne Hospital (telephone 03-347-7111).

If you live or exercise in snake territory get from your local hospital *exact* instructions on what they would want you to do by way of first-aid, torniquets, and transport in case of snakebite. (Basic ideas vary, and some measures are debatable.) Time is very important. Do not waste it, and have someone telephone ahead to the hospital to give them time to prepare and to check their supply of anti-venom. The mortality now in victims brought in quickly for treatment is almost nil. Above all, teach youngsters about snakes, where not to roam in search of lost balls, where snakes like to sun themselves, and how to give them plenty of room to move away if met accidentally. They must be told not to move towards them.

Spiders? Likewise. Regrettably many a child has picked up a spider out of curiosity and it is now clear that a lot more of our spiders are poisonous than previously thought—not just the funnel web and redback. A dash of colour is a warning of danger. Probably the urban housing spread is clearing bush where they had hidden unnoticed for 200 years. If the culprit can be killed for identification without wasting time, well and good.

Removal of ticks needs tricks, as with bee stings. The head sucks in blood and regurgitates infected saliva, so that the parasite must be enticed to release its hold and back out alive. People from infested areas know how to irritate the body with hot needles or spirits etc. If the head is left in it may have to be cut out under local anaesthetic. Cross country runners can apply suitable repellant against ticks, and other small beasties, but do not be too liberal with sprays. They can set up allergic reactions, especially in the elbow where sweat runs back and pools.

Sunburn

Anglo-Saxon skin has had to learn to live with ultraviolet rays. It is still difficult to convince teenagers that excessive exposure to the sun causes atrophy (loss of tone) of the elastic layer deep in the skin and hence much wrinkling in later life. Likewise they cannot appreciate that absorption of excess ultraviolet energy is a proven cause of malignant change (cancer) in black moles on the limbs and trunk. But it is so. In the short northern hemisphere summers these long-term factors can be almost ignored, but in the tropics or subtropics, never. Suntan is nature's protective layer and should be allowed slowly to develop by judicious exposure (avoid the hot midday sun) and protection in early summer. Remember that ultraviolet rays are reflected under hats and umbrellas and penetrate the gaps in thin woven cloth. The classic, although usually not suspected, high risk situation is a cloudy, windy day on sand or at high altitudes on snow. Very good chemical ultraviolet blocking creams of varying grades are a big improvement on the old lotions. Mild sunburn needs calamine lotion, soothing anti-histamine creams, or the magic juice of the aloe vera cactus. Severe blistering and a lesser form called prickly heat, which is sweat trapped under cornified skin, need hospital nursing like any extensive burn.

Heat Stroke

The dangers of this in tropical and subtropical climates can never be overemphasised. It is so easily prevented, and it must be. Children do not handle heat build-up as well as adults and if they are seen to be pink, sweaty, hot, and flustered, they must be made to stop what they are doing and must be cooled down. Mothers know the old adage about babies with convulsions: hold them in a cold bath. The convulsion is caused by a fever and the bath smartly drops the temperature. It is the same with bigger babies. If heat-distressed they have to be put in water or under the hose.

In severe climates athletes should be fully hydrated before beginning to train or compete, and no event should go beyond thirty minutes. In the enforced rest cold tap water must be drunk; in short events salt solutions are actually not a good idea until after pure fluid replacement.

The situation is different in triathlons and the allied iron man events that teenagers are growing fond of. There is a definite loss of sodium (salt) as the event time lengthens since sweat is produced at a steady 1.5 litres per hour containing 2 gms of salt. This must be replaced by weak salt drinks, especially during the run and cycle legs.

11. Problems Pertaining Especially to Girls

Girls don't exist, don't you know. Whitehall and Capitol Hill have officially abolished them with Anti-Discrimination and Equal Opportunity laws. There is no biological contradiction here; up to the age of puberty all children, male and female, are the same, athletically speaking. After puberty, however, nature follows its own inexorable inelectable rules and will not be denied its influence on structure and function and hence on performance.

Menstruation usually begins between ten and sixteen years, with thirteen years being in most Western countries the average. This average was higher at the beginning of the twentieth century and has dropped slowly until over the last ten years it seems to have stabilised. The cause of this decline is probably related to socio-economic factors and, specifically, to a higher food intake. Menstruation patterns naturally vary but the usual thing is for the breasts to appear a little ahead of the growth spurt, and then for the pubic followed by the armpit hair to develop, and then the menarche (the onset of menstruation). It is usual for the fast increase of height to have peaked and be on the wane before the menarche. This march to maturity may take anything from two to six or more years to complete. There will always be the problem that matching sports teams by chronological age throws together players with different levels of maturity and aggression, giving some a temporary advantage. Full adult shape is reached only after some years of influence by the hormones produced during the menstrual cycle.

The early periods can be heavy and erratic since regular predictable menstruation depends on regular ovulation, which is itself not established for up to two to four years after the menarche, but when it is, menstrual pain is a possibility. This, along with utterly normal hormone-influenced fluctuations in mood, can easily affect athletic performance.

Evidence is accumulating in medical literature to indicate that intense physical activity, initiated before the menarche, tends to delay its onset, and further, that girls thus affected are more prone to menstrual problems during later athletic life. Competitive long distance runners are obvious candidates for this problem but it has been noted after strenuous efforts in other sports such as tennis, rowing, volleyball and gymnastics. It has even been reported in a class of ballet dancers where the menarchal mean age was fifteen years, compared with twelve years in a matched age control group. If there is a common identifiable link in these diverse activities it seems at the moment to be a severe physical energy drain in pre-adolescence, reflected in the fact that, despite a high calorie intake, (that is they eat a lot!) the body weight remains low for height and age. Even more significantly, these athletes have a reduced amount of body fat, 10% or less, compared with 20% or more in average athletic girls.

This fat factor can be estimated fairly well from skin fold thicknesses, measured with callipers at such sites as the shoulder blade, thigh and lower abdomen. Parents can test this approximately by pinching up the skin fold between forefinger and thumb; they should also weigh the keen athlete regularly because continuing weight loss during training is a danger sign. It must be emphasised, however, that this weight loss is only relevant in intensely motivated and achieving athletes, not in the cheery pupil running off 'puppy fat'. In fact it is the very intensity and high motivation of budding ballet hopefuls to train and retain body shape, which provides a useful benchmark for investigators of this problem.

The physiological mechanism causing delayed menarche is not yet fully understood. Nor has it yet been clarified in a second problem group, namely, women in their late teens (and indeed mature women) who were previously menstruating regularly, and then experienced reduced blood flow, erratic menstrual cycles, and even amenorrhoea (complete loss of periods) under conditions of endurance running. Retrospective studies of such groups often reveal a past history of a late menarche and a tendency to irregular periods. Much evidence is accumulating about hormone levels and their fluctuations in such cases and it seems from the figures that athletic amenorrhoea is in some vital way different from hypothalamic amenorrhoea. This latter term applies to young women who lose their periods abruptly under circumstances of social or emotional stress and mental shock, such as war, death of a parent, or enrolment in organisations (for example, the army), where there is a dramatic change in lifestyle. It is called 'hypothalamic' because the hypothalamus is that portion of the brain which acts directly on the pituitary gland and causes it to produce hormone changes. Continuing observations may eventually show that there are indeed two mechanisms operating, one associated with technical sports and their intense mental preparation, and another associated with endurance sports that combine stress and high energy expenditure. (A newly discovered opium-like brain chemical, endorphin, is thought to be linked to the latter.)

Parents' concern is naturally: 'Will all this cause later infertility or sterility?' Actually there are two medical problems in the situations outlined above. First, in delayed puberty, will the periods ever come? Full hormone studies and clinical examination are needed to establish whether the periods are truly delayed, or absent from a definite congenital cause. Second, in the older teenager who develops scanty or absent periods, can the trend be arrested or reversed? Well, studies have shown that rowers, for example, regain their periods in the off-season, and that injured ballet dancers who cannot train resume menstruation. These favourable results can occur even if body weight is not regained.

As to proven fertility, one Scandinavian follow-up of young swimmers over a ten-year span showed that they had 'normal' fertility. However, other work has suggested that amenorrhoeic athletes do subsequently have a lower overall pregnancy rate, but it is possible that this may represent nothing more than deliberate choice. What is undeniable is that girls who do not menstruate regularly are not ovulating regularly and therefore will have reduced fertility for as long as the problem remains. Apart from spontaneous cure on cessation of strenuous endeavour, there now are powerful drugs and hormones available for quite specific treatment after proper hormone analysis. It would seem then that very talented and dedicated athletes need have no fear over the long term, but they owe it to themselves to have full, regular, physical checkups and to keep proper records for future reference.

Athletic amenorrhoea is associated with slight bone loss, most noticeable in the square bones, such as the vertebrae and the small bones of the wrist and foot. Thus gymnasts, ballet dancers, pole vaulters and long distance runners would be at particular risk of stress fractures in those bones and would be advised to have their bone density measured by special X-ray techniques.

Another rare problem is the girl who is tall for her age group, say over 170 cm at age eleven or twelve. This applies particularly if she is not yet menstruating. Such a girl will grow to 180 cm at least; her bone epiphyses are active, prone to suffer traction injuries, and will close late (Chapter 4, p. 16). Handy though these girls may be for school basketball teams, the tendency now is to stop epiphyseal growth by hormone treatment before an ungainly and socially excessive height is attained.

In the classic post puberty female shape there are design features which reduce performance in some sports or more readily produce physical stress in some girls when high achievement is doggedly pursued. A wider pelvis and tilt of the lower back affects the stride, and the thigh-leg angle at the knee joint becomes, relatively, a mild genu valgum (knock knee) which, theoretically at least, increases the possibility of chondromalacia patella disease (p. 19). The wider angle of the elbow limits throwing power. Slender ankles, a smaller rib cage, a longer neck and more delicate bones in general, but especially the facial and cranial bones, mean a greater vulnerability to injury. Compared to boys, the upper body development is also relatively less, and a smaller muscle mass and thicker body fat layer mean less absolute strength and less strength relative to body weight.

There are some benefits. For instance, not only is there a reduced total muscle mass but its composition differs from that of the average male. Female muscle has more of the pale-type fibres that contract rapidly and less of the red fibres that have a slower but stronger and more enduring contraction power. This factor gives more joint flexibility and the ability to perform more graceful, fine movements. The thicker subcutaneous fat layer provides better heat insulation and flotation for swimming.

In general, it can be said that variations and exceptions to the basic design are so many in individual female athletes that there is no medical reason to restrict their initial participation in any sport. In fact, the very opposite. Published medical articles on chronic backache and debility after the strains of childbearing and childcaring blame, as the major factor, weak abdominal muscles and lack of basic strength in the lower back, traceable to an inactive childhood and consequent poor physical development. It would therefore seem vital for girls' schools to provide opportunity and encouragement for *all* pupils actively to participate in games, sports and exercises. The more varied the exercise and the exertion the better.

Research into the functional differences (if any) between males and females is only just beginning. Whether there are real differences in aerobic and anaerobic metabolism, oxygen utilisation capacity, or sweating rates, to name but three factors, is doubtful. It is, however, clear that training will improve all measurements, exactly as it does in males. Biological responses to muscle training and body building are qualitatively the same in both sexes, but where performance depends less on skill than on mass and power, then it is impossible for the female to match the male in absolute terms. A very interesting report from the

West Point military academy in the United States in 1979 showed that the male recruits functioned at a lower level of demand on total physical capacity to meet standards, whilst the females, as a group, had to perform nearer to their maximal physical output to meet the same physical training standards. As a result, they had ten times the incidence of stress fractures in the leg, and three times the incidence of medical conditions needing hospital admission, both measures of the exhaustion their efforts produced. It was the same at Annapolis but the Navy felt that one factor was that the female midshippersons were arriving at the base in a less overall fit state than the male midshippersons.

The menstrual cycle, with its rhythmic changes in oestrogen and progesterone levels, undoubtedly affects mood and performance. Again, more research must be done to determine whether the performance is affected entirely by the mood, or whether both are due, quite separately, to effects on biochemical functions. Whichever it is, the result is a fall-off in performance in the premenstrual week with a return to normal during the period, and with possibly the best performance recorded just postmenstrually. It is still uncertain whether this menstrual effect can be overcome by a higher level of training, but if menstruation is considered a possible hindrance to a superb athlete for a really special event, then it is better for hormones to be used to bring on a period early rather than to delay it. Unquestionably, routine high school sports do not justify such interference, and it is only commonsense not to expect girls with heavy periods (always possible in the early years) to do their best on those days.

Menstrual pads are obviously restrictive. The alternative is for intravaginal tampons to be worn. There are just two problems. As stated above, the periods in the early years can be heavy, and if this flow is obstructed the blood can spill back through the Fallopian tubes into the abdominal cavity, causing immediate abdominal pain, and if the practice is repeated, it can even sometimes initiate infection and a disease known as endometriosis. Second, and very fundamental, is the obvious fact that the tampon cannot be inserted if the hymen is intact. Manufacturers' advertisements are designed to tempt you to think otherwise. Surely nobody, but nobody, would recommend that the hymen be damaged in young girls just for convenience in sport. Where it does happen, the culprits are often senior girls who gang up on a junior and 'see to it' that the tampon is inserted. The benefit to team performance is the usual excuse given. Such an abominable attitude must be detected, condemned and prevented.

Sports bras need to be chosen with care, with attention being paid to support, freedom from metal or seams that rub, ease of washing, and ventilation. Not all are suitable. To prevent tiresome breast movement some girls may even have to have binding over the bra. Blows from a ball or a stick never, repeat never, cause cancer; the adolescent breast is mostly fat with minimal real breast tissue, so that, at worst, harmless patches of lumpy dead tissue may form after injury. However (and this applies to women at any age) an injury may draw attention to a lump already there, so a medical examination should always be carried out. For martial arts specially designed rib guards should be worn to protect the breasts from unnecessary blows.

It is often forgotten, too, by coaches, that change of body shape at puberty alters the mechanical moments of inertia and the centre of gravity for that person, and the muscle strength needed for familiar movements. Performance can change despite assiduous training and this can prove frustrating to aspiring athletes. It has been said that certain countries, ever keen to add to their gymnastic successes, halt puberty for several months to prevent such changes, but the hormone doses would have to be very large.

Statistics at the moment do not give a reliable guide as to whether girls really are more vulnerable than boys to injury in certain sports. There are so many variables it may take years to determine true trends. For example, a survey in San Francisco showed that 70% of all track injuries in girls occurred in events of 400 metres or less; for boys the figure was only 30%, but this does not prove that it is safer for girls to concentrate on long distance events. Another study in Oklahoma concentrating on eight non-contact sports, showed overall rates of injury per 1000 players in each sex to be roughly the same and with a similar range of injury. However the girls did have a significantly greater frequency of knee injury than the boys, and a significantly greater percentage of major ankle injury. There was a similar finding in an earlier study of ski injuries at Vail, Colorado, where the knee strain rate for female skiers was twice that of the males, the highest risk group being that of young inexperienced females, which suggests that in this sport, at least, it would be worthwhile insisting that young girls precondition and strengthen the knee muscles. Again, in some sports in which girls predominate, for example gymnastics, statistics naturally do show an unfavourable bias in their direction. For other sports the statistics are not so clear; in fact they seem to be changing as more and more girls enter sports and receive better training and better advice on muscle conditioning.

By way of illustration, when Jesse Owens' world record for

the 100 metres stood at 10.2 seconds in 1936, Stella Walshe's women's record was 11.7 seconds, a track win to Jesse by 15 metres. Using mid 1980 records the difference between their modern counterparts has now narrowed to about 9 metres. Sport physiologists take this as practical proof that, despite the inevitable improvement in female performance with opportunity and modern training methods, they can never expect to catch up with the muscle mass capability of males.

Precise measurements by researchers at the Australian Institute of Sport, Canberra, the Philip Institute of Technology, Bundoora in Victoria, and the Australian Coaching Council, Canberra, have concluded that the structural and functional differences they found between boys and girls at around twelve years were inherent, and existed whether the groups were well trained or untrained. Their opinion is that the sexes are not sufficiently well matched in agility and cardio-vascular endurance to avoid disadvantage to the girls when there is co-competition in, for example, swimming, middle and long distance track and field, ball games, and indeed in all sports where the above two qualities are important factors in overall fitness.

Fortunately school athletes can ignore the physiological, psychological, and philosophical arguments about ultimate performance and just get on with enjoying their sport in the certain knowledge that a good schoolgirl athlete is good in her own right, and as capable of enjoying sport and reaching a high standard as any schoolboy.

Note that girl athletes about to enter any form of strenuous training should have a blood count and estimation of their iron reserves to warn of possible anaemia.

Finally, a footnote. There seems to be a genetic factor predisposing the female foot to hallux valgus, that is a lateral deviation of the big toe with bunion formation and a squeezing up of the second toe. Painful blisters and calluses form at these abnormal pressure points. Formerly blamed on pointed shoes, high heels, or ballet training in the young, it is now seen as an inherited tendency, although the other factors will no doubt aggravate it. The condition gradually limits activity and causes arthritis in the big toe joints in later life. It is advisable to think about corrective surgery early in life. The young recover from surgery better and certainly more quickly than the old and many years of discomfort can be avoided.

REFERENCE:
Telford R. D. et. al. Anthropometric, physiological and performance characteristics of twelve-year-old boys and girls: should they co-compete? *The Australian Journal of Science and Medicine in Sport* 1986; December.

12. Joint by Joint

Sport is all movement and movement is only possible through joints; perhaps we should say, through joint action, because the muscles have to act in concert with the bones which form the joint. Many sports injuries occur around joints or in muscles, either by the sudden strain of muscle power, by the accumulating stress of repetitive action, or by inadvertent leverage that the bones and joints are not designed to take. Therefore, to understand the design of a joint is to understand, in principle, where and why and how breakdowns and injuries occur. An unstable joint is a source of much future trouble, and sports medicine has been the stimulus to enormous advances in bone and joint surgery because of the demands of tiptop athletes for precise diagnosis and speedy recovery.

Bone is crystalline and would fragment with friction (in fact it does in arthritis), so where bones meet to move on one another their ends are coated with a thick, shiny, somewhat flexible gristle, the articular (joint) cartilage, which is nourished and kept in perfect condition by a fluid bathing the joint cavity. Called synovial fluid, this fluid is secreted by the synovial membrane (a lining) on the inner surface of the fibrous joint capsule (the capsule which surrounds the joint). After injury to the joint, extra fluid is secreted, visibly swelling the joint, and this state is known as traumatic synovitis. Until this settles the joint is 'stiff' and examination cannot easily tell what real damage it has suffered. The capsule, which completely encloses the joint, is often thickened along the lines of most severe strain and such formations are dignified with special anatomical names. In the final moment of joint strain however, it is the strong surrounding muscle groups or tendons that protect against disruption, and in trained athletes the muscles have learned to tense and be 'on guard' before the strain arrives.

The perfect example is in the arch of the foot. A very strong ligament, the spring ligament, unites the under surfaces of the important midfoot joint where forefoot rotation occurs, but this ligament would be inexorably flattened to the floor if it were not for the long tendon of the deep calf muscle, the tibialis posterior, that runs deliberately and directly underneath the ligament on

60 CHILDREN'S SPORTS INJURIES

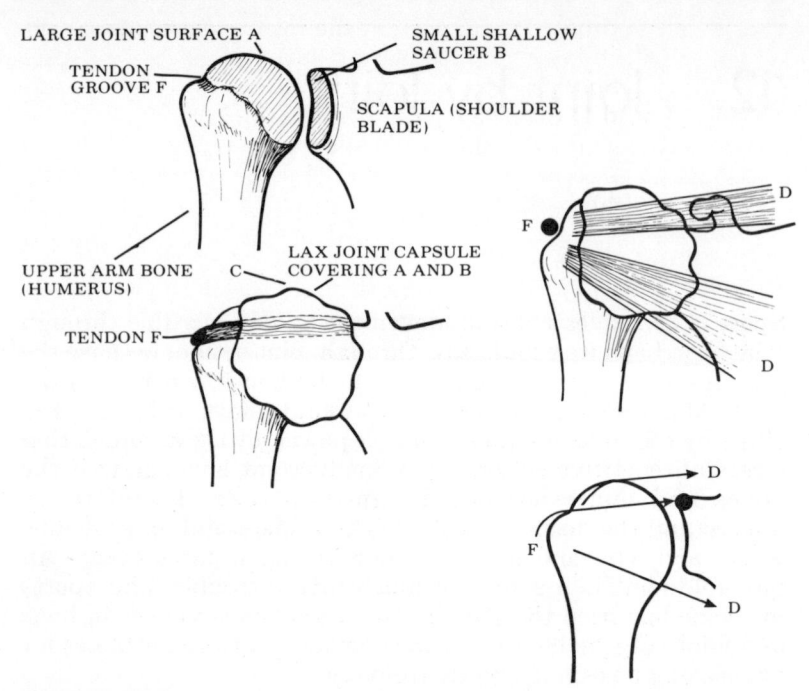

Diagram 12-1
Shoulder joint. Nature's design for mobility at the expense of strength. The joint capsule has no tensile strength.
Diagram 12-2
Shoulder joint. Closely attached muscles provide the stability.

its way to a nearby insertion, so that when the muscle contracts the arch is hoisted up.

The Shoulder

The shoulder is designed to allow free, wide, circular movements by having the top of the humerus (upper arm bone), which is a large circular head, spin in the glenoid fossa, which is a small shallow saucer. In diagrams 12-1, 12-2 and 12-3 note:

a. The very big articular surface (coated by cartilage) on the humerus.
b. The glenoid fossa, the relatively small articular surface of the scapula.
c. The lax joint capsule; if it were not so, rotation could not occur.

d. The approximate line of pull by the intimate muscles of the joints, which keep the articulating surfaces in close contact. Since the muscle fibres and the fibrous capsule blend somewhat, C and D together constitute the rotator cuff.
e. The small forward tilt of the plane of the glenoid fossa, which helps to make anterior (front) dislocation much more common than posterior (rear).
f. The groove in the humerus for the pencil-like tendon of the long head of the biceps muscle. This tendon springs from just above the glenoid fossa and runs across the top of the joint, actually in the joint cavity. This special design supplements the rotator cuff in providing joint stability.

A glance at the diagrams shows why strong sudden force can 'pop', that is dislocate the joint. The head of the humerus just slides off, tearing the rotator cuff (diagram 12–3). Athletes accept that this means time off, but do not always appreciate that this time must be set by the orthopaedic surgeon, and not by the team manager or the athlete's impatience, otherwise the cuff will not properly heal. It could remain weak, be further stretched, strained, or shredded by early return to training, and recurrent dislocation is then a possibility. If that happens then the only remedy is surgery. Although dislocation is reasonably common in adolescents, cuff tear is not, but other forms of pain and weakness caused by tendinitis, bursitis, focal haemorrhage, muscle fibre tears, or capsule stretch, all of which come under the heading 'strain', indicate that a significant problem, given time and repetitive abuse, will develop.

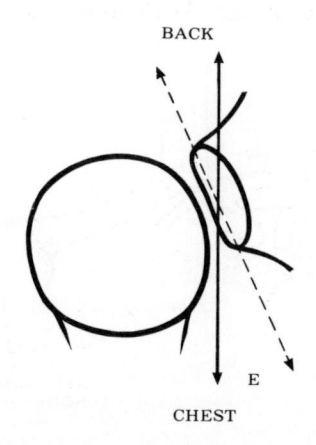

Diagram 12–3
Top view of shoulder joint. Note the forward angle of inclination (E) that permits easy forward dislocation.

In terms of precise infinitely variable movements, the rotator cuff is a beautiful design, but the work asked of it by our remote ancestors, occasionally hurling spears for food, was quite different from the demands now made on it hour after hour by athletic training. The miracle is not that rotator cuff damage occurs, but that it does not occur more often. In adolescents the plea must be repeated: please give the shoulder joint time to heal after injury! In rehabilitation the first essential is to restore mobility, gradually extending the limits of pain-free activity; strengthening exercises come second.

Finally, in describing shoulder mechanics, the first 120° of arm raising is effected by the humeral head rotating in the glenoid fossa. That is the limit of the ball and socket movement; for the arm to rise vertically the scapula has to tilt the extra 60°, which it does by the action of strong trunk muscles attached to its margins, whilst keeping the humerus steady with the rotator cuff muscles. This is why trunk muscles can get sore from jerky arm movements, and vice versa, why trunk muscle injury hampers throwing.

Acromio-Clavicular Joint

The arm is held to the trunk by muscles, tendons, and ligaments. It does not join directly but uses the clavicle or collar bone as a prop ('C' in diagram 12-4). The clavicle is itself suspended by muscles stretched between its upper surface and the base of the skull and the neck vertebrae. At its inner end, where it meets the

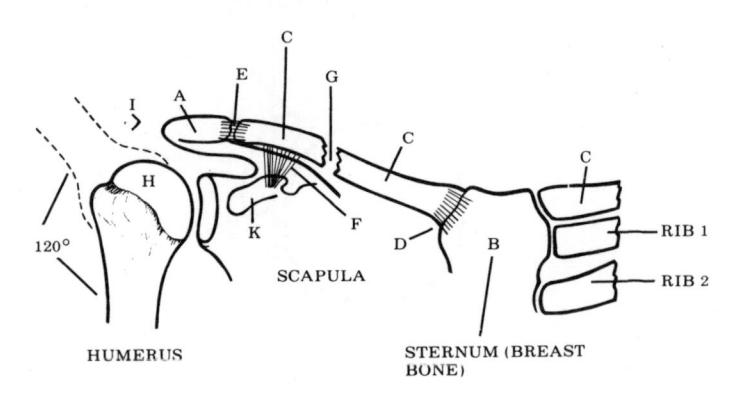

Diagram 12-4
The clavicle (collar bone) and the joints at either end.

sternum or breast bone (B), the clavicle forms a springy junction called the sterno-clavicular joint (D). At its outer end the clavicle forms the acromio-clavicular joint (E) by abutting on the acromion process (A), an outgrowth of bone felt at the top of the shoulder, which leaps from the back of the scapula and arches forwards over the shoulder joint, thus protecting the joint above as well as serving as a platform for muscle attachments. There is a second protuberance that can be vaguely felt, an anterior (frontal) knob on the scapula, the coracoid process (K), to which the clavicle is firmly tied by strong coracoclavicular ligaments (F). The gap between A and H is limited and as the arm is raised from the side the rotator cuff muscles get closer and closer to the edge of the acromion process; at about 120° they meet (point I), thus stopping further movement of the shoulder joint, and forcing further arm raising to occur only by tilting the scapula. Where there is impingement on these bone edges, inflammation and irritation of the squeezed muscles occur, a state known as the impingement syndrome. This can become a problem in all arm sports on land or water and it must be suspected when there is weakness ('I've lost my fastball'), pain in overarm action, aching after training, or pain at night due to inflammatory swelling.

Of all the possible injuries from a fall onto the outstretched palm, the most likely and therefore possibly the most common injury in sport, is dislocation of the acromio-clavicular joint (E) or the stage just short of that, subluxation, where the capsule is stretched and thereafter fails to keep the bones in cohesion. When the whole body weight is taken on the acromio-clavicular sternal prop, rupture of the coraco-clavicular ligaments (F), fracture of the clavicle (G), dislocation of the sterno-clavicular joint (D), or damage to the growing epiphysis of the head of the humerus (H), can also occur singly or in any combination.

There are thus many, many causes for a painful stiff shoulder, all lumped under the heading 'frozen shoulder', a term in use since 1934 but one that is descriptive rather than diagnostic.

The Elbow

The inner two thirds of the elbow is a simple hinge joint between the lower end of the humerus (upper arm bone) and the upper end of the ulna (inner forearm bone), whose topmost part is the point of the elbow. The lateral (outer) one third of the hinge is occupied by the concave, disc-shaped head of the radius (the outer forearm bone; diagram 12-5). The concave upper

64 CHILDREN'S SPORTS INJURIES

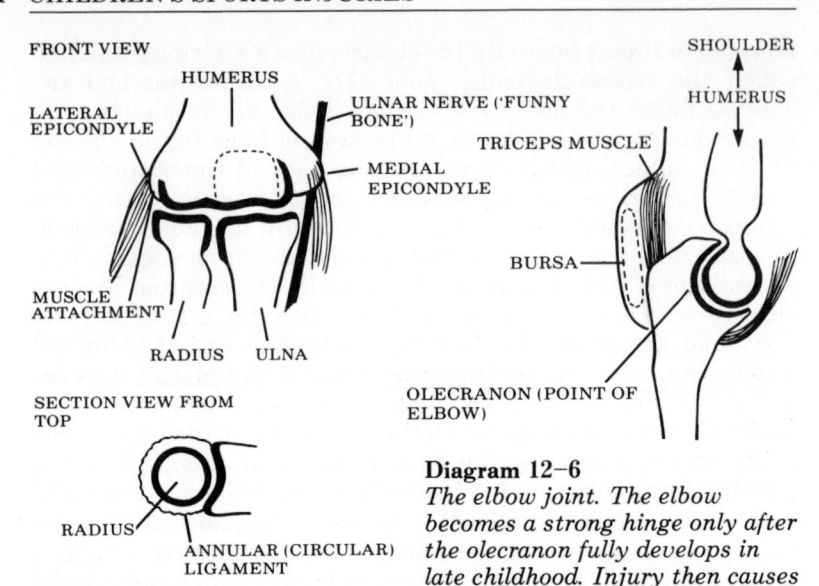

Diagram 12-5
Elbow joint. Note the basic hinge, and the circular radius kept in position by its annular ligament. Note also the large areas of articular cartilage in this mechanism.

Diagram 12-6
The elbow joint. The elbow becomes a strong hinge only after the olecranon fully develops in late childhood. Injury then causes fracture rather than dislocation.

surface of the radial head and its thick circular rim allow it to move simultaneously in two planes; it hinges with the ulna on the humerus, and at the same time it is able to rotate against the side of the ulna to create prone (palm facing back) and supine (palm facing forwards) positions of the hand.

Add to that the brachial artery running in front across the joint, and the ulnar nerve (the funny bone) running behind the inner side, and one can see that fracture, fracture-dislocation, or separation of any of the seven adolescent bone growth centres (p. 16), or a mixture of all three, could be a very complicated affair. Because the olecranon (back of the ulna) or point of the elbow (diagram 12-6), only develops into a deep socket in the years between nine and seventeen, dislocation occurs more easily in early childhood.

On either side of the hinge, epicondyles (bone projections) develop on the lower end of the humerus for attachment of the muscles that move the elbow and wrist (diagram 12-5). The larger and sharper medial epicondyle (the one which the ulnar nerve runs behind) is the origin of the flexor muscles which are torn in golf, and the chunkier lateral epicondyle is the source of the extensor muscles which are affected in tennis. These two injuries are not problems of the joint. Between the bony point

JOINT BY JOINT 65

of the elbow and the skin lies a bursa (lubricating sac) filled with a film of fluid to save the skin from damage as it slides over the moving bone. A sac inflamed and swollen with fluid is described as 'bursitis' and in this joint it is called olecranon bursitis.

The Wrist

For the wrist, the roles of the radius (outer forearm bone) and ulna (inner forearm bone) are reversed at their lower ends. The ulna narrows to a rounded peg, around which rotates the expanded head of the radius that carries the whole hand with it by its articulation with two of the wrist bones, mainly the scaphoid bone (diagram 12−7). The wrist has to be mobile, flexible, and strong, all of which it achieves through eight small bones, bound closely together and yet with each moving slightly, so that in sum considerable forward, backward and lateral bending is possible. A dense feltwork of interconnecting ligaments as well as long tendons running to the palm and fingers make for a strong structure, so strong that only considerable force will dislocate individual bones. Each tendon has its investing synovial (lubricating) sheath to smooth its movements; damage to this sheath by overuse or infection is the familiar tenosynovitis.

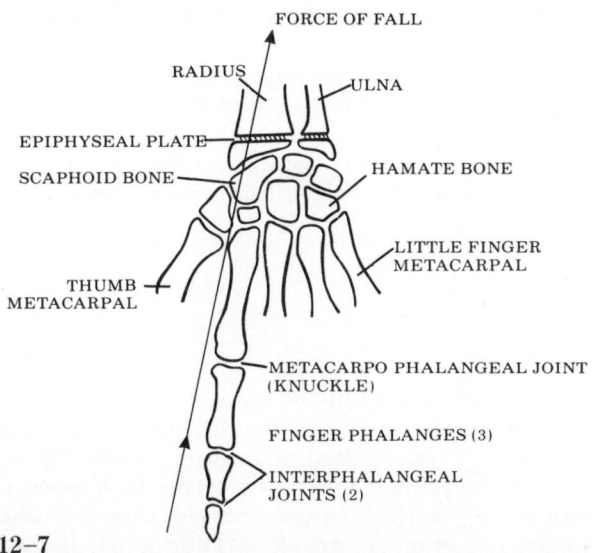

Diagram 12–7
Wrist and hand.

A fall onto the hand is taken by the butt end of the palm so that the thrust goes straight through the scaphoid bone to the lower end of the radius. Either or both may fracture. In adolescents the lower end of the radius is its growing end and hence the growth epiphysis (p. 17) can be crushed or displaced (diagram 12–7). The wrist bones are actually in the hand below the wrist crease and a sharp blow or repetitive blows to the area can fracture any of them but especially the scaphoid bone. These fractures are still only being diagnosed some time after the injury because wrist pain is so easily passed off as 'just a bit of a sprain', or as tenosynovitis.

The Hand

Between the wrist and the tip of each finger are four bones and three small hinge joints. First, in the palm, is the long thin metacarpal bone whose distal (lower) end is the knuckle, then follow the phalanges (three small finger bones) of diminishing length to give the fingers their ability to form shapes of infinite variety (diagram 12–7). As well as the long tendons running across the wrist right to the fingertips, the palm metacarpal bones are the origin of small muscles that run into the fingers where delicate attachments allow a range of fine movements. If a hand is in plaster for any time it is vital for the fingers continually to be exercised so that these small muscles do not atrophy (shrink). The whole hand is another of nature's brilliant designs. A fracture anywhere from the knuckle to the fingertip is likely to be complicated by angulations from the pull of the tendons. The thumb has only two phalanges but it has an extra set of small muscles in the ball of the thumb for all its special movements. Injury to this vital member must be expertly managed.

The Hip

The ball and socket joint of the hip is very strong when the cup is fully deepened by fusion of the growth centres at about the time of puberty; before then dislocation of the hip is easier to achieve and the perfect position for this to happen is when a child sits in a car with the knees crossed, that is with the femur (thighbone) flexed on the trunk and adducted. If the knee hits the dashboard in an accident the head of the femur is forced out of the socket. A bad landing in gymnastics can also produce this effect. The joint is otherwise hard to dislocate in sport.

Two special conditions of childhood, not due to sport but often noticed because of a sore hip and a limp following exercise, are related to the epiphysis (p. 16) of the head of the femur. In the first the growth centre is deformed by osteochondritis (Perthes' disease, p. 19), in the second (adolescent coxa vara) the centre slips from its normal position atop the neck of the femur, and the foot turns ever so slowly outwards.

Transient synovitis particularly affects five- to seven-year-old boys. It is associated with sore throat or bronchitis so it may be due to bacteria in the blood and not injury; sport will aggravate it.

The lesson is that if a child complains of hip pain, pain on full movements, or restricted movements, do not ignore it. And if the pain fades rapidly and then recurs, the warning must be doubled.

The Knee

The knee is a very strong hinge joint with a twist, an angle and an enigmatic interior. To be technical there are two hinges, medial (inner) and lateral (outer), each with cartilage-topped articular surfaces on the femur (thighbone), opposed to a similar pair on the tibia (shinbone). Between the two surfaces of the opposing bones there is a central gap which contains the attachment of the two strong ligaments, the cruciate, or X ligaments. These ligaments hold the two bones together, acting as fixed radii for the hinge, and are crucial to joint stability (diagram 12–8). It takes very great force applied in an antero-

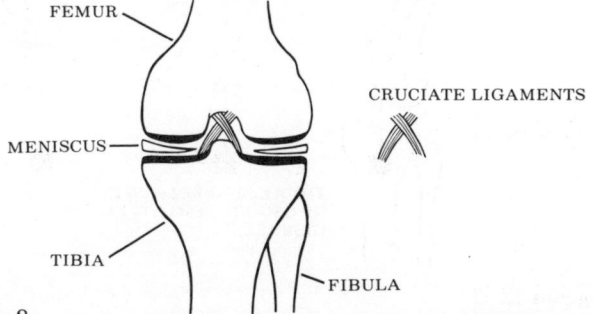

Diagram 12–8
Section of the knee joint to show the important internal cruciate ligaments.

posterior line to rupture them, and this must occur before the joint can dislocate. The articulating surfaces of the tibia are shallow dishes deepened by the two cartilages usually referred to as menisci, which are flexible semilunar-cushions attached around the rim to the joint capsule, but with a free thin inner border (diagram 12–8). The meniscus is torn when nipped by rotation forces. This occurs when the foot (which means the tibia bone) is fixed, the knee flexed, that is not fully extended and rigid, and the trunk (which means the femur) turns. The classic example is a rugby player who has all his weight on one fixed leg, having just kicked, and is tackled. The menisci and the cruciate ligaments constitute the internal mechanisms of the enigma.

The twist is the small external rotation of the leg on the thigh caused by the tension of the cruciate ligaments, as the knee straightens and the tibia locks firmly on the femur, thus making a rigid prop for stable weight bearing. The effect of this is also to make the foot rotate slightly into a toes out position.

The angle of the knee joint is an important measurement. The femur is at an angle to the vertical. It has to be, running as it does from the hip joint laterally down to the knee joint near the midline. The long powerful extensor muscles of the thigh, collectively known as the quadriceps femoris muscle and running along the femur, are attached to the patella (knee cap), which in turn has a strap-like ligament, the ligamentum patellae, running vertically downwards from its lower border to a final attachment to a tubercle (projection) on the front of the tibia, some 8 cms below the knee joint line. The angle between these two lines of

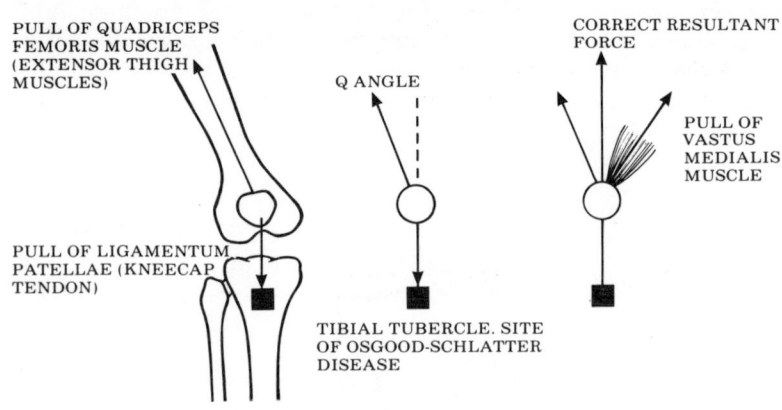

Diagram 12–9
Front view of knee of right leg. Because of the Q angle, created by anatomy, strong muscles are needed to keep the patella (knee cap) moving vertically.

force is the Q angle, which should be 20° or less (diagram 12-9). The patella glides up and down against the front of the femur as the joint bends. Their two juxtaposed surfaces are covered by cartilage separated only by a lubricating film of synovial fluid. The patella would dislocate laterally because of the parallelogram of forces if it were not for a strong medial pull from the vastus medialis muscle, seen as a rolled bulge above the knee cap of a trained athlete. In females with a wider pelvis, the Q angle can be at the extreme of 'normal' and if the vastus medialis muscle is underdeveloped, the patella glides up and down erratically flaking off articular (joint) cartilage from its posterior surface. This condition is known as chondromalacia patellae.

The knee joint is a dynamic strong hinge but very dependent on strong muscle control. In any injury with immobilisation muscle atrophy (shrinkage) rapidly occurs, so that strengthening exercises are vital during rehabilitation. It needs time, work, and constant measurement of progress, and it is now realised that muscle strength may not be restored under twelve months of endeavour. The champion athlete is the one who must beware the temptation to return too early to high output training: both knee and career may be ruined. Parents should take particular interest in the details of the exercise programme so that they can encourage, supervise and jolly along the impatient one.

The knee hinge can be strained by torsional (twisting) force created at the opposite ends of the two bone leaves (that is at the hip or the foot) by less than perfect anatomy. Sideways leverage of the leg that tends to open up the joint will be resisted by the medial or lateral ligaments to the point of strain or tear as the muscle groups are not designed to add greatly to the resistance. (Spectators have occasionally heard a 'pop' as a rugby or netball player tears a ligament and sprains a knee.) With lesser injury the knee often just swells overnight (traumatic synovitis).

The moving patella is a good example of nature's method of surrounding moving parts by bursae, that is fluid-filled sacs to lubricate the slippage of one tissue layer over another. There is a prepatellar bursa between bone and skin, which can be irritated by excessive kneeling (housemaid's knee), and other bursae between the moving tendons and bone. The one behind the patella is an extension of the joint cavity and hence swells noticeably when there is a joint effusion, either of fluid in mild injury or warm blood after more serious damage (diagram 12-10).

Constant damage to the articular cartilage of the joint causes it to flake, a condition known as chondromalacia, mentioned

70 CHILDREN'S SPORTS INJURIES

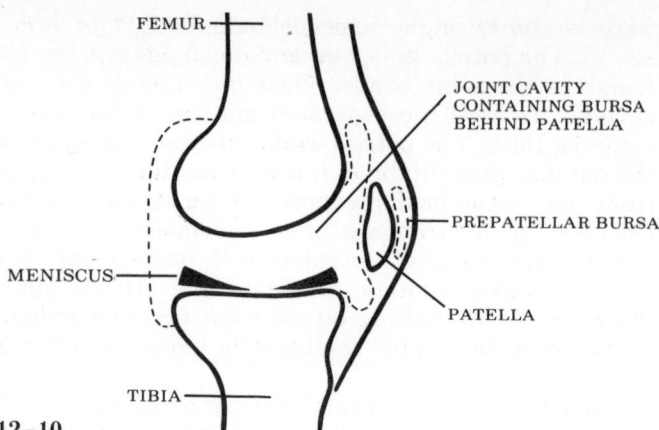

Diagram 12-10
Section through knee joint. Note that fluid in the bursa which is an extension of the joint cavity will show as a swelling above or below the patella (knee cap).

above in relation to the Q angle. This condition causes pain in the front of the knee with effusion and the sense of a weak joint. It is not so much a disease as a sequel to faulty joint mechanisms and it is these that have to be detected and corrected. Bigger chips of cartilage and contiguous bone can separate into loose bodies which block smooth joint movement and cause the knee to 'lock'. This is osteochondritis dissecans (p. 19), possibly a type of stress fracture and needing surgery. Knee braces can be very useful during rehabilitation in getting the athlete back into training but they must not be used just for pain. Proper diagnosis of the cause of the pain is the important thing and the technique of arthroscopy (looking into the knee joint through a stab hole) has led to improvement in this as well as to the development of quite wonderful surgical methods that avoid long stays in hospital.

The Swedish Insurance Co., Folksam, recorded 26,756 sports injuries (in people of all ages) between 1976 and 1983. Knee injuries predominated; further, victims of these spent the longest time on the sick list and provided the largest group with permanent disability, possibly due to a long delay between injury and surgery.

It would be ideal if an orthopaedic surgeon could rush onto the field for immediate examination and diagnosis before swelling and muscle spasm make this more difficult. In school sport no knee injury can be dismissed as trivial. Quick bandaging, ice, and later medical examination, are indicated. Along with arthroscopy, the Magnetic Resonance Imaging technique will revolutionise acute knee injury diagnosis and management.

Recent American research using an arthrometer to measure joint movement under pressure revealed hitherto unsuspected internal weakness even in uninjured (so far!) female high school athletes, that is, there was laxity of the internal cruciate ligaments. Also, there were statistically significant right to left leg differences and black girls had greater laxity than the others. Such unsuspected laxity may help explain the predisposition of female skiers and basketball players to knee injury.

The Ankle

The ankle is a strong mortised joint with the talus bone (virtually the top bone of the multi-boned foot complex) deeply recessed into the embrace of downward projections of the tibia (inner shinbone) and the fibula (outer, smaller and thinner shinbone). Each projection is called a malleolus, and strong, indeed very strong ligaments, fan out from these malleoli to hold the foot firmly in the mortise (diagram 12–11). In a sprain these ligaments stretch or tear, but may stay intact and pull off fragments of bone. Only if rupture is extensive can the talus dislocate completely.

The whole unit is somewhat like a toggle switch, allowing only dorsiflexion (movement up) or plantarflexion (movement down). Its powerful lever is the Achilles tendon attached to the calcaneus bone; this bone forms the heel and carries the talus, the two bones being firmly bound together to carry the whole body weight (diagram 12–12). This weight is spread forwards to the toes along the flexible and springy foot. Thus is created a marvellous mechanism for static and dynamic function. The anatomy is crowded with intricate detail. There are several small bones just forward of the weight-bearing calcaneus, then come the five parallel, long, thin metatarsal bones stretching forward to the ball of the foot (corresponding to the knuckles) and the toes; the big toe has two strong phalanges (small bones), the others just three minute phalanges. Long tendons from the leg muscles run in front of and behind the ankle joint to the toes and the area abounds with binding ligaments and small muscles.

In walking, and its much speeded-up version, jogging, the body weight is transmitted from heel strike, to the lateral (outer) arch of the foot, back to the ball of the foot, where it is momentarily stabilised prior to the powerful forward spring. Despite appearances this foot oscillation does not occur at the

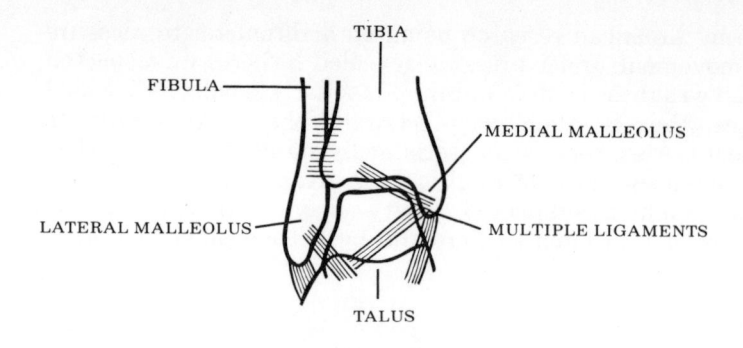

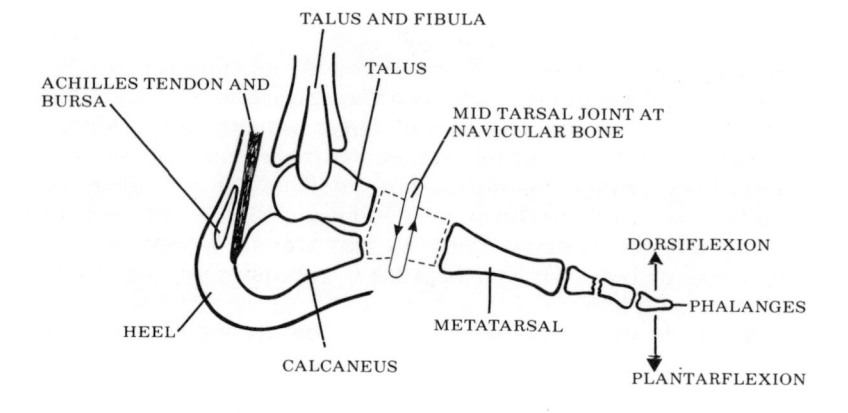

Diagram 12-11
The ankle joint, a deeply mortised hinge. The area is strengthened by many ligaments holding the bones together.
Diagram 12-12
The foot arch from heel to toe. Note the pivotal navicular bone. It alone can twist.

ankle joint which, to repeat, is as rigid as a toggle switch. It occurs at a point just ahead of the ankle, the mid foot or midtarsal joint, where the combined tarsus and calcaneus bones articulate with the small bones. The pivot is the navicular bone where arthritis and complicated dislocations can occur (diagram 12-12).

In pain from overuse, precise diagnosis of the stressed element in this interlocking mechanism is difficult, but the cure is not difficult: rest. Correction of foot problems by orthotics (inner soles or supports) should be approached warily if casual or expensive suggestions are made.

Biomechanical models of the ankle have been studied on a force platform and it was found that the Achilles tendon can be subjected to force which is in excess of that known to cause damage. There is an experimental problem in that it is difficult to measure the added influence of ground contact irregularities which would bring in other foot muscle groups to balance the shifts in weight, but it was found during experiments that a shift of as little as 1 cm in the line of force was significant. Anyway, the studies served to emphasise that because the point of attachment of each tendon to bone varies slightly, and because bone shape differs slightly from person to person, some feet can take stresses that others cannot. What did Mr Mussabini say to an Olympic gold medallist? For the answer, see p. 86.

Sprinting, where the toes claw the ground with the help of spikes, is a different foot action, and flat feet are not a barrier to sprinting. One modern national champion, record holder and Helms Award winner, D. B. Dunn of Australia, was flat-footed. In all the running movements the Achilles tendon is the prime strong mover and hence the first to squawk if the foot is overused. In ballet the long tendons from the leg muscles travelling to the toes in front of or behind the joint can develop painful tendinitis or tenosynovitis and may even rupture. The pain or swelling of tendinitis is never just a simple matter: the main question is why is it happening and the answer may reveal significant anatomical problems that affect the choice of sports.

The reactionary swelling of an ankle sprain can be minimised by bandaging, ice and elevation, Crepe or non-adhesive dressing is easy to apply, wrapping from the top of the foot, around the insole, across the sole and pulling firmly around the outer side so that mild tension is exerted to maintain eversion (outward turning), the opposite to the inversion movement of the sprain. Light thermoplastic supports can also be moulded into shape for positive protection during rehabilitation. Thereafter ankle stability must be checked; too many sprains come to surgery years later because of persistent weakness. Sprains in general should show steady improvement; if not there may be more ligament damage than expected, or bone involvement. There is danger too of damage to the growth plate at the lower end of the tibia, which if not recognised can cause twisting of the foot up to the age of twenty or so when the epiphysis (p. 16) fuses with the shaft.

If gymnasts, jumpers, or unseated horseriders land heavily on the heels, the jarring force can travel straight up to the spine, causing fractures there, which serves to emphasise that in sports needing landing mats, these must be thick and in good repair.

13. Food

Food, nutrition if you prefer, holds young athletes' attention from the moment they get up until they go to bed. There are billions of books on nutrition, a squillion of screeds on diets in magazines, advertisements, pamphlets and newspapers, and tons of temptation in supermarket promotions. All of it is mostly correct, and yet mostly absolutely wrong for *you*, and your brood. In reality you, the parent, quartermaster general of a growing platoon, must work it all out for yourself and the basic facts outlined in this chapter will help you form an indestructible, advertising-proof understanding of general principles to use as a guide. You can then flesh out this skeleton of knowledge over the years to suit your own taste and experience by scouring books and articles for practical ideas, for only *you* can judge what is best for you and your family.

Everyone knows that we are what we eat. Otherwise why are some of us so obviously akin to sugar and spice, and others made of bats and toads and skunks' backsides? Youngsters are what a parent gives them to eat until the laws governing education land them in front of the tuck shop door and they feel the tug of another lifestyle. A child's diet must always be important because family eating habits and individual tastes last a lifetime, and may (indeed probably) influence the development of diabetes, high blood pressure, obesity and arteriosclerosis or atherosclerosis (artery wall disease). The latter has been detected even in adolescence and presumably thereafter progresses every living day.

In making you own choices you will be on strong scientific ground. Research in the University of Chicago is tending to the conclusion that our cell metabolism (that is the mechanism of life and growth) is directed by DNA genes inherited from our mother alone, via her X chromosome. Father has absolutely no influence on how the cell does its job but through his genes' participation in the cell nucleus is able to dictate what the cell is allowed to do. This research indicates, by the way, that we must all have descended from one ancestral Eve (or Eves), at the moment thought to have migrated from Africa 100,000 to 140,000 years ago. Her date of origin has yet to be established. (No, we have not all remained as alike as peas in a pod, thanks to gene mutation.)

An immediate valid deduction from this research is that when it comes to selecting food for her own offspring mother is likely to know best, although if a child is as contrary as Dad or Uncle George, he or she may not want to swallow it!

The Biochemistry of Food

The average adult body is made out of about 70 kg of protein, fat, bone (which means calcium), blood (which means iron), and water (which means inorganic ions of sodium, potassium, chloride, carbonate, phosphorus and sulphur in solution, and a raft of so-called trace elements and vitamins). To get that lot together a baby first plunders mother's reserves, then makes all the rest from food, starting after birth with mother's milk that is itself a perfectly balanced diet.

Proteins

Proteins are composed of approximately twenty amino acids linked into complex chains. The basis of each amino acid is a three-carbon segment with a nitrogen fraction added. Nine amino acids are labelled 'essential' (that is without them the cell will die) and cannot be made in the body. They must therefore be in the food we eat. Any of the other eleven amino acids can be made if they are not in the diet by breakdown of food proteins into the basic short segments and appropriate recombination of the atoms of C (carbon), H (hydrogen), O (oxygen) and N (nitrogen), sometimes with S (sulphur) and P (phosphorus) added. Surplus segments can be rearranged by the liver cells into sugar or fat. A growing child, an invalid recovering from a debilitating illness, an athlete building muscle, and a marathoner needing to repair muscle all need to eat more daily protein than the average adult.

Fats

The C, H and O molecules can link gregariously to form three-carbon chain fatty acids, three of which join again then unite with glycerine to form triglycerides, that in turn combine anew in various ways to form 'animal' fats of all sorts. Three fatty acids are essential, which means we cannot manufacture them and they must be in the diet. A very important feature of food fatty acids is whether they are saturated (that is have no chemical double bonds), or unsaturated (that is have one or more double bonds). Many fats are a mixture of both. A double bond can be envisaged as two carbon atoms side by side each with an arm touching the other's nearest shoulder. In saturated form the carbon atoms are strung out in a line or closed in a circle, holding hands. In general terms the saturated acids are solid, stable and hard fats (lard, coconut, palm, butter) and the unsaturated, especially if polyunsaturated (that is with two or more double bonds) are liquid oils (corn, sunflower, safflower, walnut, cottonseed, soya-bean and fish) and unstable, turning slowly rancid. Peanut and olive oils are monounsaturated (that is with one double bond). Some vitamins are fat soluble and only by eating fats do we get them: vitamin A for the eyes, D for the bones, E for the sex glands, and K involved in blood clotting.

Minerals

Minerals and inorganic atoms have to be ingested along with very small amounts of zinc, copper, manganese, cobalt, iodine, etc. Just a trace of these along with vitamins are essential here and there, probably as co-enzymes to speed up some chemical equations. Thus every living cell (or ex-living cell) will have these trace elements.

Cannibals do it the easy way. If you want a diet containing everything a body needs, eat another one. The closest we can come and still stay within the law is to eat another animal, all of it. Eskimos are the perfect example. They hunt and eat seals, and it seems they leave only the skin. The bones, cooked and tenderised, are handed out to the children as 'sweets'. In other words, broadly speaking, by eating fat, bone, and meat (some of it raw), everything that is 'essential' can be ingested. A fatty raw T bone steak might even be the ultimate daily diet. Anyhow, lions and tigers get by on that, plus liver.

Carbohydrates

So far so good. No special mention of carbohydrates you see. They simply are not essential body builders and Eskimo kids are frisky enough without them. The body just burns them up as energy to drive the chemical equations of the cells in what they are doing—talking, running, or plain old body building. What is not immediately used in this way is stored as glycogen (see below), or as fat made in the liver cells and sent via the bloodstream to be squirreled away in all parts of the body. The liver, incidentally, is such a mighty chemical factory and warehouse that it is the perfect food source of minerals and trace elements. Carbohydrates are called protein sparers because if the diet has enough of them to keep the blood sugar at normal levels, the liver does not have to break up protein (otherwise destined for body building projects) to make blood sugars.

Like fats carbohydrates are made from only C, H and O atoms united variously to form chains of six, called sugars, that follow the old trick of merging in more complex ways to become glycogen in animals and starch in plants, the forms convenient for storage. Really complex starches (polysaccharides) make up the skeletons of plants and vegetables and are known as fibre and cellulose. They are indigestible to humans and are passed into the bowel debris as bulky 'roughage'. Maybe this is why Eskimo families locked together for months on end in small igloos frown on complex carbohydrates!

Fast Foods

So, if indeed we are all descended from Eve, all we need to know is what she gave her children to eat and do the same. It would have to have been natural products, breast milk, flesh and eggs of game and bird, fish, fruit, berries and plants. Seeds may have been crushed and cooked into gruels and breads. Cultivated grains certainly came much later. One can hardly see Adam taking a chance on milking the family sabre-toothed tigress, but eventually, domesticated ruminants would have provided milks and cheeses. And so the human diet remained, in principle, until about fifty years ago when our society discovered a new way of eating: processed, refined, prepared, precooked, modified, recombined, fast foods rapidly degenerating at the cheap end into junk scraps. This modern trend is not dictated by nutritional requirements, but by the need to save time and to feed that ogre of modern society, life in the fast lane. Given another 99,950 years to adapt the human animal may yet fare well on artificial foods but our generations are stuck with the transition problems. 'Wait a minute,' I can hear Eve say, 'don't knock fast food outlets. I sure could have done with one in this rift valley.' Well, it's certainly the case that easy snacks are here to stay and allow for them we must.

What are they made of really? Some form of protein, refined carbohydrate sugars, fried or excessively fatty items, artificial chemical colours and flavours, salt and preservatives. At first glance this seems reasonable but they warrant close study. No need to allow for waste; all is meant to be eaten and so to stimulate the taste buds that one is tempted to eat (buy, that is) more. Therein lies the real danger at school *and* if children are left to choose their own menu from the home freezer.

Good Nutrition

Everyone knows what is best for growing children and beanstalk adolescents: good quality protein milk and meat (or chicken and fish), eggs, and vitamin-rich fresh fruit and vegetables, and these they must get at least once a day at the family breakfast or evening meal. Breakfast is more important than is appreciated. By then, it is twelve hours since dinner and an enormous amount of body building has gone on during sleep! All food is energy. The junk intake, being fat and sugar in one form or another, would seem harmless if the energy is totally run off by an active athlete, leaving appetite aplenty to eat the quality food a parent has carefully thought out and cooked. But what if your child is not an athlete? Obesity, that's what, and it is no chance result that more and more schoolchildren are being labelled 'overweight for age'. Later, subtle malnutrition from lack of vitamins and essentials could occur from the sameness of fast foods or in fact from the sameness of any rigid diet; the reason why dieticians recommend variety of intake is to ensure that what is lacking in one group of foods is present in another. Science still does not know everything and the future may yet see the 'discovery' of even more minute essential factors.

The essentiality of proteins, however, is clear-cut in terms of both quantity and quality. Vegetables and seeds are labelled second-class protein foods because of their small protein content with low or absent amounts of essential amino acids. Even so, chemists can extract and concentrate what is there, and reassemble many samples into 'protein-like' products for use in what we later buy as processed foods. Animals, as they eat and grow, have been their own chemists slowly selecting and building exactly what they (and we!) want, so that fresh animal products are, for us, first-class proteins. Parents can be confident of what is in them. With fast foods, however, who knows? That is the problem of modern foods.

Classic experiments, oft misquoted, were published between 1928 and 1938 by an American paediatrician, Dr Clara Davis. She tested the preferences of three infants, all nine months old, by allowing them to select at will for each meal from a varied offering of ten basic foods out of a panel of thirty-one, and from two types of milk. It was an artificial experiment in that the foods were basic, unsweetened, and traditionally wholesome, indeed primitive. Eve would have nodded sagely at the nine preferred by all three infants: bone marrow, milk, eggs, cornmeal, whole wheat, oatmeal, banana, apple and orange. There was a low preference for all ten vegetables. The infants thrived normally. Medical texts later misinterpreted this experiment by claiming that it showed that infants have an instinct to choose a balanced diet. Not necessarily so. The test has never been repeated by widening the selection to include more tempting, less wholesome foods.

However, this has been done with laboratory rats that were still growing. Given normal, standard rations in abundance they never overate. Allowed access to a supermarket fare of salami, cheese, peanut butter, bananas, marshmallows, chocolate cookies, condensed milk and milk chocolate, they had a weight gain 250% greater than their neighbours. To draw analogies is tempting! Other research evidence supports the preference of children for anything sweet (as if that needed scientific proof), and that human animals in general will increase their intake as the choice on offer widens even though they do not need it.

The conclusion seems clear. Very young children are fortunately captive and must be given to eat 'what is good for them'. Distractions are best kept to a minimum; the odd treat will do no harm but that special bribing class, grandparents, may have to be warned off. The luckiest child in the world would seem to be the one with a French provincial housewife for a mother, and grandparents from a frugal Scottish clan. Long-term, the aim should be to educate by example in the merits of proper food, meaning that if *you* have not yet studied the topic, start now. Buy a small food guide and in a gentle but progressive way check what each major food contains. The first person to benefit will be yourself, for one important reason: junk food is only the dark side of the mirror; the bright side is the new knowledge about the significance of saturated fats (including cholesterol) in the diet, because atherosclerotic artery disease (fatty wall plaques blocking the tubes) is now thought to be the end result of deviant fat metabolism that begins even in childhood. In a few words, eat less cholesterol and saturated fats and you have less chance of dying from a stroke or coronary heart disease, a view that will cut no ice at all with the young now but if you tell them and tell them they will remember it all their lives. Hopefully, too, their taste buds will not get hooked on the less nutritious fast foods likely to be loaded with calories, the wrong fats and salt, and oh so easy to overeat. With any family history of strokes or coronary heart disease even more effort must be made to monitor and limit a child's fat and cholesterol intake; teach them, along with reading, 'riting and 'rithmetic, the three bad s's: sugar, saturated fat and salt.

The recent reversal of attitude means that complex carbohydrates are now good for you, saturated fats bad. Do you remember when it was the opposite?

'No, you cannot have all those potatoes (0% fat) and bread (0.5% fat), they are fattening.'

'Eat up your nourishing bacon sandwiches (bacon 40% fat, butter 82% fat).'

'Don't eat those lollies, have this chocolate, it's full of milk.'

It is enlightening to make a list of one's weekly diet and then look up food composition tables to check the fat and cholesterol content. Protein and carbohydrate percentages are not so important. Later, if you wish and have the time to weigh food, you could calculate the daily kilocalorie (energy) intake but this is not vital for expanding athletes; as an adult you need only weigh yourself regularly and if the weight is going up then the calorie intake is too high. Just eat less of what you are eating, as an Irish dietician might explain. Slowly, with increasing study, you can alter your diet to diminish unnecessary cholesterol and fat, and reduce the total caloric intake, by clever substitution of items that will avert hunger and testiness. Do start. Remember the old Chinese proverb: 'The longest journey begins with the first step.'

An athlete uses up a lot of energy provided, on the instant, by the glycogen stored in the muscles and liver. If or when that is used up fat has to be burned. When all that goes the muscle protein is broken down, as happened in wartime starvation. In today's terms a diet with not enough calories for activities means that the body has to cannibalise itself, so deliberate dieting must allow for slow adjustment and not court a metabolic crash. One aspect of training is that the muscles gradually learn about biochemistry, how much glycogen to store, how to burn it, when to switch to fat, and how to get ready again because if the muscle glycogen is not restored before the next training bout the session will be a poor one. Carbohydrates are thus vital and experts now say that complex carbohydrates (fruits) are better than simple sugar (glucose and sucrose). Your dentist would heartily agree, but for fear of fainting from hunger (technically a low blood sugar), any normal youngster will eat what he first sees. You can only hope that if you keep nagging he will remember that he will still have to eat the hearty proper evening meal so essential to provide the right proteins to build healthy muscle. You will know that you have won the battle for the youngster's mind when he races in and says: 'I'm starving, what's for dinner? No don't tell me, just bring it.'

A diet deliberately excessive in protein, for example steak three times a day, is not needed even by weight lifters who favour it in the belief that it will automatically force the growth of bigger muscles. It won't. Certainly muscles cannot be built without first-class protein and such athletes (endurance experts as well) will need a higher daily average, but excess is promptly converted by liver into glucose and then fat, with the protein nitrogen making an extra daily chore for the kidneys to excrete.

If muscles need glycogen so much, why not stuff them with it? It sounds logical and is called carbohydrate loading. It is done by first exhausting the muscle glycogen by severe training sessions (snag number 1) on days seven, six, and five, before the event, then forcing a carbohydrate rich diet (snag number 2) for the remaining four days with little exercise. A gentler way is just to taper down the training over seven days and increase the carbohydrates in the last three days. Snag number 3 is the harm this interference does to smooth training, and snag number 4 is the effect this artificial behaviour has on the athlete's frame of mind. In theory, this approach will benefit those in endurance sports, of all kinds, lasting over one hour, and sprinters who have no time to transport extra fuel to the muscles. But it must be judged too complicated and too serious for school and college athletes, whose metabolism anyhow is not on a steady adult plateau. Eating a diet with a high percentage of carbohydrates all the time, as a matter of habit, as many world champions now do, will keep the muscles fully primed and set a positive and disciplined goal so that the athlete will have less wish to fill up on fatty, greasy, oversalted junk.

Extra vitamins and minerals? Again the answer is that with a proper diet they are not needed although your local pharmacist might welcome the sale of expensive shotgun pellets. The body has stores of all vitamins and regular megadosing has been proved harmful. Some of the vitamins are toxic in excess. Vitamins B and C are the ones needed in energy metabolism and for really stiff sports, small, select supplements would be of psychological benefit. Iron is a special case and menstruating athletes should take a daily tablet if periods are at all heavy. (Cooking in cast iron utensils slightly increases the iron content of acid sauces and steamed vegetables.) Anorexic ballet dancers are a separate group that need expert supervision (p. 97). Salt (the sodium ion) is now frowned upon for adults but a salty tooth, once acquired, is hard to cure. It is thus in a child's long-term interest to give him or her unsalted butter and bread right from the start, and avoid adding extra to food. It is not needed because normal foods have enough. Commercial and fast foods almost invariably contain too much.

On race day remember that bulk causes bowel distension and discomfort, fat is slow to digest, rich protein is busily converted to something else, and so it is back to the complex carbohydrates again for the main meal. If the athlete has been educated to really like them the parent's task is easy, but if he craves a steak and ice cream, so be it. Better that he feels good than stoically virtuous. During long drawnout competitions water is vital. To keep up energy simple sugary solutions, seemingly ideal, are actually not so. The reason is complicated and to do with the way the body secretes insulin. Hence glucose polymers, sold by your chemist, were developed and are just the ticket.

What are these, supposedly now well loved, complex carbohydrates? Grain foods (bread, pasta, cereals, rice, corn), legume plants and their seeds (beans, peas, lentils), vegetables, and solid fruit. If potatoes or rice are fried the fat will double the calorie count of the serving, as will anything smeared on bread.

What are the unsaturated fats? Nuts, fish and the vegetable oils. Animal fats and milks, eggs and solid fats (coconut and palm oils, dripping, cocoa) are saturated. Margarine might be one or the other, so check the label. It pays to be suspicious of packets that list contents as pure vegetable oil or shortening. It is pounds to peanut oil that this conceals, legally, the fact that the fats used are the highly saturated palm and coconut oils that are cheaper for the manufacturer than the polyunsaturates. If the word 'hydrogenated' appears, you know for certain that the fat is the saturated variety you are trying to avoid. Cake mix buyers beware! Or bake your own out of the polyunsaturateds.

What is rich in cholesterol? Egg yolk, shellfish, liver, kidney, cheese, and animal fats in general. However, the level of cholesterol in the blood increases much more by production from saturated fats than by absorption of food cholesterol; thus it is vital to cut as much visible fat as possible off meat and let more drip off in cooking, to drain bacon, degrease homemade soups, and so on. No high fat foods such as takeaways, fries, pastries, some biscuits and (alas!) chocolate should be greedily golloped. Cholesterol is an essential ingredient of all our body cells and of some hormones. Why therefore is it 'bad' for us? The answer strikes at the heart of all nutritional advice. Quantity and quality. If you want to go on a binge with your favourite cheese or a fatty hamburger with everything, change next day to vegetables, fruit, and plain bread. In other words, variety.

PART B

A TO Z GUIDE TO SPORTS

Archery

This is a well-known and wonderful sport for paraplegics in wheelchairs and such is their muscle development that virtually no injury occurs to their trunk muscles. With others it is not so and the bow must be carefully matched to current strength; if not the big chest muscle, the pectoralis major, can be badly torn resulting in spectacular inaccuracy and dangerously wayward arrows. It goes without saying (or should) that beginners must attend classes and learn strict discipline for the safety of others. Arrows are lethal. To aim them carelessly over fences or in the general direction of the neighbour's dog must be expressly forbidden.

Athletics

Track and field is not a body contact sport (or should not be, middle distance runners please note!), and injuries are self-inflicted. Apart from bone breaks in jumpers, muscle strains and joint sprains are the main injuries, with an increasing number being due to the accumulating stress of repetitive action. Since athletes spend far more time in training than in direct competition, about four out of five injuries are reported during training, although many more are probably not reported at all. A Canadian survey in 1982 found that nearly one half of the injured athletes waited five days or more to report trouble, and this is far too long.

There is no need to fear the effects on the heart; it will not suffer 'strain'. Long-term research has shown that the heart may well enlarge if serious training begins before puberty, but this is a genuine hypertrophy (increase in muscle size) from effort and is not an abnormality. The heart size of those who start to train seriously in later adolescence 'catches up' so that in the end the thickness of the muscle wall is the same. Scandinavian studies on competitive endurance runners found few differences in aerobic power in the twelve to sixteen group, but after the age of sixteen major changes appeared in the heart volumes and total oxygen consumption capacity, which may indicate the natural selection of endurance types.

The importance of gradual preparation after a winter lay-off must be stressed and skylarking discouraged early in the season. Fortunately young muscles pick up quickly but will be strained if the training load exceeds their current strength. Feel for track surfaces can only be self-taught. In general grass is kinder to muscles than cinders, even if it is uneven in winter and spring. Wet synthetic surfaces are hazardous for unskilled jumpers and naturally cause worse abrasions. One oddity of training occurs with the post-exertion gulp of air. In winter the rapid intake of a mass of very cold air can cause bronchospasm, and in spring a high dose of allergic pollens will have the same effect. Wheezing has also been reported due to toxic vapour rising from indoor artificial surfaces and their glues.

Feet problems affect all growing athletes; particularly because they tend to buy cheap and poorly constructed spikes since they will grow out of them. The result is a crop of blisters and sometimes pain due to the stress imparted to the foot. Beware the shoe whose back curves forward as this can irritate the Achilles tendon and its overlying bursal sac. At some point talented young runners should invest in quality shoes.

Every category of track and field endeavour has its own special risks, with some overlapping of course, and all injuries should be carefully examined to check for minor anatomical deformities. Such deformities, although otherwise unimportant, may be a factor in recurrent injuries or may require an athlete to limit certain dreams. As Mr Sam Mussabini advised the late Sir Harold Abrahams, Olympic gold medallist and one of the 1924 chariots of fire: 'No trainer can put in what the good Lord leaves out.'

Sprinting

In sprinting, the explosive muscular contraction of the start or a desperate finish can tear one of the thigh muscles or some of the muscle fibres from their tendons of attachment. In fact, sprinters are known to have a high percentage of the rapid twitch muscle fibres. With a complete muscle belly tear, in which there is bleeding from ruptured blood vessels, the pain is worse and much more diffuse than the rather localised tenderness caused by fraying of the muscle at the tendon junction. Firm elastic bandaging should be quickly put on and, as soon as possible, cold compresses should be applied to try to limit bleeding and reactionary swelling. Water ice still makes the best and cheapest immediate compress; its temperature is constant whereas commercial gels and picnic packs may be any number of degrees below zero and could cause skin damage, especially in girls who have a blood vessel system which is super-sensitive to cold and who tend to get chilblains. Ice packs can safely be put directly on the skin for thirty minutes every two hours. Complete muscle tears sometimes heal best after surgery with removal of the blood clot and it is worth getting an early surgical opinion. If the athlete has fallen heavily check for fractures of the wrist or collar bone.

Overstriding in the middle stages of a race is notorious for tearing the posterior hamstring group. That the injury occurs at all in the young indicates either lack of basic conditioning or faulty striding at the peak speed (often around the 60-metre mark) when the sprinter urges the legs on to super-peak level instead of gliding within their established stride to the tape. Recurrence of the injury with further tearing and more scar tissue healing must be avoided or a promising career will be over. Even though active exercise is recommended for tears, full return to sprinting should be long delayed, despite the pupil's protests, whilst proper physiotherapy and muscle retraining are emphasised. Recurrence of pain must be promptly reported.

As well as muscle belly tear young sprinters are vulnerable to partial separation or complete avulsion (tearing away) of the epiphysis (bone area) to which the muscle is attached (p. 17) This is characterised by quite localised recurrent bone tenderness. If the hamstring epiphysis is wrenched away there is tenderness just under the inner side of the buttock. The detachment of one particular epiphysis, the anterior tibial tubercle, which is the point of attachment of the patellar ligament to the upper leg, is well known as Osgood-Schlatter disease (p. 19). In the treatment of this rest and perhaps immobilisation are needed, the very opposite to a muscle tear where early gentle stretching is important to prevent contracture.

Circular track sprinters have the special problem of ankle and knee strain, usually left-sided. The 400-metre athletes on completely circular tracks get acute lumbosacral (lower back) pain from the prolonged torsional ligament strain, and may even get stress fractures of the navicular bone in the foot (p. 71). (Racing greyhounds get a similar fracture in the outside rear leg.) Further testimony to the stress of this event is that rectal temperatures can momentarily reach 104°F.

Middle Distance

This is an endurance test of everything, ligaments, tendons and muscles, of the shin and feet, and of the ankle which is their pivot. Sir Roger Bannister has said that athletes today must train two to three times harder than his generation did for mile events because as seniors they now need to achieve a time of around 3 minutes 50 seconds to win. This can only increase the number of injuries due to stress.

The leg muscles are tightly encased in fibrous tissue (fascia) which protects the softer muscle fibres and guides their contraction force but necessarily limits the space for muscle hypertrophy (increase in size). The result is the painful so-called compartment syndrome, mostly felt in the front but occasionally affecting the deeper posterior calf groups. The cause is said to be restriction of blood supply to the muscles and in this case the binding fascia may have to be cut. However, Dr Almquist, who operated on Mary Decker at age fourteen for posterior compartment pain, does not in general like to operate on a growing athlete. Some anatomical factors (a high medial foot arch is one) may predispose a leg to muscle strain and thus pain. There is also evidence that some pain could be due to tiny stress fractures of the tibial bone, or to muscle drag on the periosteum (fibrous covering of the bone), thus making the term shinsplint not so much a diagnosis as a description.

Every strain pain is made worse by an uneven or hard track or very hot conditions. Tenosynovitis of the Achilles tendon, peritendinitis of those in front of the ankle, or inflammation of the various bursal sacs beneath the skin or on bone, arise from excessive friction and demand rest and a change of shoes. With better shoes these irritations will diminish.

The feet contain all structures in miniature, and strains can be difficult to diagnose, but examination, and reexamination, is needed for persistent pain of the forefoot or under the toes, or for pain on passive movements. There is no prize but serious trouble if the athlete thinks that more brave training will 'cure it'. Bruised heels result from the constant pounding that breaks down the normal fibro-fatty cushion over the calcaneus (heel bone) and causes small haemorrhages known as black heel, but there is no damage to deeper structures. Padded shoes help prevent this. Torn leg muscles, especially those in the calf, plague middle distance athletes if they put too much into the last final sprint.

Long Distance

Not surprisingly this is the ultimate foot stress and prepubertal children should probably not participate in these events. If there is pain with tender pressure points parents must insist on a full medical examination even if the athlete is reluctant, in fact especially if there is reluctance. Any stress damage will not go away and will get worse, whereas with accurate diagnosis and management modified training may even continue. The list that follows may seem too medical but has been included to show how specific the diagnosis of stress pain can be, and needs to be. The possibilities are:

- Sever's disease, a traction effect on the heel epiphysis where the Achilles tendon is inserted into bone. Statistically this seems to be most common in preadolescent boys. Leg alignment, suitable for correction by orthotics (inner soles or supports), can be an associated problem.
- Kohler's disease, or osteochondritis (p. 19) of the navicular bone in the upper mid foot. This is an important bone, being the one on which the whole forefoot rotates and twists.
- March fracture, classically occurring in the distal (lower) part of the second metatarsal bone (p. 20) close to the second toe, and so-called because it was first recognised in soldiers after long route marches. It is a stress fracture, and initially so fine that it may not show up in the first X-rays. It is often associated with a congenitally short big toe (Morton's toe) that stops the axis of toe flexion from running smoothly along the joint line from the big to the little toe; by accidentally protruding beyond this line the shaft of the second metatarsal at times and in certain positions may take the whole body weight instead of sharing it along the ball of the foot.
- Sesamoiditis under the first metatarsal head, that is under the ball of the big toe. Very small bones (called sesamoid bones because they resemble sesame seeds) develop in the young flexor tendons running to the big toe; these sesamoids strengthen the tendon against crushing pressure but, in the under-eighteen group, they can themselves develop minute fractures or softening.
- Freiberg's disease, an osteochondritis (p. 19) of the head of the second or third metatarsal foot bone near the toes.
- Plantar fasciculitis, or tender lumps in the subcutaneous binding fascia that forms the string across the bow of the medial foot arch. This condition tends to self-cure after puberty as the strengthening muscles and their tendons mould the inner side of the foot.

- Stress fractures. One in the fibula (small shinbone) 5 to 7 cm above the lateral ankle point, although not strictly of the foot, can be included here because it causes pain and stiffness in the ankle area. Stress fractures, although not really common, occur in well-defined spots in the foot but have been recorded in every leg bone (including the knee cap), and must be suspected if there is always pain during training and a persistent localised tender area on bone. They have recurred in athletes, and have been multiple, but always heal with eight weeks rest from running; normal activities are not affected. Always have the opposite leg checked for the presence of a similar stress fracture since, not surprisingly, they can be bilateral.

Achilles tendon inflammation as well as bruised heels, bruised toes, or sore toenails are a sure sign of bad shoes, a constant worry in growing children, and one which can only be solved by *very careful examination* of proffered merchandise for size and seams etc. The most common error in selecting shoes is choosing a size too narrow or too close a fit to accomodate a spreading forefoot, or in hot climates, ones made of materials that do not breathe. Check the heel for uneven wear as this may indicate a need for anatomical correction by orthotics.

Knee pain, and indeed one can extend what follows to all branches of track and field, is tricky. The initial medical report may be that no disease or damage is present. This should be rephrased as 'no disease can be found at present'. The alternative is to dismiss the pain as merely psychological, but this is risky, and indeed unfair, without reexamination and the use of special X-ray views, tomograms, arthrography (injection of dye into the joint), specialised bone scans, and arthroscopy (direct vision of the joint cavity by the surgeon). Among the rarities are stress fractures of the lower femoral (thighbone) epiphysis causing pain that lasts well after the exercise, osteochondritis dissecans (dead patches in the articular cartilage, p. 19), and the Orava syndrome which is friction of the fibrous sheet across the lateral side of the knee as it bends and straightens. Much more common, although difficult to diagnose, are chondromalacia patellae in girls (p. 19), ligament injuries from other sports which show up in high mileage effort, and hip disease. This latter is a notorious clinical fact, caused by a quirk of nerve anatomy which allows hip disease to be 'felt' in the knee, and vice versa.

Whether prepubertal children should be exposed to all these possibilities through long distance training is very doubtful. That children are capable of expending such energy is not doubted, and that they may embrace the challenge with competitive enthusiasm is granted, but how do you tell their growing bone areas, their tendons, their knee mechanisms and their joint cartilages: 'Come on, you have to put up with this, it's for your own good. You'll be better and stronger for it in the end'? Surely the aim in children's sport should be sound healthy development, not the under-ten world marathon record. The American Academy of Paediatrics in 1982 stated that long distance competitive events designed for adults were not recommended for children prior to physical maturity, and the Amateur Athletic Federation of England once said that prepubertal children's races should not exceed 3000 metres. The real danger would seem to be competitive pressure, or probably more correctly, parental or school pressure, which may in the end extinguish happy progress.

Triathlons

All the multi-endurance iron man competitions pose predictable dangers. To the risks of each individual sport add the factors of muscle cramp, exposure to the environment, and general fatigue, which all make error and therefore injury more likely. Junior competitions for teenagers and even for prepubertal toughies are too new to provide statistics for comment; one can only note what happened to adults in full-length events in Australia over a course which included a 4-km swim, 180 km on a bicycle, and a 42-km run. About one quarter of the starters failed to finish, and one half of all competitors needed treatment for injury or suffering of varying degree, all made worse by cold and dehydration in poor weather. Police expressed concern over the number of traffic breaches during the cycling leg.

Such events will always need thoughtful organisers, a large squad of mobile doctors and paramedics, and efficient transport for the injured. What place you may well ask is there for this event among the young with their relative inability to cope with dehydration, cold, or heat? Well, it will always be a challenge to some. There is the danger that race sponsors with their eyes on the press and television benefits, will schedule events at times wrong for the climate. As a parent I would take a very hard and close look at the organisers, at the severity of the course, and then at the arrangements, and tell the young hopeful: 'If you find you can't cope or get exhausted for heaven's sake drop out. It will be no disgrace.' Only parents descended from the ancient generals of Sparta would disagree.

Jumpers. Long, High, and Triple

The explosive muscular effort of the spring in jumping can rupture the Achilles tendon, but most often partially tears the junction between muscle and tendon to cause a sudden loss of power in the take-off. Jumper's knee is a mixed bag† of patellar tendinitis, osteochondritis (p. 19) of the lower pole of the patella, Osgood-Schlatter disease (p. 19), avulsion of the ligamentum patellae from the patella, or a torn quadriceps muscle at its patello-tendinous insertion, all of which cause pain after training, but only a partial drop in power because of the wide interfelting of the entire knee hinge anatomy in a broad fibrous sheet with multiple connections to bone. The cause of any of the above may be pure strain or the torsional effects of poor technique and faulty foot placement in the take-off.

As well as avulsion (tearing) injuries there is fatigue fracture of the upper part of the shaft of the fibula (small shinbone) caused by repetitive jumping from a flexed knee position. The absolutely classic example of this is the military training injury caused by jumping from a full knee-bent squat into the attitude of attack (first reported in German medical literature in the last century). Parachutists are another military group in which this fracture is well known since they land heavily on a flexed knee, as do athletes in the triple jump. As the fibula is not a weight-bearing bone, that being the role of the tibia (large shinbone), the cause of the fracture must be a sudden muscular leverage across a fatigued area. Fractures of the small foot bones are probably also stress fractures from excessive eversion (outward turning) of the feet or forced flexion of the toes, and the same tendons giving the final thrust to the leap can dislocate from their groove to cause a flash of pain behind the ankle.

The vigorous body exertions and torsions in flight can strain the ilio-psoas muscle. This muscle arises from the lower vertebrae and is inserted into the upper inner part of the femur (thighbone). Its function is to flex the thighs on the trunk, or vice versa, and strain in it results in pain in the groin or deep in the lower abdomen. Females, with their wider hip structure and rotational inertia, are more prone to this and instead of straining the muscle may even avulse (tear) the epiphysis (p. 17) of the insertion site that is developing as a bony spur on the femur. There is then a quite specific tender spot in the upper inner thigh.

† See glossary for definitions.

Bad landings can cause sprain or fracture in the ankle, knee, shoulder or outstretched hand. To avoid this the high jump landing mats for the roll and flop techniques should be bigger for inexperienced youngsters than for older contestants (watch the gaps between the mats) and the long jump pit too, should be extended towards the take-off board to catch the odd trip up.

Triple jump exponents, with two hard landings on every practice jump, are increasing their chances of knee meniscus (p. 68) damage by torsion on a fixed foot, and of fracture of the small sesamoid bone under the ball of the big toe. The strong leg faces the strain twice in each jump. In this group, too, the pelvic joints are vulnerable to rotational and jarring forces, the pubic symphysis in the midline at the front and the two sacroiliac joints at the back. Females are more likely to get this problem because nature has built into their pelvic joints a tendency for slight laxity to allow the pelvis to expand and 'give' a little during childbirth. A bone scan may be needed to diagnose stress fractures when there is vague but disabling groin pain or inablility to stand on the leg of the affected side to pull on trousers. The effort and stretch to maintain horizontal velocity, especially in the step to jump phase, creates the conditions, as in sprinters, for hamstring tears. In the knee, instead of the Osgood-Schlatter type of epiphyseal drag, complete sudden avulsion of the epiphysis can occur. Stomach muscles are easily strained (and indeed are worth special strengthening) by the stretch and distension between the trunk and legs during the step phase.

Hurdling

This combination of sprinting, jumping, and stretching (overstretching often) means strain to the hamstrings of the jumping leg, or to the adductors (the upper medial muscle group) of the trailing leg. Adequate warm-up and prevention of cold between heats is therefore essential. Bad landings and falls produce the usual crop of sprains and fractures. Rapid repetitive body flexion over the hurdles should not affect the normally supple youthful back, especially when stretching exercises are faithfully done, but nonetheless acute lumbosacral (lower back) ligament strain and the rare stress fracture in the pars interarticularis area of the vertebrae (p. 28) can occur. Stress fracture of the navicular bone (p. 72) in the foot is likewise possible. Scrapes and scratches should be protected with plastic skin.

Pole Vaulting

Strain of shoulder muscles and the rotator cuff mechanism (p. 61) from the thrust of take-off, and strain of the abdominal muscles and the big lumbar muscles with the upward twist, will occur. Strain and tear of the thigh muscles is possible when cold. All of these cause loss of power, and hence timing, and result in spectacular falls. It is in the athlete's interest therefore for any soreness or sense of weakness in the important muscle groups to be reported and checked. It is vital to keep muscles warm and stretched during work and competition.

Highspeed filming has shown that the spine goes from 40° extension at pole plant to 90° flexion in 0.65 seconds, and then reverses going over the bar. With such torque, spinal fatigue fractures are always possible and constant strengthening of the lumbar (back) muscles is vital.

The safety of equipment is paramount in this event. Pole vault landing blocks are subject to international standards in competition but at training ovals second best or high jump bags tied together are usually all that is available and dangerous gaps are ignored. Also skewing off the bar, or being thrown sideways by the pole, can mean that the landing misses the foam blocks, with drastic effects to the ankle. The proper landing area should be 5 metres square made of blocks 75 cm deep covered by mesh. Unfortunately this is expensive and time-consuming to drag out of storage and into place. To progress, a talented youth should join a club of fellow elitists that can afford the equipment and has an interest in using it properly.

Field Events

Safety to self and others must be drilled into all hammer throw, discus, and javelin hopefuls and their watching friends, and it is this safety factor that has led to the banning of high school javelin events on some fields. For maximum thrust, coordinated spin and leverage across several joints must occur and timing plus power will beat brute strength always. Leg power is vital and if the legs are sore or injured training should be suspended. Timing deteriorates with fatigue, and then errors creep into technique and injuries are more possible, so a good coach is always needed to prevent overtraining. Overenthusiastic use of training weights is another danger (p. 208). The need for leg and back strength is common to all these events, but each uses different joints and muscle groups; there is little doubt when strain has occurred and when medical help is required.

The discus puts rotation strain on the knee if the spin is ill-timed, and jerky release can harm the finger joints or the shoulder rotator cuff (p. 61). The javelin stresses the elbow joint in much the same way as baseball pitching, with pain on the inner side, but ruptured muscles and tendons can also occur. With the effort to hold back the throwing arm to the last possible moment the biceps tendon that runs across the top of the shoulder joint can be dislocated from its groove and thereafter snaps in and out of position. The planting of the front foot with knee locking (usually the left) can lead in time to all the varieties of knee strain. The thrust in traditional shot putting begins at the toes and travels right through to the fingers, with possible muscle or ligament tear all along the line, or avulsion (tearing away) fractures of bone tips or attachments. Pain is immediate at the site of injury. The wrist takes the weight of the shot and sprains are common if it is forced too far back, and, as in weight lifters, the radial (outer forearm) epiphysis (p. 17) can be damaged. A very rare result of severe effort is a fracture of the humerus (upper arm). The new rotational technique may lead to knee strain as in the discus and hammer throw.

Stress fractures have been noted in each of the field events after prolonged training so that any bone pain must be investigated.

And a final warning to all athletes: take the track suit off carefully when wearing spikes or you will trip up and gash the calf muscles!

Australian Rules

With this version of football Harrison and Wills invented a relatively safe sport for preadolescents, and even more so for juniors because of their slower speed, low weight and general suppleness of body. In Australian Rules, the coaching emphasis is on fundamental skills, positional play and team styles, and there is so much to learn that the 'win at any price' attitude (copied from adults) which produces such mayhem in body contact sports generally, is foiled. Also, with no set scrums there is almost (one can never say 'never') no risk of the neck fracture and paraplegia that so bedevil rugby (p. 159).

However, in such a fast and fluid form of football with heavy body contact in marking and scrambles for the ball, the opportunity for significant injury eventually arrives. Youngsters who have been largely standing around for instruction in the cold must warm up adequately before accelerating into action or attempting huge kicks, in order to prevent avulsion (muscle tear) of their epiphyseal attachments (p. 17). With the emphasis on leaping for a high mark, there is the risk of tendon pulls around the knee cap and arm fractures by falling in a heap.

Fingers can be dislocated in handmarking, hitting the ball or blocking it off the foot. The knee and ankle are vulnerable to sprain or strain because they are constantly involved in pivoting, swerving, jumping and landing. The feet in the young are untried and untested for heavy work, and minor bone constructions or misalignments will cause pain in the feet if aggravated by ill-fitting boots.

High marking leaves the loins exposed so that the spleen on the left and the kidneys on both sides can be bruised. Concussion from collisions (and we hope not by contact with unpadded goalposts) disqualifies the player from further play that day and usually much longer. A mouthguard is said to be some protection against concussion by dissipating the force of a head blow, and for the teeth's sake one must always be worn by serious players.

Many problems, less often met with in this code, are dealt with in greater detail in the chapters on rugby (p. 159), soccer (p. 181) and gridiron (p. 127), chapters which in any case will be interesting to national football league fans.

Badminton

A wonderful, fast, but jerky, game when compared with its cousins, tennis and squash. In a confined area sudden stops, starts, lunges, twists and leaps can tear or strain muscles in all areas, and this will require physiotherapy, rest and further muscle conditioning. Acute ankle and knee sprain can also occur. Chronic shoulder strain can develop in the rotator cuff (p. 61) mechanism from the constant endeavour for power, and from unusual actions such as the overhead backhand. A tennis elbow is rare in badminton since the shuttlecock is not causing a strong counterthrust on the end of the racquet. In doubles, young inexperienced players can collide causing cuts and bruises, and eye injuries occur more often. The net player must be specifically warned not to turn around to look at the server; he risks getting a mis-hit or a racket edge in the eye. An overhead smash can also catch the net partner by surprise, and this shot probably causes most eye injuries. If a player is wearing spectacles, they should be tied on, and in general this is one sport where eye protectors are a boon for novices. The literature also records an eye injury in a front row spectator! Older players must watch for overuse injury, especially in the back, caused by repetitive, stereotyped strokes.

Ballet

There is a big difference between allowing the really young to start ballet classes to learn deportment, movement to music, and to share all the fun of the graceful environment, and allowing them to advance towards serious levels of training (with possibly a professional career in mind) before anatomical features have developed and before strength and stamina are really adequate for the routines. Indeed teachers of long experience have noted a difference between earlier and present-day pupils. Modern teenagers, they say, tend to be quicker learners but reluctant to pay attention to detail, possibly because their enjoyment is quashed by the well-publicised rigours of advanced ballet. This may in the end make youngsters with modest aims reluctant even to start classes.

Before classes begin parents should have a careful look at the child's body form and suppleness, using the details given in the chapter on gymnastics (p. 136) as a guide since the leg and back stresses of gymnastics and ballet have much in common. One major test is the plié position. The bent knee should be directly over the toes, not on a perpendicular line falling inside the big toe with the foot rolling onto a flattened medial arch. The 180° turnout should also be checked to see that it is possible with a straight, locked knee, and that it is not being achieved by bending the lower spine. If it is, hip flexibility is poor. Either of the two bodes ill. Full ankle movements both up (dorsiflexion) and down (plantarflexion) are needed eventually. All these factors, plus the rate of growth and strength, vary even between sisters and parents must be careful to spot the danger of urging one daughter to progress 'like your sister'.

Parents must take time to visit the rooms where the classes will be held and should then have a careful chat with the teacher. Some may still believe that strain and pain are a normal part of ballet class, but pain really means that joints are being forced beyond their normal range. There is a world of difference between stretching to overcome tight muscles (rare anyhow in small children but possible as the puberty growth spurt develops), and overstretching joint capsules to increase flexibility and range of movements. Good teachers know the difference and do not advance youngsters too quickly. The bone epiphyses (p. 16) are put under such strain that pointe drills, for example, must proceed with circumspection until the early teens. This is because up until approximately twelve years of age the growth centres of the various small foot bones are still active and therefore vulnerable. Some orthopaedic surgeons are not in favour of any toe tip work until after age eleven or perhaps even later, because if the growth epiphyses do fuse prematurely the big toe can be permanently shortened. Strength of the leg and foot muscles has to be adequate for proper balance in toe work otherwise the long toe tendons on one side or other of the ankle are unnaturally strained and will become tender and inflamed with tenosynovitis. Also, it is often forgotten that without strong abdominal muscles excess strain has to be taken by the back muscles in balancing the trunk over the foot. Serious ballet work must thus include specific muscle strengthening exercises.

Obvious injury is uncommon unless the dancer falls over. Basic foot and leg overuse stress is the worry, even to the stage of stress fractures of the small foot bones. Rarely do symptoms come suddenly; the gradual onset is unfortunate because the injury is then in danger of being submerged under dedicated, passionate discipline. Poor basic anatomy eventually will strain the medial foot arch, the joints of the big toe, and the ligaments of the inner side of the knee. Where knee ligaments are under strain in the young the bone epiphyses may suffer more than the ligaments (see Chapters 4 and 12; p. 16 and p. 59). Achilles tendinitis can develop in association, or separately because of the strain of constant deceleration on landing. Bad jumping technique aggravates it. The dancer must be able to begin the jump with the heel on the ground. Excessive pointe work stresses the long tendons to the big toe, tender tenosynovitis resulting. Excessive jumping may cause patellar tendinitis or slippage of the epiphysis of attachment, Osgood-Schlatter disease (p. 19). Knee strain, and eventually osteochondritis (p. 19), develop if the knee is forced to compensate for faults in the hip or ankle anatomy in the turnout position, if the fouette is too vigorous, if there is an emphasis on weight-bearing on a flexed knee, or if the ankle lacks basic flexibility. In this latter case small congenital bone outgrowths around the ankle joint may be the cause.

Backache is a warning that parents must not ignore. It may be muscle fatigue from overzealous work, ligament strain if the back is being forced to compensate for lack of backward hip flexibility in assuming the correct attitude, or a stress fracture (p. 20) may be imminent. Rest is essential until a proper diagnosis is made.

Bone age on X-ray is more relevant than birth age in determining the possibility of stress injuries, as indicated by research among twelve- to fifteen-year-olds in the Geneva public school system, which found that delayed puberty, with its delay in bone development, was directly related to the injury rate in high level athletes and ballet dancers. National ballet schools can now use prediction tables to gauge a preteenager's eventual height before admitting them to serious training.

Balletomanes sometimes train under poor conditions which accentuate body stress. Cold draughty halls, uneven floors, nowhere to stretch and warm up, and poor shoes all spell trouble. Shoes with rough ridges, or shoes that are too small for the toes must be avoided. It is unfortunate that on stage the appearance of a shoe counts for more than comfort and function. It is a great pity that shoes cannot be designed to absorb more shock. Foot hygiene is very important. In heavy routines a body shower is not enough properly to cleanse the ankle and heel skin. The feet must be soaked, carefully cleansed, and powdered. They are a dancer's most precious possession. Ingrown toenails, corns, bruised and discoloured toenails, blisters, in fact any abnormalities must be carefully treated. A hallux valgus form of the big toe (angulation and bunion formation) and possible menstrual disturbances from excess training are discussed in Chapter 11 (p. 52). If the menstrual cycles remain poor and untreated, the blood oestrogen hormone level could drop to the point where bone strength is affected, and this is serious, especially in the vertebrae.

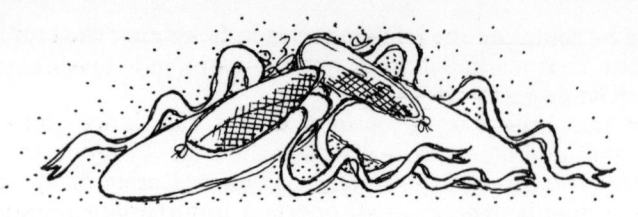

A problem developing later with some is that training emphasises hip joint abduction (leg movement away from the midline) and external rotation to turn the toe out, and neglects the opposite movements of adduction (leg movement towards the midline) and internal rotation. There can be unbalanced flexibility and tightening to some muscles and fibrous bands, causing hip or knee pain or a peculiar snapping sound as the tight structures move over bone. Stretching and muscle exercises may need a change of emphasis to overcome the imbalance.

Dieting to maintain weight and shape may also affect bone development through lack of calcium and vitamin D deficiency. Evidence suggests that where dieting becomes almost fanatical with a daily intake of 1000 calories or less the pubertal growth curve is affected. It has also been found that an increasing number of adolescent ballet hopefuls are developing anorexia nervosa.

Now let us not forget the young gentlemen. When they start their lifts leg muscle tears, avulsion (tearing) of the patellar tendon or tendon strain, and shoulder girdle tears may occur. Early back strain is an insidious cause of later adult 'trouble' so that strengthening exercises are a must, especially for the willowy. Adolescent males are inclined to be 'show-offs' in all sports, and in ballet this can lead to knee strain from exaggerated efforts and too many falls. Persistent bone pain or tender spots must be X-rayed to detect chips or hairline fractures.

Baseball

Little Leaguers are the life blood of the sport. If they concentrate on learning proper technique their risk of injury is minimised whilst their speed, strength, and ambitious play develop. Their injuries after that are basically self-inflicted or caused by the moving ball. The catcher, shortstop and pitcher collect most of the latter. If there is a most common injury in the young group in baseball it is a fractured finger or sprain of the last interphalangeal joint, and it must be suspected whenever the ball has hit the finger end on, or has hyperextended the tip as it flicks past. The bigger softball causes a 'Mallet' fracture of the finger (p. 105). Hospital statistics show that a high percentage of these injuries are seen early in the season before basic skills of catching and fielding have been honed. Little Leaguers must be coached in proper glove technique. The main points relevant to injury in baseball are:

- Metal bats will not break as often as the wooden ones but will still inflict as much damage if someone gets in the way of a warm-up swing.
- Collisions with other players or the fence can damage anything, and fracture any bone. A fractured neck with paraplegia is the worst injury (p. 22). Spinal cord shock is also frightening; if struck on the forehead by the ball the head jerks back, hyperextending the neck and bruising the cervical segment of the spinal cord. The collapsed player may be unable initially to move but slowly movement and feeling will return to differentiate this from paraplegia.
- Sliding to base must be feet first since a fractured leg is 'better' than a fractured skull. Once begun, continue the slide in a straight line. Most fractures and sprains in one hospital study occurred when the runner changed his mind and attempted something else during the slide. Friction burns are more likely on artificial surfaces or in clothes with tears and holes.
- The fast-moving ball can kill a bird, fracture a facial bone or rib, fracture the Adam's apple cartilage, or break the nose. The ball can ricochet off a foul hit to the batter's face or leap unexpectedly into short stop off a bumpy field. In the United States, from 1985, helmets were required for all softball

batters in the National Federation of State High School Associations' teams, and the National Society to Prevent Blindness in New York City recommends that children under fourteen should use helmets with face guards whilst batting.
- The catcher, too long in the squatting position, can strain the knee or patellar (kneecap) tendon. A genital protector is important. A foul hit off even a slow pitch can damage. A lightweight glove is a boon to the safety of the other hand and should result in far fewer dislocated or fractured fingers.
- Pulled muscles occur in cold or unfit runners.
- Pitching straight and smooth is safe, but excessive spells or overlong practice of fast curves will cause problems to the shoulder rotator cuff (p. 61). Probably at more risk in the young is the elbow joint because around it are seven growing centres, appearing at intervals but all being active by age ten and fused with the main shaft by seventeen. A report in 1982 noted an unusual injury, a gap in the epiphyseal line (p. 17) at the head of the humerus in twelve- to fifteen-year-old pitchers, so perhaps the epiphyseal plate is giving way before the strain can affect the rotator cuff. Adolescents must not try to be a 'horse' or dream of beating the speed gun! The Eugene League study of 1976 in the United States examined eleven- and twelve-year-old pitchers by X-ray. Some 23% had X-ray changes on the medial (inner) side of the elbow, and 5% had very significant damage to the head of the radius (outer forearm bone) on the lateral (outer) side, although none had missed a game. Sadly some players will never admit to pain, but warning signs are the inability completely to stretch the elbow, tender spots, or swelling. It has been stated that more problems are found in the southern states of America because of longer seasons and that pitching overarm is better than sidearm; a 1980 study in Oklahoma however failed to find any correlation with any factor except increasing age, which means increasing use. Tests on Boston Red Sox pitchers once showed a 5% loss of shoulder muscle strength by the end of the season. Adolescents could never play such heavy schedules but it is a warning of the need to maintain strength in the off-season to avoid shoulder strain in early games.

Strong legs play a vital role in throwing. The drive leg experiences rotation force on the hip and valgus strain (stretch away from the midline) of the knee's medial (inner) ligaments. The plant leg tends to hyperextend (lock backwards). Therefore any weakness of the legs caused by strain, bruising, or knee damage from other sports, not only slows the pitch but also causes jerky shoulder action. In other words if the legs are sore don't pitch, and if the legs are weak, strengthen them.

Accurate diagnosis of pain in the elbow or shoulder can be

difficult but it should be pursued. It is vital to decide whether play can continue or must stop. And how much unnecessary work is the pitching arm getting by pickup games and pitching endlessly to Dad *after* regular practice and games? With the undoubted cumulative effects of constant use, the young expert should learn early to conserve his best pitches, and not to let himself be pushed too hard by a coach overkeen to win a school game, or a parent too enthusiastic to see him gain selection.

A very rare problem has surfaced in Japanese players of about sixteen years of age called digital ischaemia (loss of blood supply to a finger; specifically the index finger of the gloved hand). The constant thumping of a ball into the base of the finger damages the artery of supply; the player notices coldness, numbness, perhaps a blueness, and maybe a nail deformity. The real cause is endless, endless practice. No cases were found in junior high school, but in high school teams practising seven days a week one player in five was found to be affected to mar what youngsters would otherwise call a state of paradise, playing ball for five hours every day. Catchers and first basemen were most affected. Better gloves should lessen the problem.

More recently another form of interference with the blood supply has been detected in young Japanese pitchers: ulcers of the fingertip. Coaches supplied the further observation that pitchers with flexible fingers and capable of throwing a fork ball have cold fingers. The cause of both seems to be overdevelopment of the small hand muscles and hypermobility of the finger joints, which combine to compress blood vessels. Corrective surgery is needed to release the pressure. Maybe only pitchers with small hands would be prone to the problem.

Complex electrical measurements of the sequence of muscle action in amateur and professional pitchers has shown that, in broad terms, the amateurs use more rotator cuff (p. 61) and upper arm muscles, and the professionals use more of the large chest muscles. The latter group supply most of the forward acceleration in throwing with the arm remaining more passive in the throw than previously thought. This suggests that an expert shoulder conditioning programme would help protect the amateur shoulder and elbow from strain.

REFERENCES:
Gowan I. D. et al. A comparative electromyographic analysis of the shoulder during pitching. *Am. J. Sports Med.* 1987; 15: 566–590.
Grana W. A. Pitcher's elbow in adolescents. *Am. J. Sports Med.* 1980; 8: 333.

Itoh Y. et al. Circulatory disturbances in the throwing hand of baseball pitchers. *Am. J. Sports Med.* 1987; 15: 264–269.

Sugawara M. et al. Digital ischaemia in baseball players. *Am. J. Sports Med.* 1986; 14: 329–333.

Torg J. S. et al. The effect of competitive pitching on the shoulders and elbows of preadolescent baseball players. *Paediatrics* 1972; 49: 267–271.

Basketball

It is not appreciated, but of great importance to watch out for in team selection, that strength and endurance in growing children are often not acquired for a year or two after the adolescent growth spurt. Athletes should not be pushed too far in this phase, or criticised 'for not trying' or 'for letting the team down'. In basketball, particularly, the tall young player may not at first be the match winner he was chosen to be and psychological harm can easily be inflicted. If old Father Time was the coach he would not be worried. Aggressive play is an insoluble factor in injury. In the United States, a psychological test, the Tennessee Self Concept Scale, was used following a Minnesota High School Tournament in 1980 to check injured players and it was mooted that there was correlation between the results and the tendency for those players who had been injured to take more risks or to get themselves into situations in play where injury could result. Adult wisdom may occasionally have to draw a line between keenness and unsporting aggression.

Mr Naismith did not intend his game to be dangerous or to produce a crop of injuries, but it is now doing so as it becomes f-fast and f-furious, and one must f-focus on fingers, falls, fast turns, feet, fans and first-aid.

Fingers

A three-quarter-kg ball is quite a projectile, and since fingers are accelerating towards it the momentum of collision is considerable. The resultant hyperextension of the fingertip can:

- Sprain the interphalangeal (IP) joint.
- Dislocate the IP joint.
- Fracture-dislocate the IP joint, that is dislocate it with a chip fracture.
- Avulse (tear away) the extensor tendon from the tip behind the nail. This causes the so-called Mallet deformity; the tip is bent down and cannot be straightened out because the pull of the flexing tendon running along the palm is acting unopposed.
- Fracture the shaft of the proximal phalanx (the first bone in the finger), with displacement of the portions so that it looks like an upturned dinner fork.
- Dislocate the metacarpo-phalangeal (knuckle) joint, that of the thumb being the most significant.
- Fracture the metacarpal shaft in the palm, that of the thumb again being significant.
- Fracture the base of the thumb, a complicated affair involving the joint called Bennett's fracture.

This list may come as a shock to any basketball coach of rich experience who has 'pulled dozens of fingers back'. Undoubtedly, *if* it is just a dislocation it is best reduced (put back) quickly into place by traction combined with flexion before the victim has much time to think about it and before the area cools off or develops reactive swelling. The catch is in the *if*. It is hard to provide accurate statistics, because these are based on hospital admissions, and probably most injuries are simple IP sprains or dislocations. One problem with the sprain is that it may have been a transient dislocation, spontaneously brought back into line by ligamentous recoil; the joint capsule may have thus been stretched or some fibres torn and, if so, the joint will need to be expertly splinted and immobilised. If not, proper healing is jeopardised, and the result is a stiff finger or one prone to recurrent dislocation.

Where bone chips have occurred the fragments may have to be replaced by surgery (open reduction) otherwise there is again a stiff finger. Therefore any sprain, or successfully reduced dislocation, must have a later X-ray. The thumb is so important in hand function that there is no room for error. Any injury to it must be X-rayed and expertly managed.

Falls

A bruised bottom, and ego, is hopefully all that will happen but any bone that forcibly hits the floor first should be checked for residual pain or persistent tenderness and, if there is any doubt, X-rayed. This applies to the knee cap, shoulder, elbow, hand and, of course, the head. Any fall onto the outstretched hand may cause fracture of the wrist scaphoid bone, the head of the radius (outer forearm bone), or the clavicle (collar bone), or dislocation of the acromio-clavicular joint (p. 62). If falling in a tangle the knee, ankle, or elbow can be sprained, or, with very bad luck, dislocated. One sixteen-year-old player who fell onto the point of the shoulder suffered damage to the brachial nerve plexus in the armpit and the resultant muscle atrophy (shrinkage) took twelve months to cure.

Traumatic synovitis of the elbow is common in children; X-rays will be negative but tenderness, swelling, and restricted movement will persist. In 1904 the famous Dr Robert Jones of Liverpool, England, warned that forcible passive movements or silly weight-bearing exercises of an injured elbow actually made it worse, and indeed risked permanent stiffness. The point still has to be emphasised eighty-four years later that a youngster with an injured elbow needs medical supervision and not just heat and massage.

Any fall onto the head or tumble over the back of another player causing concussion or suspicion of neck injury must be taken seriously and the rules in Chapter 5 followed to the letter (p. 22).

Fast Turns, Jumps, and Props

These can obviously strain the hamstrings, the adductor (inner side) thigh muscles, or the Achilles tendon. In the lanky and supple player rapid movements of the back, aggravated by bumps and falls, are a potent source of low lumbar (back) strain. In fact many a bad back in middle age can be traced to a basketball injury that was not checked at the time for bone damage. It is also possible that the demands of the sport will expose an existing problem in the hip or spine.

Prolonged practice around the basket can cause jumper's knee (p. 92), and cartilage tears may occur for the usual reason, twisting the body on a planted foot. It would be as well to mention here that this situation occurs particularly in netball (p. 155). In one study of professional basketball it was noted that women had 1.6 times more injuries than men, mostly to the leg joints and muscles. Men had more muscle spasm and the point was made that in training, women should spend more time on strength training and men more on flexibility exercises. In the

United States this was supported by a three-year Oklahoma secondary school study involving 130 schools and some 43,000 children. Basketball caused most injuries in girls and, in fact, when those figures were excluded the injury rate in all the other sports was the same for both boys and girls. The favoured site of injury in girls was the knee.

Feet

Bruised heels, blisters and jammed toes are common when poor shoes are worn. As players get heavier and more skilful, thus putting more strain on their feet, this part of their equipment becomes more and more important. Theoretically, different surfaces need different shoes, but it is better for young players to keep to the comfortable shoe and learn to adapt their game. The University of Illinois in Chicago once found that a vinyl-coated concrete floor was causing shinsplints and stress fractures; properly sprung wooden floors are the best.

Fans

Fans in the early days of the game were allowed close to the floor and this is still so in the older halls, encouraging fiercely competitive spirits to be aroused when players tumble into spectators. Accidental and even deliberate clashes occur between the players and spectators and, of the two, the player, being out of breath and with the eyes focused on the game, is disadvantaged and vulnerable to unfair injury.

First-Aid

Floors are always dirty and abrasions should be cleaned with soap and water and checked for splinters etc. Antiseptics are traditional and look good but should be mild; many a skin repair cell has been killed by strong chemicals, which is a pity because the repair mechanisms in the young are very active. Some sort of cotton wool pad should be built up over the wound and covered by an elastic dressing because kids are notorious for 'doing it again'.

Fingers must be taken seriously. Whilst simple dislocations

of the tip, or second interphalangeal joint (p. 66) of the four fingers, can undoubtedly be reduced (put back) quickly into place, this ought not to be attempted by anyone unable to recognise the deformity of a Mallet finger, a Bennett thumb, or a proximal phalanx fracture. And, even after a successful reduction, there is no place in school sport for the practice of strapping the stubbed finger to its neighbours and returning the player to the game. An X-ray must be organised to check for chip fracture or epiphyseal separation (p. 17), the finger properly splinted, and follow-up supervised. The same routine should be followed for what may seem to be only a painful sprain. The player should not train with the team or be reselected until an orthopaedic surgeon gives a clearance, no matter how many frustrating weeks it takes.

On resumption, the finger can be protected against further knocks by a stall made of silicone rubber, or silicone glue and seal, which are materials approved by National Councils. Figure-of-eight taping of the thumb will prevent further overstretching. If there is, nevertheless, a recurrent dislocation or sprain, the player should consider abandoning the sport. No child should be allowed to risk a stiff finger and future disability.

The first-aid attendant must be alert to the possibilities stemming from accidental fouls. A knee or an elbow can fracture a rib or the jaw and snap teeth, and the point of the elbow fits nicely and dangerously into the eye socket.

A blow on the head from a rebound was calculated by the Mayo Clinic Biodynamics Research Unit in the United States to cause a 20G acceleration to the head, enough to cause small vessels to burst; this did happen to one of their patients, a seventeen-year-old boy, who developed a subdural haematoma (p. 26) within one hour of the accident.

And it is not just flesh that suffers. Many cases of skin rash and eye conjunctivitis were once found to be due to ultraviolet radiation escaping from high pressure mercury arc lamps. And since these lamps are installed for longevity, up to 25,000 hours, there is plenty of opportunity for them to be hit and damaged.

Finally, a word to those parents who officiate at weekend games. Are you fit enough? It has been observed that the combination of running about in unwonted fashion plus the mental tension of making decisions in front of a partisan gallery produces a rapid pulse and anxiety, in other words, cardiac stress. Refereeing will not make you fit, you must get fit before doing it!

Boxing

The well-known cases of brain damage occurring in professionals later in life and the very rare, but widely publicised deaths of boxers in the ring have affected boxing as a school sport. In 1982 the United Kingdom Board of Science and Education set up a working party to study the medical effects of boxing and its place as a school sport. In 1983 the 35th World Medical Assembly recommended that boxing be banned, and published a list of practical steps that should be taken by National Medical Associations in the meantime. Many countries have long banned professional boxing. In 1984 the American Medical Association recommended that punches to the head be banned, just as those below the belt were years ago. However, organisers of the New York Golden Gloves and Kid Gloves tournaments point to a resurgent popularity under their properly supervised conditions. Four areas are vital:

Medical Assessment

This should take place not just before a tournament, but before a boy even begins training. It is very doubtful if anyone with a history of concussion in another sport, for example football, should box; the effects of concussion are cumulative. Previous eye injury, an enlarged spleen from glandular fever, or fractured fingers fall into the same category, as does anything which reduces stamina, such as past rheumatic fever or anaemia etc.

Protection

Headgear is essential although it will only protect the eyebrows and ears and will not protect the brain. Oversized gloves are now advocated and gloves with the new closed-cell foam padding may further help dissipate force. It is claimed that thumbless gloves, now used in the United States in the Kid Gloves tournament for ten- to fifteen-year-olds, are less likely to cause eye injuries. This would be true for the accidental 'poke in the eye', but not for detachment of the retina due to a direct eye hit. Such detachments tend to be of the severe variety, and even if they are remedied by laser surgery, the victim should never box again.

Mouthguard technology is improving and the latest bimaxillary type is said to reduce the pressure wave transmitted to the face and skull more effectively than older models.

Ancient Greek boxers wore leather thongs to protect the fingers, and ear guards. Plutarch recommended the latter especially for children to prevent them from hearing the bad language that accompanied the sport!

Training

This should concentrate on craft and emphasise keeping the guard well up for protection. Bigger gloves help this.

Refereeing

Butting with the head, wild punches, kidney punches, and deliberate blows to the back of the head must be penalised, with repeated infringement earning disqualification. Points should be awarded for clean punches. Bouts obviously must be stopped in good time to prevent needless punishment, and also if there is eye injury. If a mouthguard pops out hostilities should temporarily cease for its replacement.

Boxing is always quite low in the list of amateur sport injuries, but some indication of the injury rate in fit young men is given in an American analysis from West Point, published in 1980 (Welch), covering 12,000 bouts (that is 24,000 boxer appearances) with 285 injuries. The overall rate was 1.2% which is comparatively low. One in six were head injuries; head gear was worn and no brain dysfunctions occurred. A surprising one in four were shoulder dislocations indicating that shoulder strength in the young is not as good as it ought to be, and high schools should perhaps focus on it.

Most injuries, but not all, are to the head and hands.

- Face lacerations. The face has a wonderful blood supply and heals quickly but scars should be given up to three months

properly to heal and strengthen. There is no point in opening them up again in sites where they gape, such as the forehead.
- Bruised ear, that is a haemorrhage between the skin and cartilage. To prevent the cauliflower effect, the accumulated blood must be aspirated and a pressure dressing applied (the newer Insta-Mold of silicone is better as it will prevent distortion of the ear canal). If the blow leaves the boxer deaf or dizzy the inner ear must be checked for damage.
- Broken nose. With a broken nose the median cartilage is fragmented and an ear, nose, and throat specialist should repair the damage. Immediate bleeding occurs because the mucous membrane is also torn and in some cases it can only be stopped by proper packing. It occasionally happens that a blow to the nose, whilst not breaking it, will cause bleeding into the cartilaginous septum (the division between the two nostrils), which, although not immediately obvious, may cause later blockage. This is more serious than it appears because the septum can then get infected and ulcerate. In any case where nose breathing is impaired urgent specialist attention is needed.
- Fractured finger, usually the index metacarpal shaft just behind the knuckle (in a direct punch), or the thumb (when bent back in a slipped punch).
- Fractured wrist scaphoid bone (p. 66). This is always a tricky fracture to diagnose and to treat; it is doubtful whether it is worth continuing with the sport when the fracture has healed and risking it happen again.
- Fractured larynx. Uncommon, but dangerous if the airway is blocked or blood wells up. Blows to the neck may occasionally cause temporary unconsciousness by bruising the carotid (neck) artery or the vital vagus nerve (nerve controlling breathing and the heart).
- Fractured rib. If a punch capable of this lands near the heart, it may upset its rhythm, and the boxer will feel dizzy or faint.
- Kidney punches, aptly named, should lead to instant disqualification at this level of boxing. The first sign that kidney damage has in fact occurred would be the appearance of blood in the urine and the boxer must be told to watch for it.

No publicised series of brain damage or death from head injury in children mentions boxing as a cause, so that on that score it would seem safer than even, say, tennis. However, after a knockout, and possibly even a technical knockout, a CAT scan should be done to make absolutely sure no focal brain haemorrhage has occurred. Any episode of concussion has a temporary effect on the brain's mechanisms and if the youngster suffers a second such episode he should give up boxing. Repeated cerebral damage is what gives the sport a bad name. My tutor in medicine forty years ago met Gene Tunney, then a successful businessman, and came away very impressed with his intelligence. In their conversation Tunney said that after his bout with Jack Dempsey he had had amnesia for several days and decided then that he would have to give up boxing. Dempsey lived into his eighties, a respected legend with no trace of affliction. Both fighters were tough, but craftsmen, and gentlemen.

REFERENCES:
Welch M. J. et al. Case studies of upper extremity injuries in boxing. *Med. and Science in Sports and Exercise* 1982; 14: 141.
W.M.A.'s Declarations and Statements. *World Med. J.* 1982; 29: 84–92.

Break Dancing

At least the 'sport' has been accurately named. It will break the neck. The slightest miscalculation and the whole weight of the body is taken by the bent and angled cervical vertebrae. This is exactly the position described under gridiron as causing fracture or dislocation of the neck with spinal cord damage (p. 22). Such could have been predicted and cases have now been reported from accident centres, along with fractured collar bones, fractured or severely sprained thumbs, and spectacular bruising of the back. Even if there is no loss of balance the compression force is likely to cause fragmentation (collapse) of a vertebra.

Falls have torn knee ligaments and sprained ankles. Fracture dislocations of the first phalanx of the dominant thumb have needed surgery. One twelve-year-old boy, adept at back spins, developed a fatty fibrous tumour over his spine as a reaction to repeated injury. In New Orleans two young proponents each had a twisted and damaged testicle removed. Tight jeans probably contributed by squeezing the testis into unusual positions. The lucky ones only get patches of premature baldness where the hairs are continually shorn off.

Cheerleading

These open air gymnastic displays, with complicated routines, need skill and timing, and hence physical fitness and practice. Also, they are not always conducted under good conditions and during a long afternoon fatigue and cold muscles have to be combatted.

The American Consumer Products Safety Commission 1979 Report found that an average of 1% of participants were injured, and one third of these were in the five- to fourteen-year age group. The stars of the show, however, might have a higher than average risk in descending from pyramids and doing special tricks. A 1982 survey of 15,000 American high school cheerleaders between twelve and eighteen years gave a higher 4% injury rate, mostly to the ankle, knee, wrist and arm. Interestingly, some one in seven of the injuries happened at training camps.

Mild sprains, bruises and abrasions, and hamstring muscle pulls are common and, as in gymnastics, bad landings can strain the back, fracture the ankle or wrist, or dislocate fingers. The special cheerleader shoe has better arch and ankle support with flexibility to ameliorate ankle strain. As a physical activity cheerleading is as demanding as gymnastics and must not be approached nonchalantly. It needs pre-season conditioning and alertness at all times. Squads using the trampoline should read carefully the chapter on its use (p. 197).

The New South Wales Gridiron Football League has established a splendid code of ethics, behaviour and dress standards, and has adopted strict safety standards for young cheerleaders supporting their competition teams. These comprehensive safety rules are reproduced below by kind permission of Janis O'Shea, Secretary of the NSWGFL. The League holds educational clinics in the off-season and uses video tapes that emphasise safety, warm-ups and injury protection. Girls with scoliosis (spinal curvature) are given special exercises and extra attention by coaches to help them develop their confidence and enable them to reach their full potential.

Safety Regulations

a. Pyramid and partner stunt height will be measured by each complete body length as a unit. A shoulder stand will be designated as 2 units high, a shoulder straddle will be designated as 1½ units high, a double shoulder stand on thigh stands is designated as 2½ units high, etc.
b. Partner stunts will only be performed on suitable surfaces at any NSWGFL activity. Surfaces that are extremely hard (e.g. concrete, asphalt) or slippery will not be used.
c. Four high shoulder straddles will not be allowed.
d. Forearm stands that are higher than 1½ units will be double based.
e. NO dangling or protruding jewellery will be worn by bases or climbers when performing pyramids or partner stunts.
f. Climbers will wear approved, supportive athletic shoes with small tread soles when performing pyramids or partner stunts.
g. Only approved mounting techniques will be used:
   1.) Step and lock climbing technique
   2.) Back power mount technique
   3.) Assisted quick front pop technique
   There will be *no* blind mounts or unassisted back mounts.
h. All dismounts will be preceded by a verbal signal.
i. All dismounts will be conducted in an organised manner.
j. Dismounts that are 1½ units or higher will be spotted or assisted.
k. No flip dismounts will be permitted from partner stunts or pyramids.
l. No roll-off dismounts will be permitted from partner stunts or pyramids over 2 units high.
m. All cradle catches will be performed with a minimum of two bases.
n. All partner stunts or pyramids 2 units high will have at least one active spotter incorporated in the stunt or pyramid.
o. All partner stunts or pyramids 2½ units high will have at least two active spotters incorporated in the stunt or pyramid.
p. Active spotters will be alert, assertive and ready to solve problems.
q. Aerial partner stunts (flying birds, Swedish Falls, etc.) will be performed with two bases in all-girl squads.
r. Split catch partner stunts will only be performed with walk out mounts from the single or double shoulder stand bases. There will be no split catch stunts mounted with a quick pop technique.

Cricket

International fast bowlers dispatch a six stitcher at anything between 120 and 150 kilometres per hour, up to 40 metres per second, giving a batsman about half a second to do something about it, in particular not to let the ball hit him. Some school boys will have much the same problem at lesser ball speeds while their skills are undeveloped. Tests have shown that average players take 230 milliseconds to decide on their stroke. By the time a boy becomes a test star he will have got this down to 165 milliseconds. Girls' cricket rarely involves ball damage except to the fingers and the occasional bruise. Raised stitching can gouge skin with just a glancing blow but a direct hit causes real damage, even at low velocity, for example:

- Fractured wrist bone or fractured finger, caught between ball and bat handle.
- Fractured facial bone, cheek, nose, jaw, or tooth. In the latter case please read Chapter ·9 (p. 44) because time is of the essence in saving a tooth.
- Fractured rib, although the thorax is so springy in the young that just a bad bruise is more likely.
- Fractured skull. This is rare except when the ball strikes the temple where the bone is thinner than elsewhere on the skull. Note that death has resulted from haemorrhage of ruptured blood vessels which put pressure on the brain, so never ignore a comment such as: 'Got hit on the head today, mum.'
- Damaged eye. Theoretically a cricket ball is too large to fit into the eye socket and hence will fracture the bone rim rather than splotch the eyeball. This is true only for a horizontal frontal trajectory. Snicked off the bat edge in a mistimed hook, the ball zooms in from the side (or with a fieldsman bounces up from below) and on that angled path can hit the eyeball. An eye specialist must check an eye that has been hit as soon as possible for serious damage.
- Bruised fingernail, which can get quite painful if blood accumulates underneath. If the blood is let out by poking a hot needle through the nail bed it is possible to save the nail. This injury or a bruised toe (the big toe nail is too tough to be drilled by a needle), should be x-rayed if pain persists. The terminal phalanx may have been chipped or fractured.

- Bruised arm, thigh, or shinbone (ouch!). These should be bound firmly over cold compresses to limit swelling.
- Haematoma (blood clot) of the testis. Such swellings, or even what seems to be only skin bruising, should be carefully examined by a doctor. Unrelieved pressure on the testis will cause atrophy (shrinkage).
- Ruptured spleen from a blow under the left ribs.

Protective Gear

Most of the above injuries are preventable. Proper protective gear is available but expense often keeps it out of junior kit bags and the 'box' is usually not worn until after puberty. Shin pads and batting gloves are apt to be skimpy for growing lads and a common error is for lefthanded batsmen to make do with a pair of righthanded gloves, so that their right wrist and left fingertips really are without protection. It is hard to believe that helmets will become common in school cricket; they could actually be a hindrance to the development of skill in hooking which is the surest protection against being hit on the head. Also, the grading of XI's tends to keep bowling and batting skills evenly matched. Representative senior matches are another matter. The same logic that applies to helmets would apply to thigh and chest pads. Toecapped boots are out of fashion, which is a pity for the big toe.

Fielding

Fielders can suffer all of the above injuries close to the bat, but more likely are fingertip dislocations or fractures (p. 66). Slip fielders must not have long fingernails. Cut them short. Falls onto the outstretched hand, elbow, or shoulder, cause the usual fractures, and young players should be discouraged from diving at the speeding ball. Hard contact with the elbow tucked into the left side has been known to rupture the spleen. If a ball suddenly pops up on rough ground into the face, nasty cuts can occur and a knock on the tooth. It deserves reemphasis that time is important if a tooth is to be saved. Excessive explosive throwing practice can affect the elbow or shoulder rotator cuff (p. 61) as in a baseball pitcher, or just strain the chest muscles. Dr W. G. Grace, incidentally, caused national concern by straining a calf muscle in the field, or so the *Lancet* reported in 1884, in what must have been one of the first reports of a sports injury.

Sun hats or caps are advisable at all times for fielders in hot tropical and semi-tropical sun. Sunscreens should also be applied, especially to big noses.

Wicketkeeping

Wicketkeepers are certain to suffer stinging fingers from repeated pounding or poor returns, but if their inner and outer gloves fit properly and they are taught the correct, fingers pointing to the ground, technique, the opportunity for a fractured finger is minimal. Fast returns along the ground are an exception. They will damage downward-pointing fingertips (or bruise the instep). Leave them to the fieldsman backing up if you cannot get your pads behind the ball! There is a trend towards short pads for wicketkeepers, cut off at the knee to increase mobility, but this will be at a price; fractured kneecaps. Returns to the 'keeper in junior cricket are notoriously wayward.

Bowling

Fast bowling is now a problem in young hopefuls. The famous Harold Larwood, a Notts professional of immortal memory, attributed his classic delivery and troublefree career to the strength of his back and leg muscles, developed in his youth as a coalminer before he became a fulltime cricketer. The breakdowns now being reported in juniors may prove to be the result of the all too familiar modern problem: attempting too much, too early, too often. Experiments show that in fast bowling the thump onto the front foot creates a force for the knee and spine to absorb equal to between four and five times the body weight; the back is also subjected to an extension-flexion-rotation snap, since the trunk is in a partly side-on attitude to legs running at three to four metres per second. Smoothness in the run up, a true side-on delivery, and a balanced followthrough are said to minimise the vertebral strain, and it may be no coincidence that Larwood was famous for those three points in style. Boys as young as thirteen have had stress fractures of the vertebrae, or have developed Scheuermann's disease (p. 29), meaning that overbowling must be avoided. Any complaint of backache warrants an X-ray or even a CAT scan. Instead of concentrating on rhythm and side-on technique, watching their heroes on television unfortunately encourages young cricketers to overemphasise their 'strength', and this is also a good way to tear a leg muscle if they forget to warm up on chilly mornings. Once bone damage has been detected the bowler must not complete the season but use the winter to strengthen the back muscles and restudy his technique.

Mature fast bowlers wear two pairs of socks to cushion the heel against bruising but with the way adolescent feet grow this could squeeze the big toe and lead to nail bruising and blisters by the end of the season. It is possible for uneven humps or deep wear near the crease to cause a sprained ankle; at the practice nets these potholes must be looked for.

A rare event in fast bowling, accompanying the grunt of a severe effort and a rise in pressure of the lung gases, is rupture of small air sacs near the lung surface allowing air to escape into the chest tissues. As this air slowly spreads and works its way into the neck the cricketer becomes aware of pain in the midline or shoulder and some difficulty in breathing; an examining doctor may find the skin crackling from entrapped air. There is no danger and a few days of rest remedies the condition.

Another rare event is demonstrated by a young English speedster who was repeatedly no-balled. He was suspected of throwing because his elbow did not straighten for the delivery, but an X-ray showed that a congenital bone abnormality was preventing him from straightening it.

Strangely enough slow bowlers are the ones who can damage the rotator cuff (p. 61) of the shoulder in the effort to impart gargantuan spin to the ball, and they can also tear the fingernail or get infection under the cuticle margin.

Eyes

Several famous international players have always worn glasses whilst batting without any harm resulting, and although they were by then skilled adult performers, they too were once learners. This should encourage young glass wearers still to try cricket, but they should be observed carefully to see whether they develop good reflexes and can stay alert on the field. Eyeball injuries are fortunately not common; instinctive reflex movement at the last moment by the player usually puts the ball just that fraction off target to protect the eyeball, but not of course the bony margins.

Indoor Cricket

Indoor cricket is another matter and is causing more and more eye injuries. The ball used is either a leather-covered tennis ball or is made of polyurethane, hard when new and later prone to some degree of distortion. The playing area is limited by nets, meaning that wicketkeepers (and fielders) are forced to stand closer to the bat than they would in the open, especially if the players are really inexperienced. What cricketer would fancy fielding close to a slogger facing an inaccurate bowler?

Protective glasses should always be worn. An Australian opthalmologist observed that two of his patients had already suffered loss of vision in the damaged eye from previous injury and postulated that this had led to failure of eye defensive reflexes at the last millisecond. The danger would appear to be real if non-cricketers are tempted by advertisements to think that indoor cricket is a simple fun game that anyone can play, and that protective gear is not necessary.

This warning was emphasised in a report from the Royal Perth Hospital. Too many finger injuries were seen (females being singled out for special mention) because batting gloves were not worn or inexpert catchers were allowed too close to the action. One of their patients was hit by a bat wielded by an angry friend during a disagreement over the rules! Now that definitely isn't cricket.

A word of warning is apposite for fathers making up the numbers in indoor games; don't try to demonstrate your skills of yore. Torn leg muscles abound with jerky fielding and on non-slip unyielding synthetic surfaces the familiar problems of a twisted knee or a sprained ankle are more likely to occur.

Picket Fences

Unexpected, avoidable and quite bad injuries can occur by chasing a ball into the fence and children should be warned against it. A trip-up and a broken leg can occur in a twinkling, and old fence pickets are notorious for giving way under the hand, letting the face smash into the rail. Unfortunately young cricketers now see their heroes on television sliding feet first into the fence, making spectacular saves to thunderous applause. The observant will have noted that the script calls for strong legs, strong fences and smooth, smooth turf.

REFERENCES:
Coroneo M. T. Ocular injuries in indoor cricket. *Med. J. Aust.* 1985; 15 April.
Courteney N. *Sporting Royals*, Hutchinson, London 1983.
Forward G. R. Indoor cricket injuries. *Med. J. Aust.* 1988; 148: 560.

Cycling

The United States National Electronic Injury Surveillance System (NEISS) data of emergency admissions in 1979 showed that to bicycle was to participate in the most dangerous recreational activity in the United States, and that 62% of the 537,000 injuries were to children between five and fourteen years. Other figures for comparison were: baseball 438,860, football 425,000 and basketball 319,850. The United Kingdom Department of Transport 1980 figures showed that one third of those cyclists killed on their roads were under fifteen years of age. A ten-year survey in Brisbane, Australia, found that accidents on the road were most common in twelve- to fourteen-year-old boys between 3 and 5 p.m. (that is just out of school), on straight roads in clear weather. Lack of self-control and road discipline must be suspected, especially as six times more boys than girls had serious injuries. Out of 150 head injuries in twelve months only two children had been wearing helmets and the reason for this was apparently that helmets were considered to be unfashionable or 'sissy'. This stupid attitude must be actively attacked by parents and teachers because in all countries nearly all deaths involve motor cars and are caused by head injuries.

Some of these cyclists would have been serious travellers and not pleasure-bent, but if cars and cycles could be separated, the only hazard to cyclists would be falling over onto the shoulder, elbow or hand (fractures), with the leg caught (lacerations and ankle sprains), or with the thigh badly bruised between bar and road.

It behoves parents therefore to make absolutely sure that children can balance and handle their bikes *before* they mix with traffic and they must be warned time and again not to do unpredictable things that could confuse motorists or upset traffic flow. They must also be told not to lurk in a motorist's blind spots (the worst one is behind the car's near side, rear pillar). Children must be (but mostly are not) taught the rules of the road in order to be aware of what a motorist is going to do. Then they themselves can behave correctly and safely. This last point is emphasised over and over again by education committees. Some even recommend that parents should not allow children under nine years of age to ride in traffic unless accompanied by an adult, because up to that age they will not have developed the necessary skills or self-discipline to cope with traffic by themselves. Motorists should (but regrettably often do not) take especial care when they see bike-riding kids in the vicinity. A big danger is children riding in a group; one is bound to be a 'show-off', out to impress the gang, and he will end up distracting their collective attention. Night riding is definitely too dangerous for children who must be told: 'Be home before it *starts* to get dark.'

To tell children: 'Don't ride on the road, keep to the footpath', is no longer a good answer unless they are told very, very firmly that pedestrians have right of way. Children are now in the habit of riding the light, small BMX models too fast, and elderly walkers are very easily startled when they look around to see a projectile swooping down on them. Even front on, in situations where young keen eyes can see the gap, children must be told that ageing adults often cannot see very well and are slow to react. They sometimes feel the bike is coming too close and actually lurch into it. Serious and costly injuries result and parents are now being sued by victims. Police in the State of New South Wales have a bicycle safety liaison group that awards badges and commendations to careful cyclists, and warnings or even tickets to any cyclists who break traffic rules, ride dangerously, or commit common offences such as: no hands on handlebars; riding bike furiously; not having proper control (doubling); disobeying traffic signals; riding on footpath; and endangering pedestrian safety. The sale price of a bike will soon have to include a Public Risk Insurance Policy! (See Roller skating p. 156).

Beginners must beware of hopping onto unfamiliar bikes not adjusted to their size and, particularly, must not 'double up'; there is no quicker way to unbalance the bike, and then not one but two lives are at risk. Another important role for parents is to check the bike's condition and to see that it is in proper working order and that no amateurish modifications have been fitted. They should also insist on the wearing of helmets, clothing that covers skin areas, and items that reflect in dim light. Hospital statistics are beginning to show that cyclists are suffering more (and more fatal) head injuries than motorcyclists, for whom helmets are now compulsory. The conclusion is obvious: helmets should be compulsory for cyclists. The need for proper shoes is often overlooked. Bare feet can be horribly damaged and toes caught in the cogs have been torn off; thongs are little better and, like sloppy shoes, may catch in the pedals or shanks to cause a bad fall.

Losing control at speed or skidding into fixed objects such as light or telegraph poles and bus shelters could, at worst, fracture the skull or the neck. (The sight of daredevils on the new small manoeuvrable bikes rattling down flights of steps or leaping gutters is enough to freeze the blood of experienced neurosurgeons.) The strength of these small-wheel BMX bicycles must be carefully checked before purchase. There are incidents of pedals breaking, so that the genitals fall onto the bar, of front struts collapsing, so that the rider is pitched onto the head, and of handlebars snapping. It has to do with the way the bikes are ridden as much as the design, but it all adds another dimension to cycling injury. Check the design, in fact check everything about these small bikes, and then never cease to check how the youngster rides the bike because newer types of injury stem from both factors. Commercial advertising in which adults demonstrate 'tricks' are to be condemned. All the stunts are inherently dangerous. For one thing children do not have the arm and wrist strength to control the mobile front wheel if they meet an unexpected bumpy spot. In rough terrain the rider can come down quite heavily onto the saddle and break it. In one accident the saddle had rotated whilst the rider was in the air and its narrow pointed tip perforated the bowel. In another the rider fell back onto the moving rear wheel causing severe damage to the genitals. If the front wheel twists suddenly the child can pitch onto his head, fracture ribs on the side of the handlebars, or have deep abdominal organs such as the pancreas crushed between the handlebars and the spine. Always ask: 'Did the handlebars hit the pit of the stomach?' (p. 37). Grandparents may remember that military despatch riders had to wear a stiff leather corset from groin to chest as a protection against handlebar injury. Kids of course are not riding to war, it only looks like it!

A report of BMX injuries from the Sheffield Children's Hospital in the United Kingdom revealed that one child had attempted to slow the bike by putting a foot on the tyre, and another by putting a foot between the spokes! This is downright ignorance. One cannot call the children stupid, only their parents, for buying a bike, treating it as a mere toy, and obviously not bothering to give their precious offspring any tuition and supervision. It is quite a different thing if the youngster joins a proper BMX club with a track circuit. There are in fact world under-age BMX champions and some clubs even have one lap pursuit races for the under fives! To see the serious way they handle their bikes over bumps and around curves, in full protective gear, is an object lesson in controlled enthusiasm. And of course the bikes are checked by adult officials.

Parents should never ignore or lightly dismiss the statement: 'Fell off my bike, Mum, but I'm all right.' Enquire as to just what part of the body hit the ground. Even minor falls onto the outstretched hand, which would be the most likely, can damage the epiphyses of the lower end of the radius bone and seriously affect its growth (p. 17). Falling hard against projections can cause a ruptured spleen or liver. Always ask specifically, 'Did you hit your head?' There was one sad case of a little boy who said, 'I think I'll go to bed, good night, Mummy.' Those were the last words she ever heard. He died during the night of a subdural haemorrhage (p. 26). He didn't think to mention that he had decided to go to bed early because he had a slight headache.

In serious competitive racing the expert suffers fewer but more spectacular falls at speed, causing deeper lacerations complicated by embedded foreign material needing hospital management, and more fractures of limb and rib. The leather helmet cannot protect the head as well as a proper helmet unless it is thick with padding (and then the weight advantage is lost). Race clothing is also inadequate to protect the legs against bad abrasions. Nevertheless, taken overall, spills are rare under controlled race conditions.

For racing the saddle height must be adjusted with care; the weight must be taken on the bony part of the bottom, not the external genitals, and the tip may have to be dropped for women, who often find it more comfortable to fit a wider saddle. Bruising, soreness, and skin infection from sweating, demand careful attention to personal hygiene and proper choice of clothing.

Furious pedalling can cause ankle tenosynovitis or knee strain if the pedal position, the wedge, or the shoe are not just right. As with knee pain in any sport careful examination is needed to determine exactly which structure is under threat. Pain in the neck would be muscular from the hyperextended attitude but low back pain in adolescents must be checked by X-ray. Do not pass it off as strained muscles from the cramped position. Either spondylolysis (p. 28) or Scheuermann's disease (p. 29) is possible. There is a rare condition involving paralysis of muscle and loss of sensation in part of the hand. It is due to nerve pressure, which occurs when weight is taken on the hands with unpadded bars or when gloves are not worn. Recovery is the rule, in time.

Fencing

Fencing, *épée*, and the like pose no special risk of injury unless one counts breakage of the blade, when serious wounds can result, including penetration of the abdominal cavity and chest. Such injuries are acute surgical emergencies and must be dealt with in a hospital emergency centre.

The tip of an opponent's weapon should slide off the newer clothing fibres much better than it did from the older linen uniforms, but it may still catch and cause cuts and abrasions. The ring and little fingers may not be protected by the weapon hilt so the fencer's grip must always be carefully inspected. In a vigorous attack body contact may result in a fall or bruise parts of the body.

If the defender hyperflexes his back (bends sharply backwards) too often lumbar ligament strain will ensue, causing acute backache that will only be exacerbated by continued training. Weak abdominal muscles may be the real culprit causing ligament strain, but either way, a programme of muscle strengthening is indicated before technique suffers.

Long hours of competition may cause arm muscle cramp, especially early in the season or under hot conditions, as well as blisters on the hand or toes. Leg pain may likewise be just a simple cramp but constantly recurring or chronic pain may herald the onset of muscle compartment syndrome (p. 88). Torn leg muscles are possible as well as avulsion of hamstring muscles from their bone attachment high in the thigh (p. 17). Knee or ankle sprains in younger competitors should be examined with the possibility of bone chips in mind.

Overall, fencing is a safe activity at a junior level, provided proper technique is taught and developed. It is *vital* that parents check the clothing and face mask for proper fit and they must be alert to any repetition of injury; this is most likely to be caused by a fault in technique that must be detected and corrected.

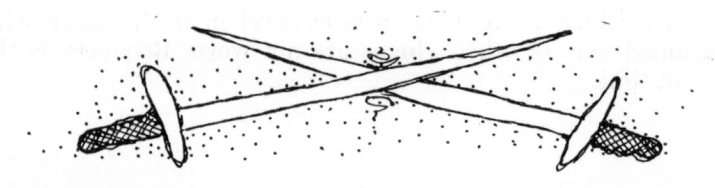

Golf

The only real problem in golf is someone else. Casual observation of the first tee or practice area on school days will show everyone doing their own thing; practice swings, chipping, throwing balls, chatting with their backs to the action, doing anything, that is, except being aware that two hard objects are moving at lethal speed around them—the club head and the ball. The author was struck glancing blows by both as a young caddy. All my own fault. My mother had not seen me walk ahead and when the ball hit she fainted. Fortunately drops of blood from my lacerated mouth revived her. On another occasion, standing at the back of the tee with two others, a topped drive rebounded at high speed off the advanced tee marker straight back between us. Seven centimetres either way and someone would have lost an eye or received a skull fracture. (Tee markers have since been redesigned to try and avoid this 180° reversal of direction.)

From tee to green everyone knows the use of 'fore!' But if a Eurokinder finds that 'fore' gets no response, by the time he has tried achtung!, attention!, and attenzione!, it is usually too late.

A thwack on the breasts in females will cause a lump, not cancer but a patch of harmless altered fat. A blow anywhere else in both males and females, except on the skull or in the eye, will be painful but not harmful.

Novice golfers must be warned of the dangers of tree roots and rocks. If the ball is on or very close to one it must not be attacked with a full swing. A slight miscalculation, the club head meets the immovable object, the hands still move forwards, the lower hand wrist is suddenly bent backwards (hyperextended) and, hey presto, something will break. Tearing the muscles of the neck or side, or those attached to the inner side of the elbow joint, will occur in the same way, or by a frightful mis-hit with the club digging in. A golfer's elbow, thus note, is on the opposite side to a tennis elbow.

The youthful golf swing with its freedom and fluidity is the envy of every senior golfer except Samuel Jackson Snead and muscle strains, tendinitis, sprains and all such things are unknown. Well, almost unknown. When they occur it is best to think of a pre-existing condition. Thus hip pivot pain may be due to Perthes' disease (p. 19): a slippage of the head of the femur on its shaft and mostly an adolescent problem. Likewise, lower back pain may be due to spondylolysis (p. 28), or fracture of the transverse process (p. 28) of one of the lumbar vertebrae consequent to injury in another sport. Knee 'trouble', from basketball say, will affect a golf swing. Occasionally, if the foot is planted firmly in the ground with long spikes, the knee will twist and over time meniscus damage can occur. Strain of the chest muscles on the side of the upper hand can follow a very jerky mis-hit but remember the possibility of stress fracture in a rib. This has been recorded although it would need much prolonged practice to predispose towards it.

Inquisitive kids ought not to cut into golf balls to see what they are made of. The author speaks again from personal experience but all I got was a sharp sting from elastic winding zipping in all directions; not so lucky was a thirteen-year-old girl in 1973 who cut into the liquid centre, not knowing it was under high pressure of around 17 MPa or 2500 pounds/square inch. The contents hit the ceiling and her eye, driving organic substances into her eyelid and eyeball.

One golf disease, if caught, is incurable: dishonesty. Close adult supervision is needed in school competitions to detect and advise those who are tempted to fudge the rules to win. Let culprits ponder the story some seventy years old now of a young American club golfer in Atlanta, Georgia, who poked his head out of the rough to announce that he had just incurred a penalty for moving the ball at address. His partner had not seen the incident and would not otherwise have known, but duly recorded the penalty on the card. In 1930, all in the one year, the same player won the British Amateur Championship, the Open Championship, the United States Open, and the United States Amateur Championship. Robert Tyre Jones was his name, skill was his game, and character was his real fame.

Finally, about natural hazards. Anywhere near an alligator is an unplayable lie, and near a snake it is a lost ball as far as I am concerned. Nesting birds get cranky and where they are about it is a protection to carry a golf umbrella held high. However, this is the most dangerous thing in the world to do if lightning flashes (p. 34). The simple rules for lightning are: do not be the highest point in the landscape and do not stand under a high point such as a tree. Lie in a bunker or hollow or if caught on an open hill lie down *well away* from the metal bag buggy or bag of clubs. The God Zeus is well known for taking thunderbolts from his caddy and hurling them about with gay abandon. The only time I ever saw a high point come in handy was when a partner decided to speed up a passing frill-necked lizard by tickling it under the chin with a 2 iron. Not being your usual sort of chummy spectator the lizard shot straight up his back, stood on his shoulders and took a firm overlapping grip on his forehead, the better to survey the surrounds for signs of further danger.

Gridiron

Gridiron jumped the Pacific Ocean to Australia in 1979. The first Australian Bowl was played in Melbourne in 1986 (Victoria won!) and made history as the first recognised collegiate football game played outside the United States. The Australian National Body now controls the Leagues in five Australian States. In 1988 New South Wales had six youth teams with not one player suffering a major injury through the season, and it is the intention of the NSW Gridiron Football League to continue this record by attaching the junior teams to senior clubs for training and instruction that will emphasise discipline, team plays and protection.

As the junior competition grows it is hoped that these dedicated efforts in education will be rewarded with a high level of safety. In every aspect of the game accumulated American experience is the only guide, so all the information in this chapter is drawn wholly from American literature to provide readers with an informative background to an important sport on the world stage and one that will recruit more and more young players to its ranks.

Gridiron is the ultimate body contact sport. And teenagers are getting bigger. School outfitters claim to be supplying a lot more 122 cm and 127 cm size football jerseys than they did even a decade ago, and a Queensland study in 1982 found that the average height of a twelve-year-old boy has increased from 138 cm in 1910, to 146 cm in 1950 and 148 cm in 1976. There is data too on Japanese children born to emigrant parents in Hawaii and on the west coast of America. In two generations of life there the offspring are now as tall as Caucasians on average. This may be due to more and better food and less infection in modern times, but nutritionists are by no means certain of this.

A freak fifteen-year-old from Fort Worth, Texas (could it have been from anywhere else!) was unable to play on team because his head was bigger than the largest size helmet available (8½), and that sat atop a 114-kg body thus raising his hair to a height of 193 cm — and no doubt making all other linesmen's hair stand on end!

The role of the coach is crucial in the important areas of selection, physical toughening, protection, avoidance of heat exhaustion, and locker room discipline. All the factors mentioned in Chapter 2 (p. 7) must be considered before selecting a player to go beyond the 'fun' stage of playing. Additionally, in this sport (as in rugby and soccer), a special watch must be kept on the long thin-necked types with poorly developed shoulder strength. Strong muscular growth will only come with a programmed and disciplined approach to off-season and preseason conditioning. Without it the injury rate has been found over and over again to be much higher than it should be. Protective gear must be worn at all times (see below), and self-protection does not end at the locker room door. Many injuries are not noticed till the game is over, so when changing the player must report to the coach any laceration, muscle swelling, bone tenderness, problems with the joints, or stiff fingers. A disciplined locker room not only detects injury but prevents needless harm. Bits of glass from broken bottles, relics of previous teams using the area, used to be hidden hazards, but now it is metal bits from drink cans. Novices have to learn about personal safety and that includes not skylarking on slippery floors.

Heat stroke should now never occur (p. 34), but heat-induced fatigue is real in full gear during an overlong practice session and it is a general principle, never to be forgotten in any phase of gridiron, that a fatigued player is the one most vulnerable to injury. The key question to ask is: are you sweating a lot? If the answer is yes cool water must be drunk regularly. A recommendation of the American Academy of Paediatrics is that children need to drink 150 ml of cold tap water per 40 kg of body weight every thirty minutes, and that this should be *enforced* in unfavourable climates in order to prevent heat stroke. In really humid climes weak salt solutions may be needed but not salt tablets; these are in fact dangerous without fluids. The taste buds will see to it that enough salt is added to the food at the next meal. Expensive formula drinks are not necessary; if they contain potassium they could actually be harmful. In severe conditions anything up to 4% of body weight can be lost, and it is therefore good discipline for the player to weigh himself, stripped, before and after a game, as a guide to the need for fluid replenishment on the field next time.

Emotional factors can be significant. Psychological tests done on a group of injured American high school players in 1979 uncovered a background of emotional tension which related specifically to their parents: their illnesses, their discords and especially divorce. The lesson is that unhappy players become either too aggressive, inattentive or preoccupied for their own good. The corollary is that the coach should have a long chat with the overly aggressive player, the ill-tempered, or the one showing persistent lack of team spirit. Adolescents hide many emotional tangles. It also must be noted here that the coach is often in the best position to suspect drug abuse; declining performance, poor coordination, defiant behaviour, abrupt mood changes, absenteeism, a change of friends or habits, sloppy personal hygiene, red eyes or dilated pupils—all the features emphasised by experts in this evil—show up quickly in team situations.

Training methods are also a factor in injury. American researchers at the Great Plains Sports Medicine Foundation in 1976 studied specific training activities. After formidable statistical analysis they were able to allocate an index of risks, to allow of broad comparisons, as follows: practice games 47, two player contact drills 19, three player drills 14, scrimmages 12, and group-controlled special drills 1.5. In other words, practice games are thirty times more likely than group drills to produce injury. The study was made at college football level but it shows that practice games must not be carelessly conducted.

Playing conditions can be a topic for endless discussion and quotation of dogma. Dry artificial turf produces more scrapes and burns than soft grass, but bare hard dirt is the worst. Prepatellar (knee) and olecranon (elbow) bursitis (pp. 69, 65) are more common on artificial turf. Rainy days and muddy grass increase leg sprains and strains as feet get stuck in the mud. Traction is so high on artificial turf that a player will fall unless he picks up his feet cleanly. The best shoe on artificial surfaces is the one with fourteen cleats. One could go on and on with such dogma but even the simplest statements must be treated as 'not proven', and the assertions of interested commercial parties as 'definitely not proven'. There are too many variables. Much, much more research is needed, although in an important recent poll of the American National Football League players, 80% voted for a return to natural grass.

If a high jumper or gymnast 'comes a cropper' the injury can usually be clearly seen but it is not necessarily so in a football melee. The prostrate figure may be revealed only when the game flows on, or in the heat of the moment the player may move on, only later to become aware of injury, A statistical analysis of injured players in 1982 showed that emergency room physicians had to refer 73% of them on to a wide variety of specialists. It has been noted that early season training is a high risk time; as well as being in poor condition, players are competing for positions and experimenting. Absolutely every injury listed in the text book can occur. It is more useful therefore to consider things by area.

Head and Neck

If a player is stretched out unconscious there is no way immediately to tell whether concussion, fractured skull, spinal shock, paraplegia, quadriplegia, or indeed a combination of these is the cause; visceral (abdominal organ) injury or even unexpected heart disease must also pass, at least fleetingly, through the mind of an experienced first-aid attendant. Apt first-aid is the critical first step, and we have come a long way since the old bucket of water in the face technique. No, the word is apt, A–P–T, for airway, position and transport.

The face mask may have to be removed with cutters but *not* the helmet. That is used to hold the head neutral for safety. The body position should not be immediately altered until some recovery indicates that spinal cord damage has not occurred. Not, as one must always point out, that movement rules out a fracture of the head or neck. Without careful observation and later x-rays this cannot be excluded which is why, in the high school arena, the player should not be returned to the game. Not even if concussion seems to have been the cause. It is too risky to field a player whose efficiency is impaired.

Concussion should never be taken lightly (p. 25). The brain tolerance to impact in football was studied with encephalograms (electrical measurements of brain waves) by S. E. Read. One player, who experienced four blows without effect, was concussed by the fifth with immediate changes to his test and abnormal brain waves were still being noted three days later. Indeed it is sometimes the second head blow, and it may have seemed only a slight blow, that has killed. The reason is not known but it seems that mild brain swelling remaining from the first concussion days before (and which is normally subsiding and reversible) is suddenly, by the second hit, made worse, irreversible and irreducible by treatment. Viral encephalitis (brain inflammation), such as that associated with glandular fever, has also been incriminated in quite serious brain damage after seemingly trivial head injury. Therefore children recovering from any viral infection must not rush back to training. Nor should they continue training after any concussion. Insist on a spell until they are their old self again, and in this keen observation a parent's instinct has to be better than a doctor's clinical examination, important though that is. In severe post concussion states only a CAT scan (computerised axial tomography) could detect any lingering brain damage. Indeed it may be this 'second impact effect' that explains why deaths still occur from head injuries despite the improved technology of protective head gear.

The American National Football Head and Neck Registry Report for 1978 indicated one change that had occurred; there were fewer cases of brain haemorrhage thanks to the wearing of helmets, but a distressing increase in cervical spine fractures and quadriplegia thanks to the wearing of helmets used illegally. At the high school level 72% of such cases were caused by illegal tackles. Catastrophic spinal cord injuries still occur despite rule changes, high standards of helmet manufacture, and education in safe blocking and tackling. In the years 1977 to 1983 the high school rate was 0.7 per 100,000 players. Nearly all these cases occurred during games, the majority were playing defense, and in most the head was lowered before contact. It would seem from the latter that at the last millisecond players forgot the coach's words and obeyed instinct. It is certain too that more force can be applied to the head and neck than adolescent muscle strength can resist, especially when the force is an unexpected rotational leverage on the face mask. A 'wry neck' must therefore always be examined for damage to the vertebral joint facets. Sharp hyperextension can cause temporary spinal shock (p. 22), or damage to the vertebral artery (p. 24). As this artery supplies the brain steam and cerebellum (hind brain), muscle coordination and the function of the eye, ear, and balance mechanisms would be affected.

It was pointed out in 1976 by Albright that a high proportion of young footballers are playing with pre-existing neck injuries, and this is clearly dangerous. Not only should such an injury be honestly admitted by the player, but also, following the injury, full recovery of movement and muscle strength must be insisted upon before play is resumed. Ideally dynamometer readings should be taken and recorded of the muscle power in the four directions of head movement.

A stiff arm across the neck can fracture the Adam's apple (the thyroid cartilage) to cause hoarseness or difficulty with breathing, but it would be incredibly rare for the nearby carotid artery to be damaged in the young even though this has been recorded in older players in whom the artery is perhaps less supple.

Forcible lateral (sideways) flexion of the neck will stretch either the nerve roots issuing through the cervical (neck) vertebrae or their amalgamated trunks further out, the so-called brachial nerve plexus, thus causing a stinging and burning sensation down the arm with later muscle weakness. In the initial episode the burning sensation may fade in ten to fifteen minutes, but in the bigger and stronger players small degrees of muscle weakness are impossible to detect. Complex electrodiagnostic studies are needed to work out the degree of nerve damage and are worth doing for recurrent 'stingers' to determine whether the player should be rested to allow full recovery. Fortunately this injury has diminished in high schools since rules were altered to outlaw head blocking.

Face masks and mouthguards used routinely will eliminate teeth, mouth and face injury, but not necessarily a ruptured ear drum, in which bleeding from the ear is accompanied by some deafness. The danger occurs in pickup games where the need for protective gear is not taken seriously.

Lower down the back do not ignore persistent lumbar (back) pain. It might not be ligament strain but one of the forms of spondylolysis (p. 00), which can only be diagnosed by x-rays or bone scans.

Trunk

The rib cage is springy and each flat rib is wrapped in muscle so that fractures may not be immediately obvious; thus persistent soreness should be X-rayed. Sharp concentrated force from an elbow, knee or boot will do the trick, and it is worth wearing the light 185-gm air-inflated jackets which have been devised to prevent this injury.

The same force can rupture the spleen (p. 37); thus ended Matt Snell's career with the Jets. In this regard glandular fever is important. It causes an enlargement of the spleen which may then rupture from trivial injury. Thus footballers who have had a recent attack of the disease must not be allowed to play until the spleen's size has been checked by ultrasound; indeed if any child keen on contact sports catches glandular fever, *ask* the doctor to pay particular attention to the spleen.

Chest pain or epigastric (midriff) pain must not be ignored. Death from heart disease has occurred even in the early teens. Fainting after exercise can also be an early warning sign of this disaster.

Arm

Dislocation of the shoulder, elbow, wrist, or finger, is obvious except for one oddity, dislocation of the radius (outer forearm bone) downwards by a sharp tug on the arm, which causes the head of the bone to jump out of its annular (ring-shaped) ligament. There is nothing but danger in on-the-spot attempts to reduce (put back in place) such dislocations. X-rays must first be done to exclude fractures or fragments, or damage to the epiphyseal line (p. 17), and reduction is a job for experts, otherwise nearby arteries or major nerves may suffer catastrophic damage. (For fingers, see p. 66.)

More insidious are the subluxations, that is, strained and weakened joint capsules. Any feelings of weakness or apprehension with certain movements, or use of the phrase 'it's sore again' indicate the need for review by an orthopaedic surgeon. It is possible for a quarterback to strain the inner side of the elbow joint with overuse, just as a baseball pitcher can. Falls onto the outstretched hand or point of the elbow are notorious for causing fractures somewhere along the line of force, and probably the most common injury when all sports are taken together is dislocation or fracture of the clavicle (collar bone).

Leg

The knee is the big problem. A survey in Oklahoma in 1978 found that 84% of surgical procedures carried out on injured high school boys were for knee injuries. Many injuries are received by running into an opponent's knee, so that to wear knee pads can be a 'kindness' to others. For the receiver of the blow, linear or rotation forces can cause a cluster of related injuries, from joint effusions which get better, to gross internal derangements which terminate a budding career. All the player is aware of is a swollen, painful, or unstable knee. It is often difficult for the physician to give a precise diagnosis, but the ability now to look into the joint cavity with an arthroscope and the availability of Magnetic Resonance Imaging has improved diagnostic accuracy. What is important is that *every* knee swelling be examined and good records kept; these are sometimes invaluable for diagnosis. The Illinois State High School League lays stress on their pre-season conditioning programme which, it is claimed, has reduced the early season knee injury rate by some 70%. A rule change in 1984 reduced the thickness of platforms used to anchor cleats to 5/32 inch (4 mm) with the aim of stopping shoes from sinking so far into the ground and hopefully this will help to minimise knee strain.

An analysis of American high school football knee insurance claims over a three-year period by Pritchett brings to light some interesting points. Ligament injury was the most common injury; one quarter of those who suffered it had a subsequent injury to the same knee and 10% developed problems in the other knee. Where the injury was to the patella (knee cap) — there is often a family history of patellar disease — there was a recurrence rate of 87% with a 34% incidence of trouble in the other patella, but it seemed to leave less athletic disability than other internal problems.

Ankle sprains or fractures are straightforward. A torn muscle is rare; such a problem is usually a complete avulsion (tearing away) of the muscle with its epiphysis (p. 17) from the main bone. The notion that a sore spot can be numbed by local anaesthetic to allow further play is ridiculous without proper diagnosis. Muscle strains or deep bruises follow their usual pattern.

Protection

The force of blocking and tackling has to be absorbed and not borne totally by the body; meticulous care in the choice, fitting, and maintenance of proper gear is so important that the sooner it is taught and learnt the better. Growing children will swap things and so attention must be paid to hygiene or they will swap infections as well. Supervision of gear should not be left to the school or coach. That's the parent's job; including selecting and fitting, mending, patching, altering the fit, repairing straps and cleaning. (Pretty simple really, just give all your spare time to it.) Young players are notorious for being lazy about equipment or for affecting a macho image, so parents will have to take a strong line until junior gets self-motivated. The alternative is injury.

Helmet technology has come a long way since Rutgers, 1896, and a proper fit with lining and face mask is achievable. Reconditioned helmets must be checked very carefully. After all, the American National Operating Committee on Standards for Athletic Equipment (NOCSAE) rules stipulate only that batch samples be tested. *You* must check every strap and mounting and lining as well as look for up-to-date improvements in design. One manufacturer says that helmets should be reconditioned every two years and discarded after five years. There can be big danger in a handed down helmet.

The helmet brace was recommended in 1979 to fasten the back of the helmet to the shoulder pads in a bid to stop hyperflexion but neck collars will achieve the same thing. Mouthguards have virtually eliminated mouth and teeth injuries provided they are worn all the time and not just in games. They can be homemade from resilient materials but individual mouths vary so much that it is preferable to have guards made by your dentist and checked annually. Quarterbacks have the extra problem with mouthguard design that voice signals must be preserved.

It takes time to check all pads for cracks, frayed fasteners or rotted fabric. Surreptitious removal of layers or substitution of light foam to reduce weight is a very dangerous practice as a skimpy pad is useless, or worse, it gives a false sense of security. A poor fit may expose bony points to injury. You are almost certain to find that built-in pads finish up in the wrong place during the growth spurt. Special pads can be fitted for extra area protection after injury. Elbow pads are now advised for artificial turf and high schools in the United States in 1984 ruled that all players must wear hip pads with tailbone protection.

To play in casts or splints is illegal at school level and so it should be. Either, to be effective, has to be rigid and unyielding. Some knee braces are permitted but not with sharp metal anywhere, nor with inadequate padding. That some players come off with their braces bent would indicate that they are of more use before injury than after it! In fact a trend is developing to equip all players except the quarterback with modified knee braces, and this will then be another item needing constant inspection. A poor or weakened brace will be next to useless, or worse, a danger as the player will have a false sense of security. In fact how far off are we from having to resurrect the armoured suits of the knights of chivalry? They might even be lighter and cheaper!

It may be of interest to Australians thinking of taking up the game to note the 1988 prices for NSWGFL approved gear:

helmet $192, shoulder pads $100, hip/thigh/knee pads $30, elbow guards $30, rib pads $70, uniform $120 and shoes $60. Mouthguard material costs only $2 but a guard made by a dentist is preferable and will cost many times that!

REFERENCES:
Albright J. P. et al. Non fatal cervical spine injuries in interscholastic football. *J.A.M.A.* 1976; 236: 1243.
Cahill B. et al. Exposure to injury in major college football. *Am. J. Sports Med.* 1979; 7: 183.
Cryan P. et al. Relationship between stress and college football players. *J. Sports Med. Phys. Fitness* 1983: 23: 52.
Mueller F. O. et al. Annual survey of catastrophic football injuries. *Physician and Sportsmed.* 1985; 13: March 75–81.
Pritchett J. W. Statistical study of knee injuries due to football in high school athletes. *J. Bone and Joint Surg.* 1982; 64A: 240–243.
Reid S. E. et al. Brain tolerance to impact in football. *Surg. Gyn. Ob.* 1971; 133: 929.

Gymnastics

A study of nine- and ten-year-old girl gymnasts in 1979 found that they were not as flexible as might have been expected, and because of their devotion to the sport were hard to treat and unwilling to rest. This suggests immediately that before fanaticism takes hold of either the child or parent, careful anatomical examination should be sought to warn of physical attributes that might become functional disabilities. The following features are not favourable:

- Lordosis (sway back), that is, an excessive lumbar curvature, convex forwards, plus weak abdominal muscles.
- A family history of 'bad backs'.
- Back pain in hyperextension, touching toes, or leg raising.

- Weak shoulder muscles, or tight shoulders.
- Wide elbow carrying angle.
- Tibial torsion (bow legs), genu valgum (knock knees), intoeing, or flat feet.
- Tight hamstrings or tight Achilles tendon with reduced dorsiflexion (upward ankle movement).

The last factor varies with age. It has been noted that flexibility is minimal at twelve or thirteen years because soft tissue development (muscle, fascia and tendon length) may lag behind that of bone during the growth spurt and during this phase there can be an increase in tendon tension. If tendon strains actually do develop training may have to be curtailed until the relative overstretch self-corrects in a year or two. Such loss of flexibility (a source of 'growing pains') is one of the possible problems occurring at puberty in this sport. Body proportions alter, muscle size increases (more so in boys), and the epiphyseal plates (p. 17) are most active and vulnerable to tight tendon traction and stress fracture. The effect of competition training must thus be closely observed and no pain ignored.

An unfortunate recent trend is for coaching to focus on prepubescent talent and even for steps to be taken to delay puberty so that a smaller and lighter figure is retained. Progress to National and Olympic standard may thus not be so much a matter of pure skill as the lucky possession of a body that can survive the strains.

Before classes begin parents should check the conditions. Criticism has often been made that in such a rapidly expanding sport the number of expert coaches and good spotters is limited. Since falls will happen, good 10-cm thick mats should be everywhere. Threadbare mats and bare floors are lethal if young Lucinda lands on her head. At competitions, spotters and mats are even more important because in gymnastics, unlike most other sports, more injuries occur in meetings than in training, no doubt due to tension and extra endeavour. (One is referring to supervised conditions; when unsupervised, training will certainly lead to more accidents.) At all times slow stretching exercises, adequate warm-up, and keeping within the limits of current strength and skill are vital. Parents may have to step in to see that kids do not skip the boring exercises to rush into tricks. Concentration and ability to cope with the more stressful challenges of competition must also be watched for. Competitors must not practice with a head cold. The dizziness and full feeling in the sinuses could be distracting.

With gymnastics it is necessary to discuss both direct injury and gradually developing self-inflicted stress. Falls or bad landings will occur, and, regrettably, sometimes due to collapse of equipment (another thing to check, see p. 199). Falls usually occur with the hand outstretched to protect the head so that arm fractures are the most common injury, or the victim lands heavily and sprains the ankle, but really any bone may break or joint dislocate. To instruct, deliberately, in the right way to fall is not good for morale in beginners. However, a suitable time will arise. Landing with the body forward on the thigh, with the feet crossed, is the perfect anatomical position for dislocation of the hip because the socket in the young hip bone is shallow and not fully developed.

Fortunately, trampoline tricks apart, fractured necks are almost unknown in gymnastics. In growing children possible damage to bone epiphyses (p. 16) around the joints is a very, very important topic and healing must be absolutely perfect before sport is recommenced. Novices are mostly injured in falls, so good spotting is vital for them and the high beam should be set closer to the floor. Beware long practice sessions and fatigue leading to loss of concentration or psychological 'freezing'. These seem to be directly related to the injury rate.

Subtle stress damage is best described by area but no matter where it strikes the symptoms are the same: pain and altered movement or reduced range of joint movement.

Lumbar Spine

Considerable stress is put on the young spine and it has been estimated in a study by S. W. Jackson that spondylolysis is five times more common in female gymnasts than in the general population. Jackson also holds that it is the result of a genuine cause and effect process rather than the worsening of an inherited trait. The continued oscillation between the extremes of extension and full flexion, with rotation, causes either osteochondritis (p. 19), or a fatigue fracture of the lower lumbar vertebrae in the portion framing the spinal cord. Such a fracture allows the vertebral body eventually to slip forward and the displacement is called spondylolysis (p. 28). Low back pain, unilateral aching muscles, or spinal curvature, all demand investigation. If X-rays are negative, but the bone scan positive, then the damage is incipient and has been diagnosed at the perfect time, early. There are other rare bone lesions, and herniated discs (yes! even in children).

What is one to do if these back problems are diagnosed? Is it worth while continuing? Well, some do. Expert advice should be sought on the degree of damage already inflicted, and this should later be followed up as to the purity of bone repair. One orthopaedic professor, Goldberg, has written: 'Our results with gymnasts who have established disease and who have returned to the sport have been disappointing. Although some strongly motivated patients did return, their level of performance was reduced.'

Elbow

This joint was not designed to bear weight but in gymnastics it has to, and girls with a wide carrying angle put excess strain particularly on the ligaments and muscles of the inner side. The possible results of this strain include traumatic synovitis, osteochondritis (p. 19) with separation of small pieces of bone and cartilage into loose bodies which cause even more trouble, damage to the epiphyses (p. 16) around the joint, strain of ligament and muscle as in baseball pitchers, dislocation, or fracture of the funny bone. Hopefully healing will occur without any further deformity.

Wrist and Hand

As with the elbow, wrist design does not favour walking on the fully cocked hand or getting a landing thump. This damaging pressure may cause: stress fractures of the growing epiphysis (p. 16) of the lower end of the radius (outer forearm bone) and thus distorted bone growth, osteochondritis (p. 19) of the small wrist bones, fracture of the scaphoid bone, friction tenosynovitis in the area, or vague pain in the back of the hand from inflammation of any of the hand's many joints. Rotational forces on the wrist in some routines and from very soft mats increase the strains. However simple sprains are the most common outcome. Tumbling, floor exercises, and the pommel horse, can strain or dislocate fingers.

Knee

Repetitive explosive jumping from a flexed knee position is a severe strain which can cause patellar (knee cap) tendinitis, epiphyseal traction injuries (p. 17), or chondromalacia patellae (p. 19) in late adolescents. Occasionally other sprains or meniscus (p. 68) damage will occur. Expert physiotherapy to strengthen the extensor muscles must follow any lay-off time. All knee problems can be difficult to diagnose but training should cease until a firm diagnosis is made of the cause of pain, swelling, or feeling of instability.

Ankle and Foot

Repetitive landings with sudden jolting deceleration of ankle flexion as the trunk pitches forwards may cause the familiar Achilles tendinitis. Unstable landings from the horse may dislocate ankle tendons or strain the posterior joint capsule fibres. Repetitive stress on the ankle joint capsule causes small haemorrhages which later form bone spurs that limit ankle movements. Stress fractures of the lower leg and foot bones can also occur. The long tendons, foot arches, and plantar fascia come under strain and although strapping is a help to continued training it is not curative and indeed the pain may be due to other stress conditions (see the chapter on Athletics p. 85 for this and related Achilles tendon troubles). Sprung floors with exercise mats reduce leg strain (and the rebound height). Shoes eventually become important. If a talented gymnast starts serious training there is every reason to change into shoes specifically designed for each event.

There are a few other conditions. Shin or calf pain as muscle develops within its tight compartment, or struggles to compensate for flat feet, is one. Leg tenderness from stress fractures is another. A common cause of both may be an increase in the level of training, in fact it must never be forgotten that high performance gymnasts are working with fine bone tolerances. Slapping against the uneven parallel bars has bruised underlying bowel and caused internal bowel haemorrhage, not serious, but if the bowel motions are noted to be black, such bleeding must be suspected and a check made for anaemia. Likewise, thigh nerve neuralgia or sore groins come from wrapping around the low bar. Padded clothing would prevent the latter, and, in mentioning protection, full skin cover on the legs is needed to avoid abrasions from the horse. Basic pommel horse routines need burgeoning strength and concentration and it is easy to bump the shins, stub a finger, or slip off straining the shoulder or back muscles. One special fear for parents is vulval injury in vaulting. Actually it is very unlikely; although bruising can look terrible nothing really vital can be hurt in that area.

Another question is : 'Will all this joint stress cause arthritis in later life?' There is no evidence that it does, provided there has not been direct joint damage or dislocation, and even then good care and time for recovery gives young bones and joints an excellent chance of full healing.

This overlong and overfull saga of medical possibilities arising from gymnastics may (and rightly) make parents wary of the sport. But what it should do, above all, is make them wary of pushing youngsters too far and too quickly into the sport, without due care, and of overencouraging those whose anatomical features are unsuitable. To proceed slowly and under the best of conditions should be the motto. That way nearly all of the above will be avoided.

REFERENCES:
Goldberg M. J. Gymnastic injuries. *Orthop. Clin. North Am.* 1980; 11: 717.
Jackson S. W. Low back pain in young athletes. Evaluation of stress reaction and discogenic problems. *Am. J. Sports Med.* 1979; 7: 364.

Handball

This is such a severe strain on elbows and hands that it is doubtful if young joints with ununited epiphyses (p. 17) should be exposed to it. Eventually, traumatic synovitis, joint haemorrhages, fragmented cartilage, and epiphyseal damage may occur, and all in the dominant arm. The constant impact of the ball on the forearm and hand can cause spastic arteries and altered blood supply to the hand as in volleyball (p. 200).

Hockey (Field)

Husky adolescents with flexiwrists can drill holes through goalkeepers with 100 kph shots. However, most novices are more likely to inflict stick bruises or cuts on one another and thus must learn to be careful. The aggressive one who gets away with it, or does not care about the backswing in the midst of more nervous players, is only developing bad habits which will impede his or her later progress.

There are few major injuries in girls' hockey, most being to the legs or ankles, along with the very occasional dislocated shoulder or concussion from falls. Abrasions hardly count! The stick causes limb bruises or face injuries, as does the flying ball. Extra attention must be focused on the ball in the glare of the sun and in free hits. Bruises to the breasts are a worry but the amount of real breast tissue in girls is small and well covered by fat; any bruising is to this fatty layer with no long-term significance. As the standard of play and level of competition rise then injuries increase and more attention must be given to protection of the shins and face. All the muscle problems of rapid jerky movement, joint strains, and leg fractures from 'mix-ups' are possible. Minor knee strains are often not noticed until the joint swells overnight, and any knee pain must be properly investigated as girls are especially prone to repetitive stress leading to chondromalacia patellae (p. 19).

The United States National Federation of State High School Associations in 1986 made face guards compulsory for all players and decreed that goalies wear commercial throat guards. Just imagine, school hockey, well on the way to needing a suit of armour instead of a gym skirt.

In early autumn 1983, near half-time in a Saturday social game between school and the old boys in Victoria, Australia, it became very dark as a storm approached, and one spectator jokingly remarked: 'Why don't we turn on the lights?' There was no wind or rain. Play continued. As Father Herbert explained in Mass next morning: 'There was no religious significance in the lightning strike but all natural phenomena are acts of God.' The 1.5 million-volt bolt threw twenty-two players to the ground. One player was killed, several were knocked unconscious and burned, one stared in amazement at the melted nylon stops on his hockey boots, and one who swallowed his tongue was saved. It could happen to any team playing sport on high open ground, and when low dark storms are about umpires are well advised to show discretion and stop play.

Horseriding

My mother learned to ride bareback. Had to. Grandfather refused to buy her a saddle until she could ride, but I think it was just a case of his Scottish genes dictating sound economic caution. After all, why spend money on what might be a transient childish whim? I forgot ever to ask how many times she fell off, but she got her saddle and loved horses all her life. Her brother, my uncle, got fed up with the whole thing, opted for a saddle closer to the ground, and became a champion road race cyclist instead.

When my time came houses no longer had large soft back paddocks where the family horse could be peacefully tethered, so it was off to the riding school on country holidays. Mother interviewed all the horses carefully, took a fancy to Amy Johnson, and I was hoisted astride. We got along famously, for two days. On the third, falling behind the group despite my every entreaty, Amy suddenly broke into a gallop down what must have been her favourite shortcut home and proved that her owner knew what he was doing by naming her after the famous aviatrix of that era! I thought of that later; at the time, when I regained my senses, I found I was still astride, legs ahead, leaning back, determined to stay where I was, and probably looking like a caricature of an old sporting print. However, I don't think it was my ancient genes springing to the rescue, just my billycart experience. I did not have the strength to hold the horse and instinctively feared I might pull myself over her head. Thereafter I was transferred to Rusty, the riding school owner proving once again that he knew his horses.

What of today? City or urban riding schools are more expensive to run and the temptation is to look for one with economical rates. Take care lest you later find that the horses are young and not properly broken and trained, or are old with bad habits, or that the instructors are inexperienced, because the opportunities for disaster begin right there. After all, if the novice stays on the horse there is no danger. Good tutors teach the importance of balance, communicating with the horse, and above all alertness. The school should have weeded out unreliable horses. United States Pony Club surveys in 1982 and 1983 found that unexpected actions of the horse accounted for 65% of their recorded accidents.

Injury can only occur if the rider is thrown, or panics and falls off. Then quite serious things may happen. We all know about concussion, fractured skulls, fractured vertebrae, vertebral disc injury, fractured ribs, and ruptured spleens with internal bleeding, but injury statistics show that these are rare. Far more likely are large bruises or any of the arm fractures that can follow a fall on the outstretched hand (p. 63). If the ground is soft probably the rider will get up and walk away, but he or she must still be closely observed for signs of concussion and not allowed back on again that day, and the lower vertebrae should always be examined and reexamined. Many an adult 'bad back' can be traced to neglected childhood damage.

A review of acute riding injuries in rural Dumfries and Galloway, shires in southwest Scotland, showed that children under fifteen made up half the total number taken to hospital, and that four out of five of these youngsters were girls. Statistics being what they are, this does not prove that girls are more at risk; rather that more young girls are attracted to horseriding and horses. A further point was that in 70% of cases the victim fell off, and in the other 30% the horse did it by kicking, biting, or trampling. The list of injuries inflicted by the horse in this way is naturally impressive. Such a report shows (yet again!) the value of prevention by proper training and supervision in the learning years, and if people are still going to fall off, the value of protective gear.

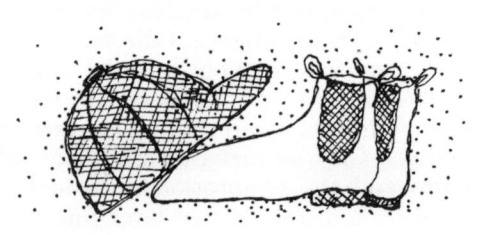

Headgear is the most important item and should be compulsory in pony clubs. Jockey type caps of hard material, with a padded lining, soft peaks, and restraining straps under the chin, are better than hats or the older style caps with hard peaks or no chinstraps. The theory that the hard peak protects the skull by hitting the ground first is wrong. The only problem is the expense of keeping up with the growth of young heads; either that or the hygiene of swapped hats. Equestrian pursuits were never ones for sick wallets! Long hair should be restrained; it must not blow about and impair clear vision. Clothing padded where it would do most good, over the shoulders and around the lower ribs, may not be fashionable but could prove valuable. Light-weight polyethylene sponge vests as used by professional steeplechase jockeys are becoming more readily available. Street shoes, jogging shoes, sneakers etc., without decent heels, are extremely dangerous in that if the foot slips unexpectedly through the stirrup and the rider becomes unbalanced and falls, he or she may be dragged along suspended by a leg through the stirrup, and a fractured skull is then a near certainty.

The ability properly to lead and handle a horse is a skill that must be acquired by example and instruction, but the small fry just have to be guarded until they learn. Mr B. Pride, for thirty years associated with the organisation of the Royal International Horse Show and the Horse of the Year Show in the United Kingdom, has never seen anyone killed in the ring, and only about ten injuries taken to hospital, but such competitors are skilled and experienced riders. In the controlled conditions of horse shows generally the injury rate is still very low amongst riders of varying levels of skill. Figures for events controlled by the American Horse Show Association and the United States Pony Clubs over 1979 and 1980, involving probably 5 million riders, show a low injury rate overall, with 63% occurring to riders under eighteen years of age. Nearly half such injuries were to the head and face. The United States Pony Club has made approved headgear, with harness and cupped chinstrap, compulsory. Daredevils might best be capped by cleverly designed crash helmets. With specific reference to riding classes, the Riding Academy in Malmo, Sweden, has an injury rate of 1 per 1000 lessons. Learning on macadam roads mixed in with horseless carriages causes big problems. The British Government's highway code and other publications address this and they should be compulsory reading for parents.

REFERENCES:
Bernhang A. et al. Equestrian injuries. *Physician and Sportsmed.* 1983; 11, 1: 90.
McLatchie G. R. Equestrian Injuries—A one year prospective study. *Brit. J. Sports Med.* 1979; 13: 29–32.
Pride B. E. Personal Communication, 1987.

Ice Hockey

Even the biggest, toughest, fastest ice hockey professionals must have started out as lovable gurgling babes in arms, but something seems to have gone wrong along the way. At some point cheerful acquisition of skating skill and finesse gives way to competitive zeal, probably in high school around puberty as strength and aggressiveness develop. Then body checking, spectacular falls, and crashing into the boards, cut a swathe through even the fittest lineup. Much attention has to be given to effective protection, beginning with the eyes.

The highest rate of eye injuries in Canada at one time was in the eleven to fifteen year age group, and 60% of these were due to sticks. (Once a player was hit in the eye by a shoe thrown by a spectator!) A variety of major eye injuries resulted, but retinal detachments in particular were seen in adolescents. Unfortunately, too, the time interval between injury and the examination averaged three years, the reason being that the detachment was often a partial one limited to the lower portion of the retina. The physics of lens optics means that the upper field of vision was thus restricted, and since one tends to look down more than upwards, it is easier for this vision loss to go unnoticed until the detachment slowly extends to affect central vision. Regrettable too is the fact that by then only 50% of operations can be successful in restoring vision.

Eye injuries declined dramatically after the high sticking rule was enforced and now that controlling bodies, notably the United States Amateur Hockey Association, have made face protection mandatory, eye injuries would thankfully disappear if it were not for pickup games where nobody 'bothers' with face masks. Plastic visors fog up; full metal masks are best, but *measure the mesh*! It is no good if the puck or blade tips can get through. Other measurements show that fifteen-year-olds are strong enough to propel the puck at a speed (about 100 kph) that can deform face masks; in this respect pre-pubertal players are still safe. Some coaches have said that making helmets and masks compulsory has increased the general level of rough play because kids lose their sense of restraint. Maybe. This is a complicated subject and the same thing has been said about helmets in gridiron and baseball. However, the unexpected is too common in ice hockey for adolescents not to wear helmets. What televised professionals choose to do is another matter.

Regrettably, Canadian neurosurgeons recently affirmed that major spinal injury is a new and increasing problem despite the use of helmets, or even because of them (see Gridiron p. 127). Older teenagers and young men playing in organised amateur league games made up all the recent cases. Most of the interviewed players admitted to lack of concern in collisions because of their protective gear and, more importantly, most were unaware of the grave risk of impact in flexion (p. 22) when either hitting the boards or spearing another player. Subconsciously to lower the head is very, very wrong. Also significant was the finding that the majority of victims had been unexpectedly checked or pushed from behind. As today's teenagers get bigger and faster, exercises to strengthen the neck muscles, and padded boards, may soon be mandatory.

The Canadian Hockey Association sets standards for face guards, mouthguards and helmets. The thickish helmet lining is important; fractured skulls have occurred when it is missing. Body pads and elastic must be checked regularly since elbows and hip bones are exposed if they slip. Gloves must be long enough. Check boots to see that they protect the ankle bones and that the tongue of the boot fits under the shin guard leaving no gap. The throat is the only part hard to protect and laryngeal fracture can therefore occur, but very rarely. The goalie would seem to be at great risk but actually suffers least; his protective gear is (or should be) impenetrable, and he is usually spared collisions with other players. The only worry a young goalie has is whether he can get his hands on enough food to grow big and loom large in the goal mouth.

What players admit to or coaches list as injuries is variable, so that medical statistics tend to be skewed towards serious trauma. Spectacular spills and thumps ought to be more productive of injury than they are, and they would be if deceleration were total, but bodies collide tangentially, they slide along the ice free of friction, and players' strong legs and skate control help to spread the force. It has been calculated that the skating velocity of the young is about 30 kph and the sliding speed after a fall can be 25 kph so that sliding head first into unpadded margins is serious. Deliberately to be splotched all over the boards, and pile-ups, remain the main sources of dislocation or fracture-dislocation of the limb joints. Lacerations by a skate above the boot rim can sever tendons and veins. Muscle strains of the groin, calf, and upper trunk occur, as do bad bruises from sticks getting between padding. There are now less stick injuries to the head or face because of protective masks.

National surveys in the United States show that more injuries occur in games than in practice due to the intense competition, and proportionately more in the second half of the season as the competition intensifies. A fall onto the shoulder or hand should be followed by a careful examination of the thumb and the clavicle (collar bone). The former can dislocate in the same way as a skier's (p. 73), and the latter is a common site for a greenstick fracture (p. 20), or dislocation of the joints at either end, the sterno-clavicular and the acromio-clavicular joints (p. 62). A group of professional players was once found to have abnormal clavicle X-rays, clear proof that their shoulders had been buffeted over the years more than they had remembered (or admitted to). For bantam and midget teams double-cantilevered air-cell filled shoulder pads are recommended, but they would not prevent shoulder dislocation in a pile-up.

Two oddities remain: skin irritation from the preparation of fibreglass sticks, and carbon monoxide sickness in young players. Tests in Boston in 1977 showed that enclosed rinks could exceed the 35 parts per million (ppm) level of CO set in the Clean Air Act, due to emissions from (old?) ice-cleaning machines. Lung tests on Harvard players confirmed a four-fold rise in lung CO even at air levels below 35 ppm due to exercise hyperventilation. Trust the Bostonians to take such care over their ice hockey!

Ice Skating

The young have it all over adults when it comes to learning to skate. They are closer to the ground and when they fall they think it is fun. Their dignity is never bruised. As in every sport, basic skill must be properly taught and beginners' classes usually concentrate on learning to turn, stop, glide, and get up; after that they either remain happy social skaters or follow their Olympic star. The only special effects needed at first are sturdy gloves, a warm jumper, thick socks to absorb pressure from ill-fitting hired boots, and waterproofing spray on the trouser bottoms, and bottom. The only initial injuries in beginner classes are sore bottoms, general bruises, and sore feet, nothing that a warm bath won't relieve, till next time!

When a new rink was opened in Oxford in the United Kingdom in 1984, patients naturally began to appear at the local Accident Centre. Out of every ten who were injured, six had fallen over, three had been pushed over or had collided, and one had been hit after falling. Whether a beginner or an expert, a fall is a fall, and likely to cause a cut, a bruise, a sprain, or a fractured arm or leg. The injury rate of the Oxford rink was estimated to be lower when the rink was overcrowded, evidence that room to speed is a big factor in causing injury. Early learners would do well to wear knee and elbow pads and gloves. Skate blades are not knives but strong blunt metal. Hands spread over the ice will be hurt by them, but not if gloves are thickish.

Figure skating, speed skating and special boots lie in the future, but aptitude, opportunity and a glimpse of Torville and Dean or Scott Hamilton are enough to fire young imaginations, and then begin all the stresses of intense training. Boots, boots and more boots, is the early theme song. If they are not a good fit, blisters, calluses and stubbed toes are a certainty, and if they are too stiff the Achilles tendon suffers. Toes must be able to wiggle. Laces can irritate and inflame the ankle tendons and may need to be padded.

Mr. J. Heater, M.C. for the United States National Figure Skating Championships, once said that a champion must have the balance of a tight-rope walker, the endurance of a marathon runner, the aggression of a football player, the agility of a wrestler, the nerves of a golfer, the flexibility of a gymnast, and the grace of a ballet dancer.

High speed twists lead to falls and the following possibilities: concussion, lacerated chin or forehead, broken elbows or fractures from falling on the outsretched hand, sprained fingers, fractured patella (knee cap), sprained knee or ankle, and dislocation of ankle tendons (p. 72).

Sharp muscle exertion in adolescents can avulse (tear away) muscle origins and their bone epiphyses (p. 17) from the pelvic bones: in front, laterally, just under the point of the hip bone, the rectus femoris muscle; in the upper inner leg, the long leg adductor (inner) muscles; and behind, from the ischial tuberosity on which you are now sitting, the hamstring group of muscles. As Micheli of the Boston Clinic first pointed out, in a child who is growing rapidly the muscles and fascial sheaths do not grow as quickly as the bones and for a year or two the back and leg muscles may be relatively taut and lacking in flexibility. (This observation might resurrect the idea of 'growing pains' and the 'gawky child'.) Stretching exercises and a temporary alteration of routines may be called for. The child may also have the added temporary problem of adjusting to altered balance from the changes of puberty (p. 53).

Fatigue increases the risk of falls towards the end of a training session and there is the ever-important topic, where young aspirants to stardom are concerned, of the time that should be given to muscle conditioning, because skating alone will not strengthen muscles vital to jumping and twisting, nor will it improve oxygen consumption efficiency. Only by alternating skating days with other training will this be remedied. Akira Kuroiwa, Japan's champion speed skater, developed his leg power and aerobic conditioning by a daily 8-km bicycle ride to school over mountain roads. One advantage of bicycling was that knees and ankles did not suffer the pounding effect of running the 8 kms. Strong abdominal muscles are another essential.

The remaining injuries are caused by stress and the cure for that is rest. Overuse leg problems are essentially the same as in athletics (p. 85). By the time a serious exponent is training six days a week, forty-eight weeks a year, he or she is exposed to low back pain, shinsplints, patello-femoral disorders, Achilles tendinitis, ankle bone spurs, foot strain, stress fractures, and frictional bursitis or tenosynovitis. The less said about cold rinks in early morning the better.

REFERENCES:

McMaster W. et al. Conditioning programme for competitive figure skating. *Am. J. Sports Med.* 1979; 7: 42.

Williamson D. M. et al. Ice skating injuries. *Injury* 1986; 17: 205–207.

Lacrosse

This is still played the Red Indian way, with little protective padding and inadequate face and eye protection, despite a 1981 report at intercollegiate level in the United States that the injury rate was 52%. Arm and shoulder pads, padded gloves, chest pads for goalies, and lighter plastic sticks are available. The top of the skull should be better protected than it is. Among the injuries that lacrosse can be expected to cause are muscle pulls, sprains of the limb joints, fractured nose or ribs from stick blows, and bruises.

There have been reports of cervical vertebrae being fractured in the face-off. These occurred in the classic way, when the head was down and contact was made with the top of the head (see Gridiron p. 127).

Martial Arts and Self-defence

There are now many varieties of the Oriental forms of combat and self-defence. Aikido, Hapkido, Judo, Jujitsu, Karate, Kempo, Kung Fu, Tae Kwon Do, with other subdivisions, are related forms of hand and feet attack. In other branches, an incredible array of weaponry is available to the advanced practitioner. Everything to do with the martial sports can be dangerous in 'free sparring'. The ideal for youngsters not yet in their teens is for the action to become an art form for learning moves and countermoves and for developing reflex habits of useful self-defence. How far they later advance is up to them for the camaraderie of the black belt brigade is remarkable. The

United Fighting Arts Federation of the United States publishes a code of ethics, a creed, and a code of conduct, which emphasise that character building and a healthy lifestyle are as important as technique and protective gear in avoiding needless injury. But accidents will happen; protective gear and padding are available in abundance and should be worn, especially as combatants grow in strength to the point where an error could wreak significant injury. Where there is kicking and twisting genital protectors become more important. For males the cricket-style box is not sufficient as it can be easily displaced by the sweeping arc of foot blows or by an upward kick. Novice students, especially girls, tend to have a higher injury rate.

Each art emphasises a different form of attack. Karate is mostly hand; round kicks are allowed to the side of the head with the instep. Tae Kwon Do allows full kicks to the head and face but not blows with the fist. Bare hands and bare feet will always suffer. It is impossible to expect otherwise. Thus the area of common injury in each differs but taking the arts as a generic sport, the possibility is that the attacking mode can be hurt, as can the area thumped. For those of a legal mind, there are penalties for both the thumper and the thumpee.

Fractured fingers, fractured metacarpals just behind the knuckle, dislocated fingers (so-called jammed fingers) and even double dislocations can occur from the thrust, or if any fingers are caught in loose garments. Thumb dislocation deserves special care; it may not be as simple as it looks. If chips of bone have come off with the torn ligament or the capsule has split then operative reduction (replacement) is needed, and the thumb is too important in the grip for it to be left in an unstable state. One must ignore folklore; karate legends of inner purity and moral strength giving to the hands supernatural ability to crack metal armour might once have been morale-boosting propaganda, but there is a limit to the force flesh and bone can absorb without injury. High-speed filming has shown that the deceleration force when breaking substances is some 400 G and that bone actually deforms like rubber. No doubt the ancients found this out by eons of experimentation and now forgotten injuries. Spectacular tricks are still best left to experts who make the development of such skill a lifetime's work. The hand does adapt to the sport over years. Experts training since childhood develop thickened skin and knuckles and thick bone along the 'chop' side as a reaction to chronic insult. That this is the correct word is proved by two other recorded changes, reduced blood flow in the palm and even damaged arteries (see Handball p. 141), and diminished range of wrist flexion-extension movement, not to mention finger stiffness after specific injury and the chance of fractured small bones of the wrist.

MARTIAL ARTS AND SELF-DEFENCE 153

The toes and feet suffer problems similar to the above but cannot adapt over the long term in the same way. Dislocated ankle tendons are signalled by a flash of pain with loss of power. Overenthusiastic effort can strain the Achilles tendon or the groin muscles, or avulse (tear away) muscle origin and attached bone epiphysis (p. 17) in those who have not stretched or warmed up correctly. The roundhouse kick may find the attacker twisting a knee or setting up the conditions for a meniscus (p. 68) tear in the planted leg. When the leg is used as a fulcrum, knee or ankle sprains may result.

Injuries to the defender depend upon where a blow lands, and whether a fall results, beginning with a fractured skull from falling back onto a hard floor and a dislocated neck from a spinning kick. Judo rules specifically outlaw choking techniques in thirteen-year-old and younger contestants but in the older, if the grip cannot be broken, submit, please. Neck injuries are not worth risking and odd things can happen at any age if the carotid (neck) arteries are squeezed, or if there is any unnatural stimulus to a juxtaposed very small but very sensitive blood pressure regulator called the carotid body. As in so many collision sports, injury to the head and neck means that one should not continue training and risk further damage. As always, concussion must be treated very seriously (p. 25).

Face lacerations, broken jaw, nose, tooth, or cheek bone, occur more often than in eyeball to eyeball boxing, especially in Tae Kwon Do, even though less blows may actually get through. Mouthguards are not as protective when sideswiped by a foot. Eye damage is the big worry. If the eye is hit the bout should stop, and alteration of vision after hard head blows must be checked. Fractured ribs, ruptured spleen or liver, bruised pancreas, kidney damage, all have happened. Haematuria (blood traces in the urine) was once found in judo exponents working on thin mats. A heavy kick to the solar plexus (p. 37) can stop the heart.

Disabling kicks to thighs and shins are popular. Deep bruises will result and if they form tense tender swellings in the tightly bound leg compartments surgical decompression could be needed; the colour of the foot is the clue to imperilled circulation. One oddity is bruising of the peroneal nerve as it winds around the outer side of the upper fibula (outer shinbone) 5 cms below the knee joint. Such bruising can cause foot weakness. Like all nerve damage in continuity (meaning when nothing is cut) it will recover but it may take considerable time. Arm nerves can be similarly damaged when blocking. Fractures and dislocations can also occur when blocking. Levered pulls cause dislocated shoulder joints, and a special dislocation occurs when the head of the radius (outer forearm bone) is pulled out of its annular (encircling) ligament. Complicated fracture-dislocations of the elbow or wrist can result from spectacular breakfalls. A hit on the side of the knee may sprain the medial (inner) ligament.

With this seemingly endless list of injury (and no doubt more freak accidents will come to be recorded), why let a youngster take up martial arts? Remember that all the above have been listed simply as injuries that could happen. With protective clothing and training we can hope, indeed aim to see, that very little actually does happen. The key is in the skill and discipline of the tutors. Choose your class and standard carefully, and above all watch to see that the show-off or the maverick is kept in order. These are the real danger to novices. As skill is acquired self-protection improves and training then reaps real benefit. Birrer in 1982 published a large survey of 24,112 injuries. Only 47, approximately 1 in 500, were serious. Mostly there were just contusions, sprains and strains.

The medical officer to the Scottish Karate Board of Control and the British Karate Board, G. R. McLatchie FRCS, has recommended that a doctor should attend competitions where twenty or more karatekae compete to advise on all aspects of injury protection and avoidance, and on the fitness of contestants. He emphasises the importance of proper floor padding, something a doctor would be quite amazed not to find, but alas, that organisers may not have provided. In this sport injury, without adequate padding, would be automatic.

Kick boxing is really a modified form of martial arts plus boxing, or vice versa. Kicks are not allowed below the belt, and knees, elbows and head cannot be used. Even with gloves and shin pads it is a punishing so-called sport with no semblance of restrained self-discipline. 'Only competent boxers need apply', should be the sign over the gymnasium door. In other words, only those who know how to protect the head should take up the sport.

REFERENCES:

Birrer R. B. et al. Martial arts injuries. *Physician and Sportsmed.* 1982; 10–6: 103–106.

McLatchie G. B. et al. Injuries in karate, a case for medical control. *J. Trauma* 1980; 20: 956–958.

Netball

This deserves special mention as a game becoming more popular, especially for girls. Although it is true that reduced opportunity for body contact and melees will lessen injury, orthopaedic surgeons regard it as a game specifically invented to cause knee injury. Consider the basic play. Catch the ball, freeze, twist, and throw. If the shoe grips the floor without a millimetre of slip or ankle movement, the ankle or the knee may twist as rotational force is absorbed. Ankle sprain may be complicated by chip fractures of bone, and fracture of small foot bones may be misdiagnosed as a sprain.

Collisions that find the receiver with a rigid leg, and the high breaking force of landing, both put great strain on the internal knee ligaments and hence are harbingers of dislocation or knee laxity.

During a season, any symptom at all, in either knee, such as pain, puffiness, sense of weakness, or loss of skill due to favouring one leg, must be examined by an expert as an insurance against serious damage. Surgical appliance technology is improving all the time and a well fitted protective knee brace could be a very good investment.

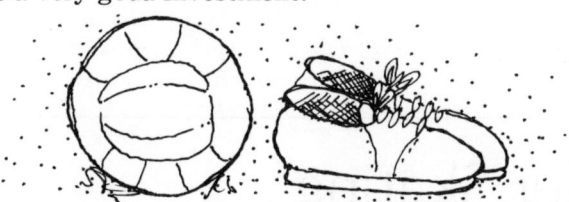

Eye injury from an opponent's finger is on the increase with vigorous defensive play. Players who normally use contact lenses should not leave them out when playing or should consider getting eye protectors with prescription lenses (p. 42). Fingers are vulnerable as the player snatches at the ball (see Basketball p. 104). High training levels and fancy gymnastics combine to cause chest, back and groin muscle strains, as well as the occasional stress fracture of the spine. It has been recorded that one half of the ankle sprains occur in training and that ankle strapping reduces the reported frequency. Knee braces and ankle strapping? In school sport? It hardly makes sense.

Racquetball

Racquetball, squash's young cousin, is more brash in style. (Royal Tennis devotees probably felt the same about squash.) With racquets bigger and heavier, the ball bouncier, and cut-throat games between three players on the court at the one time, the sport is risking comparison in safety with the those of the Roman Colosseum. The injury rate is waxing. Eye protection is very important. The greatest increase in eye injuries of any sport is occurring in racquetball, so much so that in 1984 a number of clubs in Quebec, Canada, made the use of eyeguards mandatory, and it is now estimated that more than 90% of clubs conform. This step was probably influenced by ice hockey (p. 146) and the long experience of Canadian ophthalmologists in what that did to eyes.

Court etiquette is as important (possibly more so) in this sport as it is in squash in minimising injury. If your partner ignores calls to stop wild swings the only safe thing to do is stop play. The heavier ball would tend to strain the elbow more than squash but the general range of injuries is otherwise the same (see Squash p. 186).

Roller Skating

Believe it or not roller skate dancing is fashionable in some Belfast discotheques. Presumably because some people like to fall over and that is when things happen to roller skaters. Then it is all a matter of luck and speed, unless the skater is wearing full protective gear and, going by hospital records, in nine out of ten cases none was worn. Head injury or a broken neck is the worst outcome and preventable by wearing helmets.

Compression fractures of the lower vertebrae may not be revealed until X-rays are done in later life for a 'bad back'. Fractures of the wrist, forearm, elbow, or collar bone, are the most common because of the reflex outstretch of the hand in falling. Any fractures of the ankle or leg in the tangle tend to be of the more complicated variety and to require surgery. The modern roller is unfortunately a mechanical improvement on ancient types, heavier and with better bearings, so that higher speeds are possible. As well as padded clothes and thick gloves, wrist splints are now available to dissipate the force of a fall more evenly along the arm, and hopefully to diminish individual bone fractures.

Statistics always show a preponderance of female victims but it is hard to see why unless it is the familiar problem of initially weaker leg muscles. More accidents are reported outside the proper rinks than in them, no doubt due to irregular or broken surfaces. In relation to this a very pertinent modern hazard is litigation. Children roller skating on the footpaths must be warned that more and more law suits are being taken out by pedestrians who are knocked over (see Cycling p. 120).

It is fortunate that undisciplined shopping mall roller skating seems to be on the wane. If there is a developing passion for the sport it is better channelled into championship speed skating with training sessions on proper surfaces under adult supervision. See to it also that thin youngsters do leg exercises to build up all the leg muscles, as that is the surest protection against knee injury and ankle sprains.

Rowing

The severe physical output of rowers has been long recognised and decades ago examination of rowers' urine first indicated the leakage of albumen (blood protein) and blood cells through the kidney that has since provided a marker of severe exertion in even healthy athletes. Deviation of blood from the internal organs to the muscles is a likely explanation. Replicating the situation in the exercise laboratory indicates that the albuminuria (albumen in the urine) seems not to be age or sex related and not really sport specific. As is to be expected, hot still days add to rowers' exhaustion.

Hand blisters, wrist tenosynovitis, and occasional knee strain used to be all, but now lumbar backache is a problem. To the stress element of intensive training there is added the extremes of rig now used, with new seat and feet heights. The old straight-back style has been abandoned in favour of flexion, rotation and lateral bending of the spine; when these stresses are at their maximum, rough water is the last straw.

Lumbar strain pain occurs on the side opposite to the oar and gradually gets worse. No matter just where the bone or joint stress has developed, muscle tightness or spasm ensues and this must be treated by physiotherapy. Younger crews definitely need supervised exercises to strengthen all spine movements, and to provide strong abdominal muscles. It is not often realised that without strong abdominal muscles to balance the pull on the spine and stabilise it, even more rotational twist is transmitted to the vertebrae and their ligaments.

X-rays of the spine will uncover a small percentage of congenital defects but these are not a factor in this sport because of the different source and site of the rotation stress. Until certified fit to return to the crew, skulling, which does not involve trunk rotation, is a safe substitute exercise. True spondylolysis (p. 28) seen on X-rays has been put down, not to rowing, but to weight lifting in the off-season. It might also be worth checking the set-up of home rowing machines; exercise is one thing, but lumbar strain here is unnecessary.

Lightweight women rowers seem to present a special problem in back pain and discomfort possibly because of their capacity for excessive flexion of the spine, beneficial though this is in increasing power in the drive. It is possible that such flexion excessively deforms the intervertebral discs. The back should therefore be kept in extension during rest periods, and even when sitting in a chair doing schoolwork.

Canoeists, kayak enthusiasts, and the like are prone to overuse injuries of the elbow, shoulder and wrist tendons, and they will need to take tender care of the skin on the bottom.

Crews racing in estuaries with access to warm oceans, please don't throw the cox off the wharf if you win. Once in Western Australia when a cox was heaved over, a shark resting in the cool shadow of the wharf could hardly believe its luck.

REFERENCE:

Green E. A. W. Comfort to contortion: The last 10 years of rowing. *Brit. J. Sports Med.* 1980; 14: 109.

Rugby

Teachers beware. A learned English judge has ruled that you must not tackle pupils if playing with them. (Legal buffs can refer to R. A. Abednigo Affutu-Nartoy versus R. Clarke, 1984.) His Honour ruled that teachers could take part to keep the game and the ball moving, and to demonstrate skills, but it was wrong and a breach of duty for a teacher to have any physical contact in such a game. One wonders however how many of the 1st XV would just love to have a teacher join in a game now and then!

The Rugby Football Union published and distributed the following recommendations to all United Kingdom schools in 1980:

- 'Greater attention should be paid to pre-season preparation; boys need to be fit to play rugby rather than hope to become fit by playing it.
- 'Coaches should be fully involved in fitness training and injury prevention and should be aware of materials such as posters and wall charts. They should be encouraged to attend suitable sports medicine seminars to further their knowledge of the basic principles of physical preparation and of first-aid.
- 'The teaching of the current play techniques, for example in tackling, scrimmaging, and rucking, must begin at the earliest moment at school level, because faulty application of such basic techniques endangers not only the boy himself but others with whom he is in contact.
- 'In school rugby up to six replacements for injured players may be allowed in a match in order to minimise the risk of boys playing out of position.
- 'Levels of experience must always be matched, because the body, as a result of modern techniques, is now required to accept heavier strain.
- 'Teams should be reasonably matched as to age, strength, and rugby maturity, and all matches and games must be authoritatively controlled by a referee well versed in the Laws. Traditional matches between School and Old Boy teams may continue provided supervision and selection are in the hands of the School coach, but normally matches between Clubs and Schools should only be played if there is a strong element of coaching in the match.

- 'The spirit of the game is ill served by coaches and others "psyching up" players and this must be resisted at all costs.
- 'A player who has had severe concussion should not be allowed to play until he has reached full clinical recovery and only after he has been cleared by a medical examination. Firm discipline is necessary by School Staff and coaches, as great disservice may be done to a player who is allowed to return to the field before he is fully recovered.
- 'Mouthguards minimise face, jaw, and dental injury, and also reduce the risk of concussion but must always be fitted by a dental surgeon.
- 'Studs in future should be of composition rubber and the fifth, the toe stud, should be eliminated. It will take time for manufacturers to develop a satisfactory moulded sole with adequate heel support, but such a type should be sought when replacing boots.'

What more needs to be said?

J. P. Sparks published statistics in 1981 analysing thirty seasons of play between 1950 and 1979 at Rugby School, England, where adolescents had notched up half a million hours of rugby. There were 9855 injuries, a rate of 197.7 per 10,000 player hours. Interestingly, the rate per five year period remained fairly constant at between 189 and 205, despite many changes over time in training and technique. (Comparable indices of injury for other sports at Rugby were: basketball 103, everything else in the 20 to 30 range, down to squash at 10 and tennis 7.)

At the top of the list of injuries were: concussion 513, torn thigh quadriceps muscle 327, fractured finger 183, fractured teeth 157, torn hamstring muscles 131, torn medial (inner) ligaments of the knee 119, and traumatic synovitis (fluid collection) in the knee joint 156. None of the four cervical spine injuries led to paraplegia. But every conceivable injury and fracture occurred at least once, including the unusual fractures involving joint surfaces, a warning that any joint injury or tenderness must be x-rayed to search for fracture lines running across the bone ends and involving bone growth centres.

An antipodean set of figures collected in 1981 by Sugerman, covering thirty-three schools, 3059 games, 45,885 player games, and 541 injuries leading to school absence (and probably underestimating a lot of bruises and lacerations), concluded that the incidence of severe injuries in these well supervised games was 'very slight'. In round figures there were 50 concussions and 400 musculo-skeletal (muscle and bone) injuries, a different ratio to the England series above which may reflect the harder pitches in Australia and the way players learn to fall. There were no injuries in the ten years and under sides but after that the number increased every year as muscle power and momentum increased. There were no head or neck fractures.

Headgear is uncommon in rugby. Players criticise it for being uncomfortable and claim it may even encourage butting (see Gridiron p. 131). Photographs of one of Australia's all-time great league internationals in the 1930s, Dave Brown, always show him in headgear, so perhaps it just needs redesigning to gain wider acceptance. Light shoulder, thigh and skin pads seem to be a thing of the past. Rarely mentioned in past decades, mouthguards have been developed with new technology and are now an important item (p. 135).

Neither of the above sets of figures mentions herpes simplex, a viral skin infection causing blisters, but it has been reported as spreading from an infected player to others in a scrum by vigorous skin contact (see Wrestling p. 211). A neat piece of detective work by the pathology department of St Thomas' Hospital, London, traced the path of a footballer's nephritis (kidney inflammation) back from his severe skin infection to his teammates', thence to its origin in the beard of an opposing team's forward. They had all met in a scrum and swapped organisms. It is now recommended that antiseptic be applied directly to cuts and abrasions and reapplied for two more days in case organisms have survived in surrounding skin.

Concussion heads the list of injuries at Rugby School and is a condition that must be taken more seriously than it usually is (p. 25), but cervical spine fracture remains *the* big worry of administrators. Indeed, between the years 1953 and 1982, in the United Kingdom, there were sixty-three serious neck injuries in rugby. J. R. Silver, consultant in spinal injuries at the National Sports Injury Centre at Stoke Mandeville, wrote a most detailed analysis of the problem in 1984 which pointed to an increase in spine injuries with paralysis, particularly ones involving schoolboys. Collapsed scrums, overboisterousness and piling on in the rucks, faulty tackling techniques, multiple tackles and illegal tackles are pinpointed as the causes. Unfortunately even the expert player, according to the statistics, is not protected by his skill. He is more at risk of paraplegia, either because of more vigorous play, or more deadly marking and an overall excess of competitive effort. The close inspection of Internationals' brawls by the television lens must also have a subconcious effect on young gladiators. In earlier times one had to depend on rumours from midfield as to how who did what to whom.

In the mechanics of this injury the common factor is always

that the head is fixed whilst the body is forced in any old direction. Multiple or illegal tackles must be immediately spotted *and* penalised by referees; Silver makes the point that otherwise the perpetrators sneak away to do harm another day. Trying to tackle head-on is brave, but dangerous nonetheless. Collapsed scrums may be a matter of gross disparity in weight and strength, and are most likely to occur at puberty or when boys are opposed to adults. Rough rucks are a problem for the Rules Committee, indeed at a meeting of the British Orthopaedic Association in 1984 the point was emphasised by several consultants that the 1970 rule changes had caused an immediate rise in the number of broken necks. In the final analysis school coaches will have to get the game back to a fast open spectacle if paraplegia is to be eliminated, indeed everyone associated with rugby should read the article by Silver for its careful analysis of the game and the eyewitness details of how neck fractures happened. Donald Macleod, honorary surgeon to the Scottish Rugby Union, claims that until their mid teens boys are not powerful enough to hurt themselves or others. Maybe, but teenagers seem to be getting bigger in each generation. Also, in the school structure there is occasionally a senior boy who repeats final year, and that extra twelve months' maturity can put him far above adolescent opponents in strength and aggression.

It must be emphasised over and over again that the long slender-necked boy has no place in a forward line-up at any age, and that a programme of exercises to strengthen neck muscles is very important as a boy advances through the age teams. Important, in fact, for *every* keen rugby player. Parents must listen carefully to any comments a player makes about a game or the position in which he is playing. With forwards especially, experienced neurosurgeons have noticed that many injured players commented that they never had felt 'comfortable' or 'confident' with their place in the scrum. They may in other words have had a subconscious feeling that they were not strong enough, or did not have the instinctive reflexes, for the position. Coaches could brush such comments aside, but parents should not.

The enormous influence of proper first-aid in suspected neck fracture cannot be explained better that it was in a letter by J. Piggott and D. S. Gordon of Belfast, published in the British Medical Journal, 20 January 1979. Four victims transported in the 'recovery position', with uncontrolled head movement, are permanent quadriplegics. Three other players, initially quadriplegic on the field, were seen at once and accompanied in the ambulance by a doctor who held the head in a 'neutral position' with light traction right into hospital and until caliper traction was there applied. Two of the three made a full recovery and the third is partially paralysed, but walking. Minor neck injury is a misleading term to use. A neck injury is *never* minor on the field, it has to be *proved* minor by subsequent medical examination. A rotation force is the one to fear and a 'wry' or 'twisted' neck means that the player in question must leave the field. There is a very real danger that the joints of the neck vertebrae may have been displaced or made unstable (p. 22) and it takes only a minor bump after that to cause complete dislocation. The result? Paraplegia. A Jordan frame (p. 24) and inflatable neck collars should be available at every rugby ground.

It would be wrong to overemphasise the question of paraplegia. In fact, overall it is in the region of 1 per 1.5 million player appearances, according to the New Zealand and South African figures covering all ages. It is only the current *trend* that must be watched, and parents in turn must watch training methods, playing habits, and playing position.

Seven-a-side games played as touch rugby, are a new and growing version of the sport, rather like 'tag' games, and theoretically quite safe as they emphasise skill and running rather than rugged defence. However spectacular falls can still occur if footwear does not supply proper traction. Probably the greatest danger may be to keen fathers who join in wearing street shoes, forgetting how slippery these get in a short time on grass.

Gaelic football is in a class of its own for the variety of ways of creating mayhem; only the speedy turnaround in the direction of play, a genuine desire to get hold of the ball to kick it the length of Ireland, time out for the combatants to shake hands, and soft green ground stop anything more than the usual fighting injuries; it's when the spectators invade the pitch to join in the celebrations that real danger to the players looms.

Regrettably we must finish as we began, on a legal note. In 1987, in the New South Wales, Australia, Supreme Court, a schoolboy quadriplegic sued and was awarded heavy damages in a case against the Department of Education. He claimed teacher negligence in playing him as hooker between two shorter props, in failing to instruct him in neck strengthening exercises before choosing him in that position, and in failing to instruct him in the technique of scrums. In evidence the boy said that he was looking down and to the left to watch his half back (would you, the reader, now please stand up, bend forward, and do just that), when he felt a sharp pain in the neck. Are you surprised at what happened? Imagine if a heavy weight had fallen on your neck in that position. Force platform measurements have shown that the speed of impact generates the significant force, not the steady pushing in the scrum. It has been estimated that in a collapsing scrum 0.5 tonne force can be transmitted to anyone caught off balance.

To the contrary an English High Court Judge in 1988 dismissed a claim against a school for a 1980 paraplegic injury to a pupil in an interhouse game. In judgement His Honour rejected the player's version of the accident and preferred the evidence of the opposing wing three quarter and the master in charge of the game, to the effect that the plaintiff was not injured by attempting a head-on tackle. It had been side-on from a wide angle and when his head hit his opponent's hip, he had tried to tackle correctly by getting his head behind the other's thigh, but mistimed. Further, that the plaintiff had been well taught and coached in the basics at his previous preparatory school and he had not needed much more instruction in the basics from his senior school, although he had received it since the school was one that 'deserved its high reputation for the quality of its rugby, and had a high standard of supervision'.

This legal trend (it is the same in school gridiron) is very important and only parents can eliminate it by uniting to impress upon administrators the need for rule changes at junior level and for referees to be given more power to send off the thugs who are ruining a good game. The current legal requirement for parents to sign permission for their sons to play school rugby and to take out accident insurance leaves them no option but to make sure that referees also enforce the International Rugby Football Board Rule 20 which aims to minimise the force of impact at engagement on the front rows; and they need to watch carefully for any evidence of gang tackling, spear tackling, playing the man rather than the ball, and dangerous techniques in general.

REFERENCES:

Silver J. P. Injuries of the spine sustained in rugby. *B. M. J.* 1984; 288: 37.

Sparks J. R. Half a million hours of rugby football, the injuries. *Brit. J. Sports Med.* 1981; 15: 30.

Sugerman S. Injuries in Australian schools rugby union. *Aust. J. Sports Med. & Ex. Sci.* 1983; 15: 5.

Taylor T. K. F. et al. Rugby must be made safer; preventive programmes and rule changes. *Med. J. Aust.* 1988; 149: 224.

Scuba Diving

Decompression sickness (the bends) cannot occur in dives of less than 10 metres but lung overpressure can, *even in 1.5 metres of water*. Death has resulted from a 5-metre dive. Therefore *even divers in training* are at risk.

The pressure on the outside of the chest wall, that is on the lungs, must equal the pressure of the gas inside the lungs, otherwise the lungs will either collapse or burst. On land, the pressure is atmospheric, adjusted for altitude. Under water, this pressure is atmospheric plus the weight, that is the height, of the water column, measured naturally as 'depth' of water. At 10 metres depth in sea water the extra water pressure equals one atmosphere, meaning that the chest walls externally and the lungs internally are in balance at 2 atmospheres of pressure; breathing apparatus must therefore deliver air accurately to the lungs at 2 atmospheres, or else! On ascent to the surface the internal lung pressure must drop back smoothly to 1 atmosphere again. If it does not the lungs will burst. It is as simple as that. During ascent, with the mouth passively open, a stream of bubbles indicates air exhalation and hence pressure equalisation, but this latter will not happen if the diver keeps his mouth, nose, and especially the larynx shut, and it will not happen in all parts of the lung if air is trapped anywhere behind a plug of mucus. The bursting pressure has been measured experimentally in dogs and found to be at 80 mms of mercury, equal to just under 1.2 metres of sea water, thus showing how narrow the tolerance is.

If the lung tissue bursts air bubbles may trek anywhere, but the worst outcome is if they enter the bloodstream as emboli (small particles), and travel about blocking arteries in vital organs. The effects are immediate. The diver may suffer a stroke, go blind, or have a coronary heart attack with death underwater. In fact many cases of drowning in scuba diving are probably from lung overpressure and air embolism (disease caused by emboli lodging). The gas bubbles remain as a physical entity because the nitrogen will not dissolve in blood even though the oxygen will.

It is clear that some youngsters are not medically fit to dive: asthmatics, previous pneumothorax (air in the pleural cavity) sufferers, chronic bronchitics or those with chronic ear, nose and throat disease. Others are disqualified by diseases liable to complications at any time which must not occur underwater: epileptics, migraine sufferers, and diabetics. Those with poor vision must buy quality goggles with bonded prescription lenses. Surely nobody with claustrophobia would want to try scuba, but if they do, be hard-hearted enough not to go in with them. What you do not need underwater is hindrance from an unbalanced person or a disturbed personality. Such people, as firefighters or divers, have been observed to pull off their mask under stress. If a surreptitious rise is noticed in the breathing rate or the heart begins to thump, carbon dioxide build-up is occurring and the diver *must* have the self-discipline to surface at once.

One must *never* dive with a common cold. Not only is the virus activated by lowering the body temperature but also mucus is driven down into the lungs by pressure, and localised blocks in the lungs are set up, perfect conditions for air embolism to occur. The importance of steady exhalation during ascent to equalise lung pressures can be emphasised again, because this also automatically equalises middle ear pressures due to the ear's communication with the throat by way of the Eustachian tube, provided of course that all three are healthy. If not, such as when the ubiquitous infected mucus is blocking the tube, the eardrum will rupture outwards. It might even have ruptured inwards on descent because equalisation could not be achieved. Any diver who notices blood trickling from the ear, deafness, dizziness, loss of balance, or ringing in the ear, has suffered some damage and must see an ear, nose and throat specialist. In the same way blockage in one of the sinuses will cause pain, or bleeding into the nose; indeed thorough ear, nose and throat examinations, including a puretone audiogram, would be an excellent insurance for any youngster before taking up scuba diving or deep skindiving with flippers. Only in this way can defects in the sinuses or nose which will interfere with pressure equalisation be detected *before* there is trouble. Fanatical divers ought to have an annual examination and test.

The temptation to override a common head cold with decongestant drugs is strong but fraught with danger. If the effect wears off before ascent all the evils of barotrauma (injury due to high pressure) reappear. Barotrauma ruptures the eardrum, causes bleeding in mucous membranes and ruptures the lung. It may not be a 'cold' limited to the nose, in fact sinus and bronchial mucous membranes are sure to be involved to a degree. And the sprays or drops used may include an antihistamine that causes drowsiness, or an adrenalin type substance that just might alter heart rhythms. Above all the rule should never be broken: Do not dive unless 100% fit.

Pain in a tooth after diving means a visit to the dentist; air under pressure may have crept into a cavity or leaky filling and expanded on ascent. Unequalised pressure exists under the mask when it only covers the mouth and not the nose; a red eye or skin haemorrhages can result. Gas in the bowel (swallowed air, or loads of cabbage for lunch!) will cause abdominal pain as it expands on ascent, and will need to be passed one way or the other for relief.

Decompression sickness is not a normal scuba danger. For it to happen, it needs diving depth and time, conditions that favour its development, and then a fast ascent that breaks all the rules. Government bodies such as the Navy, and National civilian associations, put out tables to cover deep diving and *they must be obeyed*, in fact more than obeyed. Study them, understand them, and then allow a personal safety margin of up to 20%. It is a recommendation that adolescents up to age fifteen should not go deeper than 12 metres, and sports dives should end short of 30 metres. Below that special training and equipment are vital.

There have been odd cases of divers suffering the bends even when following the tables strictly, the cause probably being individual variations in fitness or body function. The pressure at depth gradually forces some air nitrogen into solution in the bloodstream and slowly, over time, it is absorbed from the blood by body fat. On ascent the process has to reverse and if time is not allowed for it the gas bubbles accumulate causing the characteristic limb and back pains of the bends, and spinal cord paralysis. The condition is very serious and the onset deceptively insidious. It all has to do with the high solubility of nitrogen in fat (five times the rate in water), and thus its slow release; in fact it may be a flight home in an underpressurised aircraft that triggers off the decompression. Do not fly for at least two hours after any dive, and certainly not for twenty-four hours after a decompression dive.

If a diver surfaces in obvious difficulties suspect air embolism from lung rupture because the effects of that, unlike the bends, are instantaneous. Put him on a stretcher with the feet high to encourage the gas bubbles to travel 'up' to the feet, that is away from the brain, give 100% oxygen to breathe, and hurry to hospital. Have someone telephone ahead to allow enquiries to be made about the nearest pressure chambers (either a Navy facility or specialised hospital unit) and means of pressurised aircraft transfer, in case the emergency centre deems it necessary.

When surfacing a diver can be run down by passing craft if he has strayed from the marker buoy. Danger from local denizens of the deep must also be most carefully considered. Those who belong to clubs will be taught all this, indeed, self-contained underwater breathing apparatus (s-c-u-b-a) or compressed air should not be sold to anyone who is not a certified club member. One ought not to accept compressors and tanks on sight either. A serious scare was once caused by the use of sanitary napkins, just because they were cheap, as filters in private compressors. Such napkins are made of wood pulp that in the presence of compressed air and oil can produce lethal carbon monoxide. Theoretically this gas can also get into an air compressor intake from a nearby car exhaust so the purity of every commercial source should be checked at regular intervals.

The diving tables, remember, were formulated for fit commercial and naval men divers. There is practical evidence that female divers are more susceptible to decompression sickness and there are good theoretical reasons to support this. The adolescent increase in body fat percentage means that more nitrogen can be stored. Therefore girls should be very careful to stay well within the limits set in the tables, and not just copy what the boys do in depth and time. The body fat layer also means that they will feel hotter on land in the wet suit, and yet lose heat more quickly underwater through conduction; they will thus feel cold more quickly. Menstruating girls should not dive. They may not feel in tiptop condition, which is an absolute must for underwater safety. The idea that the menstrual blood will attract sharks has been discounted, but who can guarantee that? There is simply no point, when it is just sport, in giving sharks a scintilla of encouragement. Overweight fat boys would do well to lose weight if they want to dive, a matter again of nitrogen absorption into fatty tissues.

In the final estimate one's life may depend on foresight and equipment. Thus care and maintenance of equipment must be 101% perfect. It is worth repeating that any sense of dizziness, disorientation, or deafness underwater is a danger sign of inner ear damage and the dive should be promptly aborted. Confused divers or those in panic are in great danger of drowning. For that reason—reduced efficiency and risk of confusion—dives should end well before physical fatigue sets in, and should not even be attempted if the diver is not in top physical condition or feels 'below par'. The one most at risk is the holidaymaker who has paid a lot of money to get to a tropical resort, and hates to waste a single hour for such a silly thing as a cold.

REFERENCE:
Unsworth I. P. Director of Diving and Hyperbaric Medicine, Prince Henry Hospital, Sydney. Personal communication, 1987.

Skateboarding

Skateboards are really the roller skate updated. Junior stands on a narrow platform travelling at speeds up to the legal limit for motor cars, 50 kph, with no means of stopping, no way of steering, going too fast to jump off, and in nineteen times out of twenty wearing no protective clothing. Motorcyclists are not allowed by law to behave that way. Why should street skateboard riders?

Kids have fallen for them in a big way. Unfortunately they then fall off them, fall across the hard edge of the board or the gutter, fall in front of cars, cause pedestrians to fall over, or their equipment falls apart. Worse, parents fall off if they try to imitate junior; they fall harder, do more damage to themselves, and risk a broken neck and paraplegia, because their sense of balance and their falling skills are not honed.

The United States Consumer Product Safety Commission 1977 Report on skateboard injuries noted, inter alia, that of the accident victims:

- One third had been on the skateboard for less than one week, and most of these fell off at the first attempt.
- 45% had been skating for less than one month.
- One third hit some irregularity on the surface.
- 40% were on borrowed, unfamiliar boards.

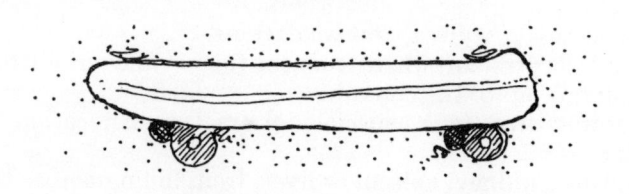

- Very few wore protective clothing.

The danger to beginners is thus obvious; they will go too fast and use city streets. If they cannot learn balance and control in skateboard parks it is doubtful if they should be allowed on boards at all. The Safety Commission has recommended that skateboarders should:

- Emphasise *control* not speed.
- Do warm-up exercises.
- Not attempt difficult manoeuvres early.
- *Not be towed.*
- Learn how to fall(!!!).
- Wear protective gear.
- Keep equipment in working order.

Product failure was held to account for 2% of the reported injuries; newer models are said to be safer, with wider nonskid decks made of laminates and larger and better wheels with sealed bearings. Protective clothing can be obtained: padded trousers, elbow and knee pads, ankle guards and gloves, and helmets which should be equivalent in strength to a motorcycle helmet. It is no wonder that kids will not put on all this for what they call fun. If they were using boards as a serious means of transport on public highways the law would make them. So they are going to get injured. As with children who bicycle or roller skate, police and the law are looking with a jaundiced eye on skateboarders weaving along pavements, and dodging between pedestrians.

Assiduous readers of this book could by now almost guess the injuries which can be caused by the inevitable fall.

- Concussion.
- Fracture of the spine, usually of a transverse process of one of the lumbar or thoracic vertebrae (p. 28) bent across the edge of the board or the gutter. Children are quick enough to protect their head and neck with the outstretched hand, but adults are not, so please, another plea to parents, don't jump on to share in the fun. Your job is to be very cool about skateboards.
- Bad scrapes, bruises, and lacerations.
- Arm fractures, anywhere from the fingers and wrist (the most common), up to the collar bone.
- Leg fractures, and especially a fracture-dislocation of the ankle.
- Ruptured kidney, spleen, or liver, from falling across things.
- Falling under a car? It does not bear thinking about.

Skiing

Downhill Skiing

Racing downhill at speeds up to 120 kph is very much a young person's sport and intensive training for it has to begin in adolescence. A Swedish survey published in 1976 showed that 40% of all skiing injuries occurred in the under fifteen-year age group with three quarters of these happening in downhill skiing. Many of these were probably due to inexperience in the dangers of varying slope surfaces and inability or unwillingness to adapt speed and technique to changing weather conditions.

An analysis of 42,245 injuries in Japan between 1956 and 1979 showed, in round figures, that 42% were sprains, 27% lacerations, 6% contusions (deep bruises), and 2% dislocations. The commonest leg fracture was, and remains, a fracture of the inner shinbone, the tibia. However, over that period the injury pattern has changed with the design of safety bindings and modifications to the boot; ankle injuries have diminished and knee problems have increased. The same trend was confirmed on analysis of 17,300 injuries in the Black Forest region of Germany between 1936 and 1980. Note that both these sets of figures are for all age groups combined, and there are differences based on age. Children's bone, being immature and less strong, breaks with less force and thus they still have relatively more of the common tibial fractures. But they seem to have less arm breaks.

One thing has not changed: the devastating effect of high speed collisions with fixed objects. Figures from Denver, Colorado, showed that two thirds of such collisions caused a ruptured spleen or kidney, or both, needing surgery, and that the chances of survival were improved by helicopter evacuation with treatment of shock en route to hospital. Multiple fractures, penetrating injuries from broken poles, closed chest injuries to the lung and great vessels, a fractured skull or a broken neck, often complicate the rescue. Nordic skiers, far from a ski patrol and therefore further from swift rescue when they may most need it, must remember to ski with the caution commonsense and isolation demands.

Newer freestyle trends, ballets, aerials, moguls and the like, are producing more upper limb, spinal and head injuries. This could have been predicted! The risk was estimated by the United States Ski Association (USSA) in 1981 to be 2.8 injuries per 1000 skier days in competitions under USSA rules, but clearly it would be higher if ill prepared skiers were allowed to 'give it a go' in poorly supervised competitions. Nor do statistics reflect how many must have been injured whilst learning, or worse, casually practising at a remote spot. Any parent, let alone any doctor, watching films of the spectacular spills from this orchestrated mayhem would freeze in the chair from fear and disbelief.

Ski jumping has a low injury risk *provided* conditions are carefully checked. A five-year survey in Norway (where in the 1981–82 season there were 2238 licensed jumpers over twelve years of age) revealed a very low incidence of injury (.003%), but when it did occur it tended to be serious. It was felt that danger signals were seen in: the fifteen- to seventeen-year age group attempting to jump further than their capacity or skill allowed; the beginning and end of the season in attempts to better the previous best; the first jump of the day (the most likely time for injury); the use of more than one standard heel block (and falling off in the run-up); uneven snow conditions in the run-in; loose snow in the landing area; and rails and fences that could catch the ski in a fall. A formidable list indeed, but from it parents can deduce that if they see the young preparing a jump, it would be an idea to stroll over and check the smoothness of the run-in and take-off, the firmness of the landing area after fresh falls, and to make sure that goals are quite modest.

Acute mountain sickness is possible for those living in lodges from 2500 metres upwards, as the oxygen partial pressure drops closer to a level that begins to interfere with oxygen transport in the blood; by 4500 metres most skiers will be suffering within twenty-four hours from headache, nausea, irritability, fatigue, and poor concentration. The occasional victim, and it is more likely to be in the young, progresses to dangerous pulmonary oedema (fluid in the lung) with distressed breathing, a rapid pulse, and a bluish complexion. Without absolute rest, extra oxygen, and urgent return to lower levels, death threatens. To prevent this the body must be given a chance to acclimatise. Skiers who live at sea level would be wise to spend forty-eight hours at 1500 metres on their way up to 2500 metres, and certainly above that level should ascend slowly and extend their exertion gradually.

Specific problems when skiing that are preventable by taking proper care include:

Sunburn or Windburn

These injuries are self-inflicted, or in the case of the very young, parent-inflicted, by lack of time-consuming care. Lips, ear lobes, and exposed face skin must be covered by good quality blockout sunscreen. So-called snow blindness, a red, inflamed, bleary, discharging eye (acute conjunctivitis), caused by sunburn, is very painful and should never happen. Eyelids and the eyeball must be protected, not only against the sun but also against scratches from twigs, by good quality sunglasses. There is an unfortunate trend towards cheaper, disposable, or cheap lens fashion-framed glasses. Pubertal skiers think of appearance and fashion first, instead of quality and function in choice of gear! Young eyes, if too long unprotected against ultraviolet rays, will form a pterygium (p. 41) at the inner angle when adult. Mirrored sunglasses can cause nasty burns to the nose, so cover it. Also radio headphones must not have metal in the earplugs; this could cause painful spots and even frostbite in the ear.

Cold sores, due to the herpes simplex virus activated in cold temperatures, must be covered by cream. They are contagious so be careful with balaclavas, making sure they are washed and not swapped around the family.

Frostnip

These numb white patches on the exposed face or hands are really the beginnings of frostbite. Children, whose body temperature regulators are inefficient compared to an adult's, are very vulnerable. Never ignore a child who says: 'I feel cold.' He or she must at once be taken indoors to warm up and thereafter more attention must be paid to self-protection by wearing proper gloves and a balaclava. Silk is the best material but more expensive than cotton polyester.

Skier's Thumb

This dislocation of the metacarpo-phalangeal joint (knuckle) should be a thing of the past in snow (but not on artificial runs, see below). It is caused by catching the web of the thumb in the ski pole strap when falling, although this as the sole cause is still debatable. A series of such cases treated in Switzerland showed that the best cures came when there were avulsion (tearing away) fractures as well which were treated surgically. Simple strapping of dislocations had more failures; in other words was the initial diagnosis correct without an X-ray, was the immobilisation time long enough, or were the ligaments so torn that surgery should have been carried out? Expert advice is needed for injury to such a vital structure as the thumb. Strapless poles (or webbed gloves) will eliminate this risk but new flared hand grips are posing another hazard. If the thumb will not bend around the handle, the tip thus protruding may hit the ground head-on and dislocate in a fall.

Fractures

Falls on hard-packed snow can cause fractures to the outstretched hand and wrist, or to the collar bone. High-speed falls can also cause sprains or dislocations, wounds, and nasty facial abrasions. Beware wrist cuts made by one's own sharp ski edge or runaway strap. Deep vital tendons can be severed. The need for proper gloves and ski brakes is obvious. Newer sharp-edged skis can also cut the inside of the calf above the boot.

An analysis of Australian children's injuries in the Perisher Valley resort showed that they were more prone than adults to leg fractures, and these were more likely to be of the serious type since children's tibial (inner shin) bones are relatively weak until maturity. Whatever the contributing cause (inexperience, soft snow, speed, slope etc.) *if the bindings had been correctly adjusted and released*, the bone would have been protected. Unfortunately, this was found not to be the case. Significantly, few of the children's bindings released as they fell. The choice of a good ski hire shop is a vital step for parents. For example, the Snowline Ski Centre, Smiggin Holes in the Perisher Valley, takes three times longer in fitting out children than it does adults, in order to make sure that their boots fit well, before attending to the boot to binding fitting. Extra care is taken to set the binding at the correct tension. The setting is recorded for reference and parents are advised to return to the shop if it seems wrong. There is a temptation to save time and trouble by adjusting tension hastily on the run; the odds on a broken leg then shorten rapidly!

That children are more often involved in collisions and ski-lift injuries is a clear indication of the vital need for adult supervision at *all* times, even though the result for the parent is less time on the slopes! Interestingly, in a Perisher Valley study no child wearing a helmet got a head, neck or back injury.

Leg Strains

Edging conditions put great strain on the medial (inner) ligament of the knee, and that this is more of a problem in girls must indicate that it is a matter of thigh muscle strength. Children with knock knees also must watch iced slopes.

In deep snow pitching forwards may cause boot top contusion (deep bruising) or strain the Achilles tendon attachment to bone. Another rare outcome is dislocation of the tendons that run into the foot along a groove behind the lateral ankle malleolus (p. 71). The victim will feel an intense flash of pain in that part of the back of the ankle and the tendons will thereafter be heard snapping in and out of position.

Outwardly turned feet or knock knees can cause difficulty in learning the technique of parallel skiing and in achieving good edge control. The effort may well cause foot, knee or hip pain as the skier struggles to compensate. Over time Achilles tendinitis and chondromalacia patellae (p. 19) can then occur, as in any sport where the legs are under strain. To reemphasise, properly fitted ski boots are vital to ski control. Before the children even leave home make sure they have a good pair of warm woollen socks and that you know what size of school shoe fits over them. If they have knock knees, tell the fitter, as bulky clothes may hide them. Girls have special problems in changing from light shoes to heavy ski boots, and adolescents with muscular calves may feel uncomfortable in high boots. Those with problem feet should quietly think about boot selection before leaving home instead of leaving it all to pot luck in a crowded ski shop in haste to get onto the snow. When feet have stopped growing addicts can have custom boots made with leg angles and torsions (twist) accurately measured for cants (footbed inserts) to improve the fit and comfort. Boots with built-in cants are unlikely to be just right for the individual even if the shop's electronic machine says so (when was it last checked for accuracy?). Since young developing feet can be between sizes, pad out pressure points and pay even more attention to the bindings. And do not overencourage children if their boots are affecting ski control. One year may make all the difference!

The past five years have seen a change in knee injuries; there are less medial (inner) ligament strains and more of the serious internal cruciate ligament (p. 67) ruptures. The reason is probably that much attention has been paid to toe-release bindings to prevent tibial (shinbone) fracture in a twisting fall, but little to heel designs that could release in sudden deceleration before the force is transmitted to the internal knee mechanism. The novice skiing straight-legged is most at risk, rather than the experienced flexed knee skier. Boots that are too stiff and high at the back will also make internal knee damage more likely if the skier falls backwards.

Wheezing

Asthmatic-like attacks (p. 86) can be triggered by exertion and hyperventilation of cold air. This problem seems unrelated to allergy but asthmatic aerosols cure it if there is acute distress.

At an International Conference in 1974 at Rikogransen, Sweden, the question was seriously posed: is downhill skiing too difficult a sport for children? Age is obviously important in the development of concentration. Over the years many factors have been debated: inexperience, weak leg strength, unrecognised deficiencies in the slope, skiing too fast and beyond their ability, and becoming tired, hungry, and frozen. Significant points raised by the Swedish 1976 statistics were: most injuries were seen in boys aged fourteen to fifteen years; the most dangerous time was the third hour of skiing (fatigue?); and 95% of the injuries came from falls. Many suggestions have been made to remedy the situation. Expert tuition and professional supervision are obvious needs but *only parents* are in the position unceasingly to insist on the following safety precautions whilst children are learning.

- Lubricate and check bindings and clean off debris and dirt. This is just as important for the expert whose bindings are rarely called into use for quick release as it is for those who rent skis. Hired equipment chosen for youngsters is often of poor quality in the interests of economy and the feeling that 'they don't need it'. Nothing could be more wrong. Budding racers who have good equipment must not use release bindings set for stronger adults, and must never overtighten them in the belief that they will stop the bindings accidentally releasing when they attempt to go faster.

- Do not rent skis that seem too long. Statistics from Waterville, New Hampshire (1966 to 1973), show that even among experts using longer skis more accidents occurred, so the point must be relevant to novices.
- Avoid wet and heavy snow, ice on the slopes, and deep snow. Experience must be gained in these conditions, but carefully!
- Do not ski when visibility is poor.
- Be extra careful when there is heavy traffic on the slope, for example on weekends.
- *Never* skylark, go across slopes in the wrong direction, or imitate show-offs. Keeping to the beaten packed track is the only way to avoid rocks, fallen timber and soft snow.
- Take more care on the first few days of a ski holiday.
- Do not ski in late afternoon or be tempted into 'just one more run'.
- Strengthen the legs by pre-holiday exercises and herringbone up the slopes for the first few days instead of whizzing straight to the top by lift.
- If somehow stranded on a chair or in a gondola *never, never* try to climb down a tower or go hand-over-hand along a greasy steel cable. Skiers trying this have lost their grip and dropped to their death. Just wait patiently for the rescue team. Also, do not try to jump onto a passing vacant T-bar to save money or time.
- If young skiers or tobogganers fall over and get wet insist that they go back and change to stop any chance of hypothermia (dangerous drop in body temperature). It only needs one other factor, change in weather, waiting too long in lift queues or hunger, and wet youngsters are particularly likely to slip into that insidious state. It may not even be noticed but suspect it if the child begins to feel unwell, or is beginning to do or say strange things.

The first and last points are probably the most important. The athlete who learns to care for and understand his equipment and himself, develops a better attitude to any sport. Pre-season conditioning benefits all, particularly inexperienced girls. A study at Vail, Colorado, in 1981, showed that the girls' knee injury rate, especially for mild ligament strain, was twice that for boys, and this must be due to lower average leg strength.

There is not universal agreement with some of the time-honoured injury factors given above. Garrick, studying the injury patterns among 3500 Seattle students from five high schools, confirmed a higher injury rate in girls, but otherwise found only age to be significant. The under-ten group had the lowest injury rate of all; it then climbed steadily up to thirteen, levelled off by fifteen, and decreased slightly through seventeen. It was also noted that the fourteen- and fifteen-year-olds were less likely to report injuries to anyone. Perhaps Benjamin Franklin deserves the last word: 'Carelessness does more harm than want of knowledge'.

Langlauf

Skiing has been a normal means of cross-country travel in Scandinavia for 4000 years, maybe longer, thus the modern recreational touring is known as Nordic or Langlauf skiing. It does not harm the wallet as much as downhill and is much safer in terms of pure injury; tree branches may hit the face but otherwise the main worry is ankle fracture-dislocation or sprain because the boot heel is not attached. For persistent ankle pain or sense of instability X-rays should be done to detect fine fracture lines or chips in the area. Heavy falls onto the bottom can fracture the coccyx (the last bone in the spinal column), and spills can cause the usual fractures to the outstretched arm. There is also the possibility of catching the pole in a tree and wrenching the hand or shoulder. Odd results from the exertion of poling include low back strain, shoulder strain, transient wrist weakness from ulnar nerve (funny bone) inflammation, fracture of a very small sesamoid bone in the thumb, and a 'squeaky wrist'. This latter also causes a weak wrist and pain from inflammation of long tendons criss-crossing the back of the thumb. Severe damage can of course happen in spectacular speed crashes during a race, as noted earlier.

The special dangers of cross-country competition are:

- Inexperience of wicked conditions, especially the sudden snow squall. It takes years of experience before novices appreciate the treachery of alpine weather so it is imperative that the trails be carefully marked and monitored and that children be instructed in self-preservation.
- Wrong clothing. Further from home and hearth than in downhill races, cold becomes a greater danger. A risk is to overdress, sweat into cotton, overheat, strip down, and then become hypothermic as the sweat rapidly evaporates. When wearing thin racing uniforms, note that even though the body under exertion produces more heat it will dissipate rapidly on stopping. Wonderful modern lightweight fabrics

almost make the choice of layers difficult, beginning with the all-important long underwear. Polypropylene is good for whisking away sweat (but do not forget to wash it). In general, use multiple layers that can be taken off or put on at will, and outerwear materials that breathe to stop sweat condensing.
- Emphasis on speed instead of safety. It only wants one other factor added to the wind chill effect such as lack of clothing, sudden wind, falling into wet snow or water, or immobilisation due to injury, and frostbite can rapidly occur on exposed parts. For example, racing in zero ambient temperature at 30 kph means that the face is hit by a $-15°C$ blast, such is the wind chill effect. At 65 kph, a speed which might be reached on long downhill sections, the wind chill factor lowers the skin temperature to $-22°C$ and at this level frostbite occurs in minutes. Tight uniforms and tight gloves heighten the risk.
- Whole body hypothermia. This is serious. It is obviously present in people who are plucked out of icy water, but with general overexposure the suspicious signs are shivering plus odd personality changes. If the rectal temperature is above $33°C$ ($92°F$) rewarming in the hut is safe. Below this *do not rewarm rapidly*. This is a task for hospital experts. On the way there keep the victim's trunk, neck and groin warm but leave the limbs exposed. The rationale behind this is that the core body temperature must be maintained and big blood vessels are near to the skin in the neck and groin. To warm the limbs would take blood out to them and deprive the vital centres; hence victims can be taken out of the icy sea alive, paradoxically to die 'in warmth'. In a warm bath leave the four limbs right out of the water.
- Inadequate breakfasts. In a long race the blood sugar drops to a very low level producing dizziness, sweating, disorientation, and strange behaviour. The effect of cold is thus made much more potent. Contestants must be up in time to eat a hearty breakfast!
- Inadequate preconditioning. This is more important in langlauf, both for shoulder and lower back muscles, and the heart. Measurements of the maximum oxygen intake, in Sweden, called the Kundy factor, show that cross-country skiing is more demanding than even rowing or marathon racing, which will not be news to someone climbing uphill.
- Overuse injury from enthusiastic summer training. Shinsplints, foot, ankle and knee strains, any running damage, in fact, is possible to legs that have spent the winter mostly standing or gliding, factors that normally eliminate pure wear and tear from the sport.

Back country or wilderness skiing adds another dimension to survival equipment. Surely no group of youngsters would be allowed to attempt it except under the leadership of not just one but two very experienced adults. Extra equipment must be carried such as extra ski tip, extra binding with glue, extra screws, extra food, spare clothing and anything else that experience in the area indicates may be needed. Maps, matches, compass, two-way radio and lodgement of a plan with the rangers are also important. Experienced lone skiers know to stay in the basin and not to go over the ridge where brilliant sun can change swiftly to advancing bad weather. In emergencies skiers can be trapped in inappropriate clothing so it is essential to give instruction in how to build a snow hole. This has saved many lives where otherwise the skier would have carried on getting more and more lost.

A new activity on the slopes, promising excitement in a simple way, and hence likely to be taken far too lightly, is sliding down in or on rubber tyre inner tubes. It is really a case of sliding out of control and if several riders link up it is certain that the lot will swivel around, a danger to themselves and anyone innocently nearby. Approaching a tree or any fixed object means serious injury will occur unless the rider(s) bail out, and if they do bail out, likewise! Full protective gear and padding should be worn and the possibility of frostbite not forgotten. Some ski resorts have installed alpine slides as a summer attraction for kids. These asbestos-fibreglass troughs have potential for injury if the sled jumps out of the trough or rams the one in front.

Last but by no means least remember that there are thousands of snowmobile injuries each year. A report from the Mayo Clinic in the United States, in 1979, describing the injuries of a boy aged seven who caught his foot in a track while helping to push a machine, indicated that of all such injuries treated in emergency rooms 20% involve children and that their injuries tend to be severe and lengthy. (Adults would do well to remember that snowmobile accidents kill, and cause spinal injuries, every year.)

Artificial ski slopes are not always happy playgrounds for children either. Edinburgh, Scotland, has the largest one in Europe with a main slope 400 metres long made of plastic squares framed by bristles. In complete reverse to what happens in snow, analysis of injuries there showed that arms were injured four times more often than legs, with particular emphasis on sprain or fracture of the thumb. In a fall the thumb tends to get caught in the matting as well as the ski pole. As in snow skiing failure of the bindings to release in a fall led to knee ligament strain. One sixth of the injured were skiing for the first time, clear warning that children cannot be sent off for unsupervised fun.

REFERENCES:

Blitzer C. M et al. Downhill skiing injuries in children. *Am. J. Sports Med.* 1984; 12: 142–146.

Eriksson E. Ski trauma and ski safety. *Orthop. Clin. North Am.* 1976; 7: 3.

Garrick J. et al. Injury patterns in children and adolescent skiers. *Am. J. Sports Med.* 1979; 7: 245.

Kuriyama S. Trends in ski injuries and boot top fractures. *Jap. J. Phys. Fitness Sports Med.* 1980; 29: 177.

Sherry E. et al. Children's skiing injuries in Australia. *Med. J. Aust.* 1987; 146: 193–195.

Wester K. et al. Serious ski jumping injuries in Norway. *Am. J. Sports Med.* 1985; 13: 124–127

Limbrick A. Manager, Snowline Ski Centre, Perisher Valley. Personal Communication, 1987.

Soccer

This is a worldwide sport and probably the most popular. It was estimated in 1977 that 50 to 60% of all sports injuries in Europe were from soccer so study of the game and its dangers is of economic importance if nothing else. However, it has an injury rate one fifth that of gridiron, and the injuries are less severe; the cost of insurance claims in 1981 by American high school soccer players was only 16% of that of an equal number of injured football players. Indeed, it has been said that if gridiron injuries are not reduced soccer may replace it. An American study from Indiana by McCarroll, of 4000 players in 250 teams, listed 176 injuries. Although the average injury rate was thus 4.4%, the highest was in the nineteen-year-olds' age group at 8.7%, decreasing as the ages went down. Nilsson collected data from the Norway Cup carnival played in Oslo, for the years 1975 and 1977, when 25,000 youths in 1549 teams played 2987 matches, and in them suffered 858 injuries at a rate of 3.4%. Two thirds of these injuries happened to the legs. Proof of the safety of the game is that in this premier meeting 95% of these injuries were bruises, abrasions, strains and minor sprains. There were only twenty-nine fractures, mostly of the wrist area, and four dislocated knees. The final rounds produced more than the qualifying rounds, partly because of fatigue, but mostly through greater striving. Girls had twice the injury percentage rate of boys, thought to be due to their fewer numbers and smaller groupings, and hence greater chance of small girls playing against big ones. Parents will be interested in one other statistic from this carnival: a further 485 injuries happened away from the playing areas!

Heading the ball looks dangerous, especially as youthful skull bones are not firmly united with one another until about eighteen years, and correct technique is vital. Heading is safely done with the forehead (that is using the thick frontal bone), with tensed neck muscles to keep the head fixed and to prevent rotation and acceleration forces on the skull. Experiments have always shown that it is rotational force, not just a blow, that causes brain damage. Nonetheless a player wandering about dazed should be rested; mild concussion has probably occurred. After a game inability to concentrate on schoolwork, irritable conduct, headaches, or seeming loss of memory must be carefully investigated. The first recorded death from soccer was in 1925 when a twenty-year-old German lost consciousness in the locker room and died from a subdural haematoma (p. 26). Thus the risk is always there.

The danger is greatest when trying to head the short-range fast kick, because of its speed. Players showing excessive zeal in heading should be coached in other tricks to use. It is not just a matter of the ball, but aerial collisions with other players, and the chance that a lowered head will meet a rising boot to cause more severe head lacerations and injuries, including a broken neck. In any head injury and especially lacerations of the face, remember the possibility of an eye injury; the ball may have hit the eyeball (see Chapter 8 p. 40 and Ice Hockey p. 146).

The long-term effects of heading the ball have been studied in retired international players. The bad news is that X-rays showed degenerative changes in the neck vertebrae ten to twenty years earlier than similar changes were to be found in a non-football playing control group. The good news is that those players who considered themselves 'headers' were not worse affected than other players.

Teeth are frequently hit and this is more serious for the tooth than is commonly realised (p. 44). Loss of a front tooth can be devastating and routine use by all of mouthguards should be insisted upon. Newer plastic balls have the advantage of not absorbing water, which can add 20% to the weight of a leather ball, an extra the receiver can do without.

The twisting, turning and leaping must occasionally cause lower back strain, which may be just muscle and ligament strain, but bone and disc damage has occasionally been recorded (p. 28). After direct blows to the back watch for blood in the urine from kidney damage. Collisions, falls, and fouls leave the usual trail of injury to muscle, bone or joint, and must be considered part of the game. Children under ten seem rarely to feature in accident reports, perhaps because the trouble doesn't really start until their speed and skill increase. Taking into account every possibility, the ankle is most affected, followed by broken legs, and derangements of the knee. Shin pads should be worn. Why suffer a painful kick on the shin when it is so easily nullified? Older readers who are familiar with the *Boy's Own Paper* will remember the sneaky advice to wear the shin guard on the good leg to decoy the opposition! Tight laces will occasionally cause inflammation around the Achilles tendon.

Leg pains in general are often dismissed as 'growing pains'. Never so! Muscle strains or avulsions (tears) of the sites of bone attachments occur as in any running sport (p. 17), but soccer adds the stress of twisting with jerky kicking of a weighty object and there is, therefore, also the risk of overuse and cumulative small damage, noticeably to the hip joint and the toes. Pain in either spot must be checked, not that the sport has necessarily caused bone problems but rather that it may uncover them. Special cinematography reveals that young players have a faster foot speed than the professionals, but achieve a lower ball speed, so that slower and smoother is better both for the tissues and the team. Soccer training balls, the ones staked to a spring, are to be watched in this regard. A fast faulty technique will easily strain rather than train and strengthen the leg. Give *both* feet a turn at kicking to promote balanced muscle exercise and development and to avoid one-sided back strain.

Goalkeepers must add to all the above damage to the fingers (p. 66), collisions with the fixed posts, and balls hitting the nose or eye, all of which may need hospital first-aid.

Soccer fields for junior games are very likely to have had horses grazing over them in earlier centuries leaving tetanus spores in the ground. Anti-tetanus injections are a must for lacerations, and immunoglobulins have now replaced the serum that used to cause the odd case of severe allergy. Lime and other chemicals cast on the grass have also contaminated wounds from time to time, wounds and abrasions made more likely if the playing surface is rough, poorly grassed, and left with holes and ridges.

In Saudi Arabia, where soccer is now a popular and burgeoning sport, it causes two thirds of all the sports injuries in the country. One lesson noted was that many injuries in the young occurred in recreational play after school and not in organised and supervised games.

Indoor soccer cannot be regarded as a simple aerobic fun activity. Hectic activity in a confined space, leniency in applying the advantage rule, and the desire for excitement, have seemingly combined to promote collision and yield an overall injury rate five times higher than that seen in the outdoors.

REFERENCES:

McCarroll J. R. et al. Profile of youth soccer injuries. *Physician Sports Med.* 1984; 12: Feb. 113.

Nilsson S. et al. Soccer injuries in adolescents. *Am. J. Sports Med.* 1978; 6: 358.

Sadat-Ali M. et al. Soccer injuries in Saudi Arabia. *Am. J. Sports Med.* 1987; 15: 500–502.

Softball

Slow pitch softball is advancing by leaps and bounds, with so many adherents in America that it has become the most popular recreational sport in all age groups. That it is now more prominent in sports injury statistics is the result of player numbers and not of any special hazards peculiar to the sport. It is a means of introducing youngsters to baseball. Teachers must be alert for finger dislocations and injury to those with little ball sense or catching ability (p. 101). Beginners should play on well grassed areas and not on hard surfaces that make falls more hazardous.

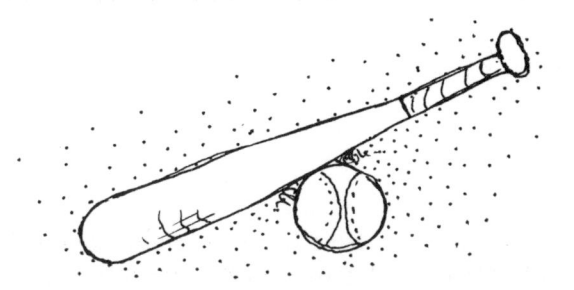

In general, being a recreational activity, levels of expertise, physical fitness, aptitude, and ambition are highly variable; add to this the fact that more than the regulation number of fielders may crowd the playing area and it is clear that collision and injury are real possibilities.

Ankle and knee joint sprain, and thigh muscle strains, predominate. Torn ankle ligaments are worthy of an x-ray if pain persists because the presence of small bone chips will complicate healing. The shoulder joint suffers in players (shortstop and centrefielders beware!) constantly trying for spectacular plays or hoping to keep a special position in the team. Repeated attempts at fast throwing will cause overuse strain in amateurs with relatively low levels of muscle power and skill. It is unfortunate that minor shoulder strains with mild pain are so often ignored at the early stage; proper physiotherapy and instruction are important, especially in those youngsters eager to progress to baseball.

Thigh strain with pulled muscle fibres is usually a reflection of similar overexertion (parents, stars of yesteryear, beware!). Recreational players cannot maintain a high level of muscle stretch-contraction capability, but as happens with the shoulder joint, there is an inclination to ignore muscle soreness and press on.

This amateur level of expertise and fitness is also reflected in reports that falls and sliding account for most of the significant dislocations and fractures, including those of the hand when sliding head first, a dramatic spectacle always to be condemned (p. 101). Some medical authorities have recommended that sliding be banned altogether in softball, or at least that fixed bases be replaced by releasable models.

Squash

'Very fast, squash', as Noel Coward might have said. Things happen in the twinkling of an eye, and to the eye in a twinkling. Ball and racquet speeds have been timed at over 160 kph. Reminiscing with players of long experience, none could recall an eye injury and indeed had never given it a thought. All had been taught to give the other player room to play his shot. Possibly this meant, although it was not then exactly stated, that one should station oneself back from the path of the opponent's racquet and not well in front looking back for the return. It is players in this last position who are receiving so many eye injuries. Published reports are many and eye damage can be serious and permanent (see Ice Hockey p. 146). In any case of possible eye injury an opthalmologist should be consulted as speedily as possible.

Apart from sensible court manners only eye guards will prevent damage. Open frames theoretically allow freak penetration by a fast ball or the edge of a racquet and hard glass lenses make things worse by shattering. In fact squash is one game where to wear one's own glasses is a risk. Such is the speed and force of direct contact that glass fragments can be driven into the eyeball. Polycarbonate or CR39 lenses with 3.00-mm centre thickness, in rigid frames with a rubber bridge, are recommended for complete protection. Padded frames would be ideal if it were not for sweating. Players who need prescription glasses should consult their specialist about contact lenses or modification of the protective lens. Children with only one eye are really not suited to squash except for a game with a considerate expert; it is not so much a question of damage to their only eye as their lack of visual depth and field of vision which would restrict their capacity for enjoyment. Games against lefthanded players need extra care until one gains experience in them. The forehand has a wider racquet arc than one is accustomed to expect from the backhand of a righthanded opponent.

It has been said that beginners and low-ranking players get more facial injuries from a wild racquet, or injuries from running into the wall, whilst experts get more ankle sprains, twisted knees and muscle tears, but in practice everything depends upon the speed of play, level of fatigue and inattention, and whether evenly matched players are struggling hard. Elbow symptoms akin to tennis elbow are caused in the same way: by a stretched-elbow bent-wrist backhand. It's a pity they no longer emphasise the old maxims 'keep the wrist cocked' and 'hand below the racket', which had the effect of keeping the elbow bent and hence reduced the stretch on the forearm muscle group. The constant wrist twisting can cause pain in the small wrist joints, especially in the one immediately below the wrist crease on the inner side.

Basketball or volleyball shoes, designed for twisting turns and ankle protection, are a big improvement on the traditional sandshoe, but jogging shoes are unsuitable. Apart from anything else, they may have dirty soles with pebbles in the tread which one does not want squeezed out onto the floor.

Swimming

Everything that can result from repetitive use of muscles, joints and bones will be seen in competitors with high training levels. However, for the average child, swimming is very safe apart from neglect of upper respiratory tract infection and blockage, and water pollution.

The Water

Bacteria and viruses thrive and multiply in water. The United States Centre for Disease Control and Environmental Agency reported eight outbreaks of water-related diseases in 1981 from recreational activities. One outbreak was of pontiac fever of the Legionella genus from a motel whirlpool, one was due to algae toxins of the blue green *Microcoleus lyngbyaceus* in the ocean beach on the windward side of Oahu, Hawaii, and six were of dermatitis from the *Pseudomonas aeruginosa* organism. This same organism caused otitis externa (ear infection) in eighteen out of a team of twenty-five competitors in Aberdeen, Scotland, and investigation showed that all those affected had trained in the early morning when water chlorination levels were inadequate. The United States Agency advises that outbreaks should not occur at pH levels between 7.2 and 7.8 and when there is a free residual chlorine level over 1.0 mgm per litre. If the swimming pool water has a cloudy or opaque look and the bottom cannot be clearly seen, contamination with algae and bacteria must be suspected, with the possible development of skin rashes or infected abrasions, conjunctivitis, earache, sore throat, or fever within forty-eight hours. Shallow wading pools in the sun and whirlpools are just perfect for making warm bacterial soup so check them even more carefully. Walkways and dressing sheds are notorious for spreading tinea spores and plantar wart viruses.

Chlorine levels normally fluctuate and would be slow to eradicate a heavy bacteria load, so that from time to time a wide variety of organisms has been detected by laboratory culture from swimming pools, including staphylococcus (skin), streptococcus (throat), coliform bacterium (bowel), mild respiratory and gastrointestinal viruses, and the viruses causing poliomyelitis and hepatitis. Symptomless carriers unknowingly shed viruses but it would be commonsense if pupils with obvious nasopharyngitis, septic sores, or bowel pains and diarrhoea, were temporarily banned from swimming; either that or hyperchlorinate the pool after use.

And a final reminder to Tom Sawyers everywhere. The United States Environment Protection Agency warns that 'water in natural springs and creeks even in isolated high altitudes should be considered undrinkable and must be disinfected by chemicals or boiling before being drunk'. Rafting down rivers may be great fun, but it won't be if you swallow the water. Does anybody know any swimmer who does not accidentally take in water? Thirty-two outbreaks of illness in 1981 ranging from parasites, bacteria and viruses, to chemical toxins, prove the Agency's point. As a specific example, half the freshwater lakes in Orlando, Florida, and some inland waters in Australia, contain amoebae of the genus Naegleria which multiply in hot weather and cause outbreaks of amoebic meningitis if ingested. And note that young travellers on rivers such as the Mississippi or the Nile should not cool their bare feet in the river. A parasite (bilharzia) lurks there which breeds in snails (look around for evidence of them or their egg white froth). It penetrates the skin around the ankle leaving a distinct itch, then migrates around the body and causes the disease schistosomiasis. Bilharzia is widespread in equatorial regions.

Shallow Pools

Neurosurgeons shudder if they see children dive head first into the shallow end of a pool. Any child seen doing it should get a strongly worded lecture on safety, and all pools should have a warning sign at the shallow end to indicate its depth. Pool fences should not be close enough to allow dives from off the top. The danger is greatest, not in supervised training, but on family holidays. A 1981 Canadian report listed one victim of paraplegia from diving into a swimming pool, but thirty-five from diving into shallow lakes, significantly, in summer's late afternoon when presumably the water was darkening. Australia, per head of population, used to have the world's highest reported incidence of diving accident paraplegia, but by 1982 had sharply diminished the number of victims after intensive school education programmes, media campaigns, and wide use of municipal signposts at dangerous sites. Children must also be educated to observe beach and river tides which alter water depths and create sandbanks, be told *never* to dive into pools of unclear water, and to remember that last year's marvellous swimming spot may now have a submerged tree trunk in it. Paraplegia is tragic, and so easily avoidable. One last point, nearly all recorded victims are male. Showing off?

Tumble Turns

Transient spinal shock or cervical fractures can occur if the head hits the wall whilst turning. It is very important to observe all the rules in moving such a victim (p. 23), and it is best if they are floated onto a board. With the cough reflex probably absent and the throat possibly filled with water there is a real risk of drowning and it will not be easy to drain out the fluid by tilting, whilst at the same time keeping the head and trunk in line, unless a board or stretcher and several intelligent helpers are available.

Ear Infections

Otitis externa (inflammation of the skin-lined external canal leading to the eardrum) has been mentioned and will occur in swimmers in serious training unless soft ear plugs are used, because chlorinated water is a chemical irritant over time. The best protection is cottonwool balls rolled in vaseline and covered by a cap, with spirit ear drops being instilled after training to dry the canal. However, if wearing ear plugs do not dive deep in fun (see Scuba p. 166).

Middle ear infection is still serious—earache, recurrent temperature, and hearing loss are the symptoms—but the dreaded mastoid (infection in bone behind the ear) is a complication of the past thanks to antibiotics. The cause of middle ear infection is bacteria travelling from the nose or throat up the Eustachian tube, or infected mucus being forced along it by pressure when swimmers take a deep breath and hold it. Divers are more prone to it because of the added pressure changes of hitting the water and plunging to some depth. The problem occurs more often in coastal than inland areas, possibly because of air temperature variations which activate throat viruses and hence cause more throat infections, but it is best if parents stop children with infections from swimming until they are well again.

Eardrum Perforation

The end result of middle ear infection can be a perforated drum, discharging pus. Rupture can also be caused simply by pressure thrusting along the external canal (leading to the eardrum) if the Eustachian tube (joining the middle ear to the throat) is blocked, if its internal opening into the pharynx (throat) is obstructed by enlarged tonsils or adenoids, or if the mucous membrane is swollen by allergy or a bad sore throat. It is clear therefore that water sports should be banned for any child with a 'cold', sore throat, running nose, or sinusitis, until examined by a doctor. Nose drops or inhalants may be of help but nose clips are a trap. They make it harder for the Eustachian tube to equalise ear pressure—try it yourself, hold your nose and swallow! Modern jet travel in under-pressurised cabins by itinerant competitors is a new hazard in Eustachian tube blockage.

One study of water polo players revealed that 18% had ruptured drums and it is a risk after a tumble in water skiing or board riding unless ear plugs, ear protectors, or caps with built-in ear covers are worn.

Eye Problems

High chlorine or faulty pH levels irritate the conjunctivae so that for long spells in the pool goggles should be worn, preferably ones with Velcro straps. Kids, being kids, tend to pull goggles off carelessly and eyeball damage has occurred with elastic straps when rims catapulted back from slippery fingers onto the eye. Contact lens wearers should act on advice from their ophthalmologist; it might be best to have prescription lenses bonded onto swim or scuba diving goggles.

Serious Training

Many of today's stars and record holders, especially the females, are teenagers. Shane Gould, at age fifteen, held all the major world women's records in 1973; Michelle Ford, a seventeen-year-old 1980 Olympic gold medallist, had spent an average of four hours a day in the water from the age of thirteen and had to live with shoulder pain; a fifteen-year-old schoolgirl, ranked 8th in the world and winner in the 1984 Australian Age Championships, swam 90 to 100 kms per week in training, using a mere half million strokes per arm in a year. The psychological, physiological and mechanical stresses of this are not to be wondered at and there are many studies in progress. To give three brief examples. Fifteen elite young performers in Florida undergoing three years of intensive training during the adolescent growth spurt period, improved their lung capacity and maximum oxygen intake level beyond average expectation by the second year of training, the males showing consistently higher values than the females. Echocardiograms (measurement of heart size) done on children on both sides of puberty who were swimming in regular daily training, showed that their heart size and muscle wall thicknesses were greater than in non-athletic children. These improvements can only be to their long-term benefit but that such training can be stressful was proved in nine girls in Italy aged thirteen to eighteen. Over six months the levels of two important pituitary gland hormones, the prolactin acting on body growth and the menstrual cycle, and the adreno-cortico-trophic acting on the adrenal gland, increased for the duration of training. The old problem of children attempting too much, too soon, or of being pushed too hard in training, is a difficult one for parents to solve if they find they have a gifted swimmer on their hands. Lucky, perhaps, is the child with many interests.

Tests on elite teenage swimmers have shown that a large number have laxity of the shoulder joint capsule and that many have weakened relative strength in the external rotator muscles to the point where selective corrective exercises should be done. Prolonged training in any style may lead to shoulder impingement syndrome (p. 63) and disability but there are added risks in each event, for example: deformity of the upper arm growth centres in overarm freestyle; Scheuermann's kyphosis (an exaggerated thoracic spine curvature) plus low back strain from the butterfly stroke; knee ligament or meniscus (p. 68) strain in the breaststroke; shoulder dislocation or ankle strain in the backstroke, and, also in this event, finger injuries (p. 66) and head injuries due to misjudging the wall. Water polo adds the chance of ball injury to the nose, eye, and eardrum, strain to the hip and knee adductor (inner leg) muscles with vigorous throwing, plus the hazard of roughhouse tactics underwater that the referee does not see.

Comparisons of the physiques of female swimmers and divers from the 1976 Montreal Olympics showed substantial differences; each event seems to demand special qualities. Of interest too were the differences between the event finalists and the non-finalists. The diving non-finalists were heavier; presumably their acrobatic skill was thus affected. The swim finalists were taller than those they eliminated. When you think about it the taller swimmer covers a lesser distance, not to mention the advantage in the turn. This might indicate to parents that no matter how skilled a tiny (or even average height) adolescent is, high training levels to excel may prove at the very end to have been better discouraged, or at least not blindly encouraged. One is speaking here of an attempt to progress to state, national and international titles, not of someone bursting with determination to do well in the school sports. Of course, one cannot take any notice of height before the pubertal growth spurt and, to sound a philosophical note, what a dismal thing it would be if analyses of this kind were allowed to influence school coaches and a child's own choices too far down the ladder of life.

Diving

The competitive diver faces special injury hazards and the need for gymnastic flexibility puts extra demands on muscle and joint, especially in the low lumbar area. A vital part of early tuition is to emphasise that locking the hands in the high dive protects the head on water entry. Eardrum rupture by barotrauma has been mentioned and it must be reemphasised that practice diving should be forbidden if the youngster has a head cold, sore throat, or an unexplained temperature (see Chapter 2 p. 7 and Scuba p. 166). Diving deep into cold water can cause temporary giddiness if the cold rinse down the ear canal disturbs the inner ear. Neophytes must progress carefully and not be tempted to exceed their skill on the tower or have the springboard fulcrum too far back. Divers have hit the board, which may cause injury, but, more importantly, the imbalance ruins water entry, so be prepared to dive in to assist in case there is concussion. Advanced training pools have foam making equipment ('air') under the platform to soften the water barrier so that errors on water entry do not cause damage, very useful if new and complicated dives are being developed.

Learning to Swim

Possibly the most important and lifesaving present a parent can give a child is the encouragement to learn to swim, and it will need more than just words. My father simply ignored the complicated time wasting schemes I evolved to evade swimming lessons and thoughtfully organised for the early morning so that afterschool homework would not be curtailed. The municipal pool, so seemingly huge and deep, was frightening, the water, not yet touched by dawn's early light and in the shadows of the dressing shed and diving tower, was cold, and I was very young, thin, and shivering. I hated it. But learn to swim I did. Instinct for safety in the water and in the surf followed easily, reinforced by never-ending paternal patter during summer beach holidays on tides, currents, cramps and cold, what to do if carried out to sea, how to cooperate with lifesavers, the importance of never swimming alone and, oh, a whole host of things. Schools, the Royal Lifesaving Society, governments, and municipal councils now run programmes and classes and parents should enquire about them. Children are far happier learning in their own age group. Today danger is much closer to home, in the shape of neighbourhood private swimming pools, and every year youngsters who cannot swim or float are tragically drowned in them. Young children are much safer playing on a beach.

It would be difficult for a parent to act calmly when pulling a drowning or drowned (there is no way of being sure in an instant) infant out of a pool but memorise two words over and over again: *airway* and *breathing*. Try now to remember what you read in Chapter 6 on resuscitation, and reread it (p. 31). The first thing, indeed the only thing you can do by yourself, is to get air into the child. Start it at once and whilst you are doing it collect yourself, shout for help, and begin to think of the situation the child is in. In a few words, pull the angle of the jaw forward and mouth-to-mouth insufflate at your own breathing rate.

It would be very unlikely for the child to have a fractured neck so lie him on his back, lift the chin up to open the back of the throat and the mouth, hold his nose shut, breathe *slowly*, and watch the chest rise and fall. It will not take as much of your breath as you think because a child's lungs are not large. Then the sooner you get him to hospital the better. If you cannot feel a pulse and you know about cardiac compression do it too, but *air* is the main thing for parent first-aid, and keep it up until experts take over. Of all the chapters in this book, Chapter 6 is the one you should read regularly and indeed, rewrite the essentials in your *own* words, to keep your mind alive with the ways to revive young children. You never know when you will have to do it.

REFERENCE:
Mrs F. B. Hutchins, née Singleton, Australian Olympic Team, Melbourne, 1956. Personal communication, 1987.

Tennis

In doubles the player at the net can be hit on the face or the eye by the ball, and so can an inattentive spectator from a wild shot. Occasionally the player will fall, but otherwise this worldwide prime racquet sport is virtually free of incidents except those self-inflicted by overexertion or overuse of the limbs.

Therefore, the better prepared the muscles are by warmth and stretching for a serious game, and the better the equipment, especially the shoes, the less chance there is for unexpected injury.

True tennis elbow, pain aggravated by gripping, is a strain or tear of the muscle fibres from the epicondyle (outer spur) of the humerus (upper arm bone). Arising there are the muscles that extend to and dorsiflex (bend back) the wrist. If the elbow is straightened, a fist made, and the wrist bent backwards, the extensor muscles can be felt to harden. That position, reproduced somewhere in the backhand stroke, causes tennis elbow. Whether it is faulty technique in not keeping the elbow bent and forward, whether the racquet is heavy and large-headed, steel-shafted or made of synthetics, thin-handled and gripped too hard, whether the strings are over-taut or synthetic, are debatable items which may be worthy of scrutiny and change. All these factors probably do modify the split second kick of the fast ball on the racquet, which, counterthrusting against the tense muscle on stretch, must be inflicting microstress over time. Tennis elbow statistics have been accumulating since the first report from Berlin in 1873 and it is actually not common in adolescents although there is a transient peak incidence in girls aged eleven to fifteen years which may have something to do with relative muscle weakness and the use of 'standard' size and weight racquets. Thereafter, graphs show a steady linear rise in the number of victims with age, that is with continued play. The most important fact about the condition is that the best time to cure it is the first time it is noticed, by rest, physiotherapy, and muscle strengthening, and when the game is resumed, by adoption of the two-handed backhand. This not only spares the elbow but also trains the player to move more quickly and get closer to the ball for the stroke.

The other muscle strains or torn fibres of tennis occur in the lower back and around the shoulder joint from excessive twist or effort, in the medial (inner) side of the elbow (a different tennis elbow) from huge serve attempts, and in the thigh and leg from stretching wide. Wrist tenosynovitis has been attributed of late to· metal racquets. Maybe. It is hard to see why that feature alone is blamed when there have been so many design changes since the old days of the familiar 'junior' wooden models. It is more likely to be just a matter of too little force being absorbed by exotic racquets, and too much being transmitted to small muscles and tendons.

The joints affected are the shoulder, knee and ankle. If there has been dislocation of the shoulder from other sports or unrecognised subluxation (capsule stretch), the serve or smash may redislocate the joint or cause it for the first time. Rotator cuff injury (p. 61) or impingement syndromes (p. 63) are theoretically possible but adolescents would have to play an enormous amount of tennis or be trying to serve too hard. This latter can also cause lumbar (lower back) disc damage. As a matter of interest radar gun tests show that average social players serve at about 95 kph, well short of Martina Navratilova, once clocked at 149 kph. The knee can be struck by the usual problems of twist and strain, so that traumatic effusion (pain or swelling) must be promptly investigated.

Shoes exert a positive influence. The old sandshoes prevented sprained ankles by just slipping a bit but the new soles with high grip co-efficients do the opposite. They should have high lateral (side) support and no lateral roll to the sole otherwise they will facilitate a twisted ankle, and if the size is too big it is the foot that slides with dire effect on the toes. Choose with care. Buy the socks first and wear them when buying the shoes. Blisters can be prevented in new shoes by using powder or Vaseline around the heel. Black heel (bleeding into the fatty heel pad due to repeated injury from friction and thumping) is a warning sign of poor shoes.

Aspiring youngsters are playing or rather, practising, much more than their parents ever did, and it is nothing for some to notch up thirty hours of play each week. This means that the future will probably bring to the foot and leg muscle overuse problems, shinsplints, and stress fractures, more perhaps in girls because of the prolonged rallies. Such injuries will also be more likely to occur on hardcourts as opposed to grass. There will also be opportunity for damage to the elbow epiphyses of which there are seven, so any pain or stiffness resulting from intensive use must be checked (p. 17). In the subtropics remember to protect against sunburn and hand blisters.

Touch Football

Do not assume that touch football is just a friendly J. F. Kennedy family game. Inadvertent collisions do cause serious injuries to anyone caught unawares and in one 1980 study everyone injured was wearing light soccer shoes, suggesting that these caused either too much speed or poor control. Knee injuries predominate, again.

Trampoline

This has no place at all in the backyard or hectic playground where active youngsters may try to copy new tricks unsupervised. It has proved to be a dangerous toy, whatever else it is to experts giving exhibitions.

In 1973 in the United States a report stated that fifty cases of spinal cord injury were occurring annually. In 1976 the Consumer Product Safety Commission reported 19,000 people of all ages being injured each year. In 1977 the American Academy of Paediatrics advised against the sport because of brain and spine catastrophies from poorly executed somersaults, and in 1981 the American National Collegiate Athletic Association eliminated it as a national competition.

The Paediatricians' 1977 statement was designed to stop it being a compulsory part of physical education classes and to stop its unsupervised use. In 1983 the following revised statement was issued:

The Academy does not endorse the trampoline but a revision of its position to allow for a trial period of limited and controlled use by schools seems appropriate. However careful assessment of the incidence and severity of injury must continue during this trial period. The trampoline is a potentially dangerous apparatus and its use demands the following precautions:
1. It should not be a part of routine physical education classes.
2. It has no place in competitive sports.
3. It should never be used in home or recreational settings.
4. Highly trained personnel who have been instructed in all aspects of trampoline safety must be present when this apparatus is used.

5. Manoeuvres, especially the somersault, that have a high potential for serious injury should be attempted only by those qualified to become skilled performers.
6. The trampoline must be secured when not in use, and it must be well maintained.
7. Only schools or sports activities complying with the foregoing recommendations should have trampolines.

In Germany a 1981 report revealed that 7000 school children had been injured and 64 of these were now quadriplegics. In the same year the Danish Ministry of Education advised local authorities to stop the sport in Danish schools and the Board of Health recommended that the ban be permanent.

What then goes wrong? In a Danish review by Hammer, half the injured children did not know what had happened and reported 'black out' or 'dizziness'. It can be postulated therefore that the jump creates an acceleration force sharp enough to drag blood back down from the brain, or at least to impede the flow upwards, so that there is a genuine split second of unconsciousness. One hundred and forty-five children were injured in jumps of 1 metre or less and in 40 of these the injuries were permanent, so technique error or clumsiness must be a big factor.

What are the injuries?

- Fingers or hands jammed in the folding frame. The heavier and bigger it is, the more care that is needed, in fact adults should set it up.
- Fractured teeth, and torn toe nails in the sockless.
- Collision of knee with face.
- Dislocated knee, ankle, shoulder or elbow in falls.
- Torn knee menisci (p. 68). In a kinetic analysis of the

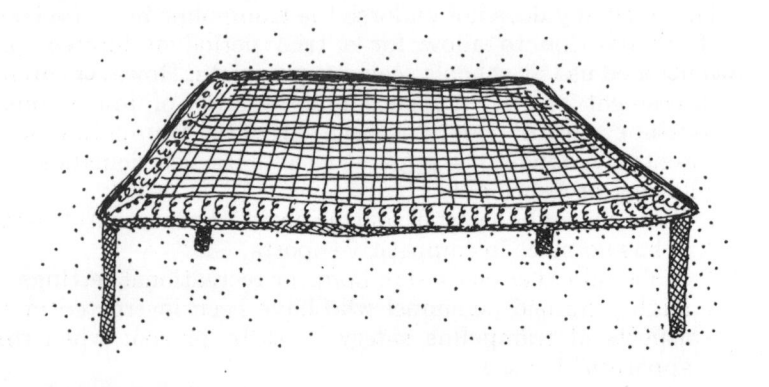

trampoline spring, Vaughan measured the upward thrust of the bed as five to seven times the body weight, and this force has to be absorbed by the hip and knee joints.
- Fractured limbs or damage to the vertebral epiphyseal plates (p. 17).
- Concussion.
- Fractured skull or neck. These are the real reason for such concern as to the safety of the sport. The usual cause is loss of balance and falls onto the frame or the floor, or attempted somersault finishes. The potential for catastrophe is always there and training with a harness, of the type used for divers and gymnasts, would seem essential.

More recent statistics point to catastrophic injuries to skilled performers, even on the minitrampoline, so perhaps there really is insufficient margin for error in all the techniques. That said, the fact remains that World Age Trampoline Championships are held. A 175-cm, 63-kg, fifteen-year-old Australian boy won his event in 1986. When he had shown skill and great interest at age six, his mother took him to an expert coach who wisely insisted on perfection at each stage before letting him advance the order of difficulty. He trained in a gymnasium with a harness and four spotters, one for each corner of the mat.

Playgrounds may be no safer for the very young and parents ought to look them over with a very critical eye. Too many children need medical attention every year after injuring themselves on play equipment; swings and slides account for half the injuries. Fingers and heads get trapped, slides are too steep, rust weakens the structures and the metal welding, metal edges are too sharp, sand blows away from supposedly soft landing areas, ladder rungs get slippery, guardrails are inadequate, and there is always one funnyman on a roundabout (the author vividly remembers, age seven, being pushed underneath and having to crawl to safety!). The list of injuries and fatalities is terrible. Regrettably Christmas gifts of backyard swings and exercise rings are just as likely to be of faulty design and should be checked very carefully. The price of safety is eternal vigilance and crafty suspicion.

REFERENCES:
Hammer A. et al. Trampoline training injuries. *Brit. J. Sports Med.* 1982; 16: 27.
Trampoline 2 Statement, *Paediatrics* 1981; 67: 438.
Vaughan C. Kinetic analysis of basic trampoline stunts. *J. Human Movement* 1980; 9: 236.

Volleyball

Ankle sprains, knee sprains, muscle strains, and jumper's knee can all occur, the latter said to be more likely if the floor is unyielding (for example, if it is cement). As in any ball game dislocated fingers or fractures are possible (see Basketball p. 104). A review from Italy in 1981 found the little finger to be the one most often fractured and, just to show that really every injury possible can eventually happen in sport, a stress fracture of the ulna (inner forearm bone) has been reported in a fourteen-year-old girl. High school players can now use braces and supports in play provided they are padded with 1.5 cms at least of foam rubber. A very special problem involves the effect of the constant impact of the ball on the forearm, the constant blows to the hand, and the impact on the hand when slapping the ball to the floor. The forearm arteries can go into spasm with the hand getting cold, numb, or blue, and more so in cold weather. The problem seems reversible with adequate rest from the sport, and thereafter protective pads should be worn. A rare non-reversible injury to an artery has also been noted, an aneurysm, appearing as a pulsating lump in the palm.

Height being such a vital aid to volleyball superiority, prediction of a child's final height is taken seriously in some countries. Two popular equations used in Czechoslovakia are, for a boy's height: (father's height + mother's height × 1.08) divided by 2, and for a girl's: (father's height × 0.923 + mother's height) divided by 2.

REFERENCES:

Gangitano R. Volleyball injuries. *Ital. J. Sport Traumatol.* 1981; 3: 31.

Kostianen S. et al. Blunt injury of the radial and ulnar arteries in volleyball players. *Brit. J. Sports Med.* 1983; 17: 172.

Water Sports

Surfing

An analysis of injuries which occurred at Waikiki, Hawaii, in 1977, highlights the severe injuries caused by a runaway board, which were only to be expected, but the current wide use of the leg rope should stop danger to others. Not necessarily, though, to the user. Duke Kahanamoku set the original fashion with a huge slab of wood (he could lift it!) that could slay any wave, but the modern light portable boards are not stable in choppy seas and have had to be stabilised by multiple long fins, with curved pointed ends. These have damaged eyeballs, cut ears, and speared into the chest, legs and throat, oft-times on recoil from the leg rope.

A 1983 set of Australian statistics indicates an overall significant injury rate of 3.5 per 1000 surfing days, not high, but it might well be higher for inexperienced surfers and occasional riders. These statistics were gathered from dedicated day-long expert riders and include the penalties of overuse and stress to the shoulder and lower back from kneeling on the board and furiously paddling. Four stress fractures of the lumbar spine probably came from the repeated hyperextension strains of some manoeuvres, the rapid nature of which can also strain the neck. Falling off the board flat onto the ear will perforate the eardrum, and in big seas spectacular falls and battering on the back of the neck have dislocated vertebrae. In such situations a sore or wry neck must be examined at a hospital emergency centre. Apart from the odd limb sprain or dislocation, and fracture of the face, rib or teeth, lacerations to the face and leg are most common. One penalty of long hours in the sun and spray is the growth of a small skin-like pterygium (p. 41) at the innder angle of the eyeball if protective goggles are not worn.

It has been observed that warm-up exercises are rarely done except by experienced riders, but then afficionados are a nonchalant and hardy breed. The author was once looking over a bunch of youngsters with an impressive range of cuts and bruises and said: 'That must hurt.' 'Nah' was the reply, 'it only hurt when it was cut.' Bad lacerations should be stitched and covered by plastic skin. Chronic immersion in water has a macerating (softening) effect on wounds and causes indolent (slow to heal) infection. Some lacerations are caused by recoil of a leg-roped board, but that is minor really compared to the havoc a loose board can wreak on someone else.

Riders are also at the mercy of one of the most dangerous creatures of the sea, other board riders. With two or more trying to get onto the same wave and thinking only of their own movements collisions are an ever-present risk. The odd death is still reported from a fractured skull or ruptured spleen in bad collisions or impalement on a fin where riders and bodysurfers are admixed. Eyes have been damaged by the board and have had to be removed. This should *never* happen. In the matter of control, with the way in which waves shift and change, the board rider, watching the narrow area of the breaking wave, has limited manoeuvrability in the immediate area of the white and blue junction. He has to see the bodysurfer in order to abort the ride. If he cannot the surfer has to dive deep to clear the fins. As a matter of practical safety, quite apart from legal responsibilities, bodysurfers must keep clear of boards, and vice versa. One hopes that riders will not be cheeky, and further that they will take the trouble to warn lone bodysurfers of their danger. Bodysurfers can forget about the tide and drift, or, if new to a beach, may be unaware of the flags or the tacit division of areas. Riders may be chasing shifting wave patterns. Either way, both groups must keep alert on mixed beaches.

Young enthusiasts can get quite neurotic about the quality of the waves. They seek them here, they seek them there, they seek them everywhere, in battered jalopies laden beyond the Plimsoll line. Motor injuries getting to the waves are almost the biggest hazard of the sport!

Young surfers standing on a beach at Newcastle, Australia, were so enthralled by the sight of a spectacular storm at sea that they failed to notice a mass of low cloud on the land side hurrying to catch up with the action. Their feet in salt water, clutching their boards stuck upright in wet sand, and the highest point for hundreds of metres around, they became perfect lightning conductors. One youngster literally came back from the dead after two weeks in hospital. The moral of the story? Don't watch just the storm, look hastily all around.

It also seems hard, when your gleaming-faced youngster is racing to the beach on a Saturday morning with his prized board, to delay him every time to protect his eyes, ears, and skin. If he does not take notice, keep trying. I still remember as clearly as if it were yesterday my mother's warnings over fifty years ago about the sun's rays, and now when it is too late I obey her!

Boogie Boarding

Unfortunately, these are very popular. The long forgotten rubber surf-o-plane was corrugated like iron of that name and held its direction as well as bouncing harmlessly (well almost!) off someone else, but the boogie board does the opposite. Light, smooth and erratic, it has to be stabilised by small fins, and that is the snag. Long and curved, or multiple and a little smaller, they make the board a menace to bodysurfers in the confusion of a breaking wave. The first adult who devises a foolproof method of making children aware for others' safety will earn eternal applause.

Skimboarding

This is the latest craze. You run into the shallow surf, drop a small circular board onto the swiftly receding film of water, and do a handstand as the board skims out. It is another testimony to the skill, enthusiasm, and ingenuity of the young with impeccable reflexes, but the tyro will have spectacular falls. Hopefully there will not be a rash of ruptured eardrums from water pressure or broken necks. Experts wear half length johns as all the sprinting into the surf heats them up.

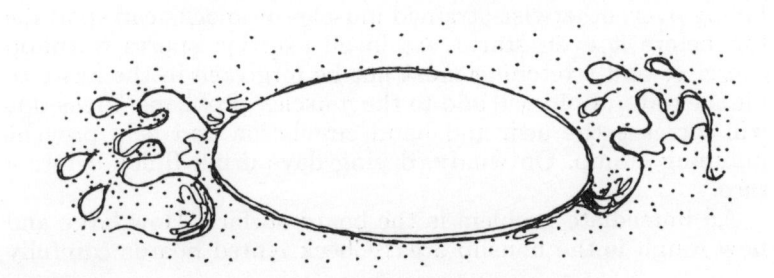

Waterskiing

To fall off at high speed with a caught foot can break the neck, with instant paraplegia and drowning. At lesser speed the eardrum may perforate. Fracture or dislocation of the knee and ankle are possible in a fall at any speed. There is the odd shoulder dislocation, rope burn, torn finger and thumb strain. This latter must be taken seriously as it may in fact be a dislocation or chip fracture with later disability if not properly treated (p. 152). At fast speeds goggles should be worn and carefully tied on since if they are dislodged in a spill the water wall can still damage the eye. Apart from the above, the big risks for waterskiing are hitting a buoy or a wharf, and being run over by another boat. Nasty and quite serious injuries obviously result. As in all water sports, especially mechanical ones, youngsters must be disciplined and taught safety until it becomes second nature. This is not really a sport to try just as fun on summer holidays in a crowded commercial zone. Everyone should wear a life jacket. The author shudders to recall that he (a doctor!) never thought to wear one.

Girls must be aware of a special danger. If their bottom hits the water at speed, water can be forced straight into the vagina and even right back into the peritoneal (abdominal) cavity, causing peritonitis (inflammation of the peritoneum). They must wear an occlusive wet suit or at least something more than a skimpy bit of material.

Windsurfing

The first thing to learn is how to get on and the sail up after falling over, otherwise strained muscles or knocks can spoil the fun before it even starts. As in all exertion sports warm-up exercises and stretching must not be forgotten in the haste to hit the water. Cold will add to the muscles' problems. Press-ups will increase the arm and hand circulation and help prevent numbing cramp. On windy, drying days drink fluids before a race.

An immediate problem is the board surface. How large and how rough is the nonslip area? Check rented boards carefully for sharp edges or rough fibreglass repair patches. Special shoes are a help and knee guards or a wet suit will preclude unnecessary abrasions. Cuts and lacerations aplenty plague the advanced surfer who skims across reefs in exotic resorts. Cold numb fingers can get caught whilst fiddling with the dagger board. The mast foot should have a pressure release spring to avoid the danger of the leg being trapped and crushed in a spill. Hands can get cut or burned on the rigging, so wear gloves to give a better grip and add to control and safety. A scuba diving wet suit is too tight and restrictive for the muscle activity of windsurfing and may cause aching and fatigue. Skin gradually toughens but use cream to protect against windburn.

Please learn all the right-of-way rules and the habits of boat traffic in your stretch of water. Power boat skippers know that they must give way to sail but windsurfers have been killed by turning suddenly, probably due to inattention on the blind side, across the path of boats. Never take your eye off catamarans in the area; unlike power boats the cats bear down silently, and very swiftly. Be especially careful of river mouths; outgoing tides are tricky and sandbars more so. Knowledge of local wind conditions is vital. Sydney Harbour is famous for its sudden summer 'southerly buster' that destroys masts and sails, and gives the water police much rescue work. Always listen to weather reports or, better, telephone the boating forecast service. If there is a strong wind warning even experts should not set out.

There have been suggestions that sunscreens made from lanolin or other animal oils create a scent trail in the water that attracts sharks. Much more dangerous however is the food trail left by picnickers throwing food scraps overboard, or fisherfolk cleaning fish nearby. This really will attract sharks to the area.

Finally, learn to *watch the weather*. In an emergency, *never leave the board*.

REFERENCE:
Lowdon, B. J. et al. Surfboard riding injuries. *Med. J. Aust.* 1983; 2: 613.

Weight Lifting

The United States National Electronic Injury Surveillance System figures for 1979 show that one half of all weightlifting injuries occurred in the ten to nineteen age group. Significantly, 50% of all injuries happened at home, where presumably there was no supervision and probably poor techniques were used, or unfit youths were fooling around with adult equipment. Home gym equipment should therefore not be bought until *after* everyone who is going to use it has had proper lessons. The sport obviously needs expert tuition at all levels.

Training statistics gleaned from seventy-one contestants in the 1981 Michigan Teenage Powerlifting Championships showed that the coach was not present for half of the training time, and that one quarter of the contestants had developed their knowledge of the sport by trial and error. Help was often not sought for the muscle pulls that were high on the list of injuries, emphasising that possibly secret and undisciplined training *must* be detected. Muscle pulls plus tendinitis, sprains and cramps, were overall the most frequent problems. The lower back was the site most often injured or painful and yet was responsible for a disproportionate lack of time off training. Elbow injury was the opposite; training had to stop for twice as long as for the average injury. This strongly suggests that back strain was not taken as seriously as it should be at this early stage in life. Statistics also revealed a high level of pain incidence and severity: in round figures, 60% for the lower back, 30% for the upper back, shoulder, and knee, 25% for the wrists, 20% for the hips, elbows, and hands, 15% for the stomach and groin muscles, and 5% for the ankle. Nobody found fault with their feet! Many of the trainees got pain in several areas and this provides clear proof of the stresses of this sport, stresses which, if ignored, can only end in injury as follows:

The Back

Muscle and ligament sprains are common. Lack of muscle development, lack of lifting skill, and failure to warm up, are factors that must be continually monitored. X-rays show damage to the vertebrae far in excess of what one would expect if using only low back pain as a guide to the possibility. In Aggrawal's set of figures from India all those injured were adults, rather than weaker-boned adolescents, yet unexpected stress fractures appeared in the lumbar vertebrae (pars interarticularis) after five years in the sport. Spondylolysis (p. 28) is an ever-present risk in powerlifters. Weight lifters can also tear the pectoralis major (big chest muscle). There is a sharp tearing feeling with obvious deformity. Surgical repair is needed.

The Shoulder

Rupture of the biceps tendon is a special risk during the lift, and the joint can dislocate downwards when the arms are vertical.

The Elbow

Muscle origin tears (somewhat akin to those in tennis and golf), strained ligaments and even dislocation cause more days off training than any other injuries, lower back strain included.

The Wrist

If control is lost overhead the wrist is bent sharply backwards and the lower end of the radius (outer forearm) fractures; up to the age of twenty or even later the epiphysis (p. 16) will not have fused with the main shaft and therefore may be damaged. Spotters should be there to catch the bar and prevent this injury.

The Larynx

Again, if control is lost overhead, or if the foot slips and the lifter falls over, the bar can fall across the throat and fracture the larynx (hollow passage to lungs containing vocal cords). Special shoes to promote frictional grip should be worn, not just any old gym shoe.

The Knee

The leg extensor muscle group is called on for terrific momentary force, thus risking a tear of the quadriceps muscle or its patellar (knee cap) tendon. In the rare event the knee cap may dislocate and this should lead to a full orthopaedic assessment. It may be that the Q angle (p. 68) is unfavourable. An unbalanced state will twist the knee and perhaps the meniscus, tearing it. Chondromalacia (p. 19) can slowly develop. The need for a proper muscle warm-up is often forgotten in the belief that lifting smaller weights is a warm-up.

The Hip and Ankle

These powerful hinge joints can have their attached muscles torn or detached from their bone origins, but the joints themselves are safe from strain until the contestant begins to wobble or collapse.

The Cardio-vascular System

Breath-holding must *not* be allowed to happen and training must ensure that lifting is synchronised with breathing. The ideal is to inhale deeply and exhale whilst lifting. Otherwise the rise in chest pressure impedes blood return to the heart and the athlete faints. In this sport to fall over is dangerous! A special danger time is in the clean and jerk when the bar is resting momentarily across the shoulders and possibly pressing on the trachea (windpipe) and the carotid (large neck artery) going to the brain. Incidental, transient headaches which may result indicate tension or spasm of the neck muscles, and there will also be a temporary rise in blood pressure during the lift. The sport is therefore not recommended (nor are isometric activities in general) for adolescents with high blood pressure. Any headache accompanied by dizziness, speech or coordination problems, or funny vision must be checked as soon as possible.

Such injuries indicate that it is doubtful if pure weight lifting should be a serious activity for pre-adolescents or that they should be allowed to test their current maximum. Weight training may be safe with submaximal weights to aid muscle endurance rather than pure strength. The American Academy of Paediatrics has stated: 'Weight lifting is a competitive sport with a high injury rate that should not be practised by a pre-adolescent. Teenagers who wish to participate should have proper safety precautions and capable supervision.' Some orthopaedic surgeons would not allow it at all. Not only are muscles underdeveloped and incapable of gaining bulk until pubertal hormones are released, but also bone epiphyses (p. 16) are very vulnerable to the strong pulls and heavy load and can be torn off or damaged by the shearing stresses. This is so up to seventeen years, even up to twenty years of age. Only then do the growth centres cease activity and coalesce. Always to be condemned is unsupervised activity in the weight room.

Most in danger is the 'big boy', that is one tall or stout for his age who possibly feels that he ought to be able to shine, but it has to be explained over and over again that size and age are *not* a measure of maturity of development, and this latter is the critical factor. Adolescents are often tempted into the sport because weight training is included in some high school conditioning programmes, and they impress themselves with the large weights they can manage even without tuition. It is vital that weight training meant to develop muscles for another sport should err on the easy side with light weights. However, if pupils do become serious good tuition is also vital, with careful supervision by a trainer approved by the National Weight Lifting Association to ensure the emphasis is on technique, and that the build-up of strength is slow and deliberate to protect the bones.

Weight Training

Weight training, now so popular with all sportspeople in the off-season, would involve all the above hazards if lifts were attempted in the same way, but pumping iron should be approached differently. It is designed firstly for general muscle development and endurance, secondly to strengthen special muscle groups for individual sports, and thirdly, if circuit training is skilfully programmed, to combine with aerobic exercising. Injury should not occur unless faulty or ill-fixed equipment breaks or falls over. In the early stages it is important to strive for gradual improvement in the back muscles (something pure weight lifting will not do), and then to add other muscle groups. Many routines have been written for specific sports but at all times variety is important in the young so that they achieve a balanced body development. Muscle endurance can only be built up gradually. Overtraining is bad; it merely overstrains and denies the muscle the time it needs to recover, repair, and set about building fresh tissue fibrils (small sprouting fibres). There is further debate as to whether pre-adolescents benefit from weight training (as distinct from weight lifting), but many youngsters find it fun and a challenge. Certainly it must be done with extra care if in groups, because of individuals' wide range of bone strength, level of muscularity, and general maturity. Apart from this it is hard to see why pre-adolescents should not benefit provided they are carefully programmed and set modest goals. It has been claimed that high school athletes who follow a comprehensive training programme have fewer injuries and need less time in rehabilitation than the less fit, but this is only to be expected. However, overuse of the equipment or overenthusiasm will be rewarded, not with super fitness, but avulsion (tearing) of muscles (and their bone epiphyses in the usual places, p. 17), neck sprain, or shoulder dislocation.

Girls particularly should not straight away attempt a high level of endeavour. They should proceed slowly. The physique and body composition of top female body builders when measured proves that regular heavy resistance training does increase upper trunk circumferences and reduce the mean body fat below the female average of 20%. There is nothing scientific in the phrase 'muscle bound'. There is no such thing. There will however be a loss of harmonious symmetry in overdeveloping one set of muscles. Avoid this by a good routine that exercises all muscle groups.

Before any of these activities are begun make sure that the boy, or girl, does not have a hernia!

REFERENCES:

Aggrawal N. D. et al. A study of changes in the spine in weight lifters and other athletes. *Brit. J. Sports Med.* 1979; 13: 58.

Brown E. W. et al. Medical history associated with adolescent power lifting. *Paediatrics.* 1983; 72: 636–644.

Rians C. B. et al. Strength training for prepubescent males. Is it safe? *Am. J. Sports Med.* 1987; 15: 483–489.

Wrestling

Wrestling is a contact rather than a collision sport, and statistics do show that football has a higher total injury rate than wrestling, but in the latter more serious incidents are likely to happen, for example dislocations and fractures, especially at times when one of the wrestlers is at a disadvantage. To minimise the possibility of such injury and to give the one disadvantaged at least the benefit of a sporting chance, particular attention must be paid to the following:

Good Referees

They are needed to spot quickly and break up illegal holds. Unfair leverage increases the opportunity for more serious fractures and dislocations. In training arenas a good coach to pupil ratio is needed to spot injury situations in time, and if an injury occurs bouts should be stopped. One wonders who was the Olympic referee when Leontsikos won the Olympic crown in 456 and 452 B.C. He used a neat trick, bending his opponents' fingers back until they dislocated!

Matching by Maturity

In wrestling, it is not a question of size, age, or weight, but of maturity, a quite different measure. Maturity compounds qualities of speed, toughness, determination, aggression, and mental aptitude, and it coincides with the full production of male hormones and adrenal steroids which allow muscle growth to really leap ahead. For a year or three a boy may run rings around even his bigger friend. One measure of the (variable) rate of pubertal change is the Tanner Index. Full maturity is reached at stage 5 when the pubic hair assumes the adult triangular shape with clear lateral angles. At stage 4 the pubic hair is still rounded out above with no lateral angle and it has been said by some that school wrestling should not begin below stage 4.

Previous Injury

Over a third of all injuries are aggravations of old ones, especially in limbs, and of course the original dislocation or fracture may have happened in another sport. Rehabilitation after injury must never be a nonchalant afterthought, but must be expertly supervised with proper conditioning and gradual redevelopment of strength. Wrestlers are notorious for dodging medical instructions, if they get half a chance, in a desire to rush back to competition.

Mats

Quality, number, and hygiene are important. They easily deteriorate from overuse and unless regularly cleaned, ingrained dirt and organisms menace mat burns and even minor lacerations. Remember too that the virus of plantar warts and the spores of tinea will be shed onto mats. Resilite mats are better than old canvas ones and easier to keep clean.

Personal Hygiene

Herpes simplex (cold sores), herpes zoster (shingles) and chicken pox viruses will be spread if sufferers are allowed to indulge in contact sports of any kind. Such players must be banned from training until their skin has completely healed. Staphylococcal skin lesions (pimples, pustules, acne, and beard rash) are unpleasant too, and the infective bacteria will be passed to others. Athletes should shower before a bout and keep their gear clean out of regard for their opponents' welfare. And naturally they should wash and clean the skin after bouts, and treat cuts with mild antiseptics for forty-eight hours to stop entry of lurking bacteria.

Protective Gear

This is available for the head and ears, elbow, and knee, and there is no excuse for not using it, particularly in the early years.

Proper Instruction

High school statistics published in the United States in 1981 showed a decline in the overall injury rate in the second year of competition, in all sports, but particularly in wrestling. This indicates the benefit of experience, and the development of correct technique by good instruction. Supervision may well further improve the statistics.

Weight Reduction

This vexed question! It is a confused scene. State and National rules vary, weighing-in rules vary, and competition classes are subject to debate and change. Let us therefore try to proceed logically.

- The athlete must get a copy of the rules, study them, appreciate the problems, and then resist all temptation to fudge (the verb, not the sweet!). Everyone wants to wrestle in the lowest possible class but it is absolutely inevitable that a lad will grow over the season so that reducing weight ridiculously to be smart with the pre-season classification will certainly lead to frantic efforts later to keep in that class.
- Try to assess the level of body fat. Underwater weighing once or twice a year is the most precise method, if it is available, and ways of doing it are improving. Mathematical equations based on some specific body measurements have been established for the purpose but are not completely valid for some ethnic groups, for example Negroes, who are said to have a heavier skeleton. Skin fold measurements are simple and can be done, in fact should be done, weekly, with good quality callipers. After practising with them to develop uniform pressure, measurements of the skin fold at the thigh, iliac crest (hip bone), abdomen, chest, shoulder blade, and back of the upper arm, can be checked against tables to estimate body fat percentage. When recording the value remember that the accuracy of the method varies by up to 5%. Results for fit wrestlers can be surprisingly low and may indicate that there is *no scope for forced reduction*. The underwater weighing experts in Minneapolis in fact reported a wrestler who quit the sport rather than follow instructions to lose more weight;

on test he had only 3.3% body fat! Further, records over a season may show that weight gain occurs when skin fold is static or even decreasing; that is, the lean body (muscle) mass is increasing, hardly an undesirable trend.
- After establishing the body fat percentage with skin callipers, subsequent eating habits can be calculated. Many young parents today are expert calorie watchers and they must appoint themselves wrestling weight controllers. A 45-kg lad needs 1500 kilocalories a day, minimum, just to live; an 84-kg one needs 2000 kilocalories. No less! Exercise requirements are extra, but with daily hard workouts and an intake of 2000–3000 calories, excess fat can even be lost. The quality of the diet is also important. It seems from careful physiological estimates that the best diet is one with 60–70% carbohydrate to maintain adequate muscle glycogen stores (p. 80); otherwise lethargy develops. All high salt foods such as chips, hamburgers, and the like should be banned. In the occasional person the sodium ion in excess might just affect the blood pressure, and certainly it can lead to fluid retention. Computer software is now available which is specifically addressed to the intertwining of menus and calories. Choose carefully however. Make sure the list of foods remains sufficiently wide to provide variety even after you have excluded the ones your family is allergic to or does not fancy.
- Keep proper weight records, preferably twice a day, so that normal daily variations can be observed, and the effects of food and activity learned.

The optimum body fat percentage is not really known. The figure adopted by the American College of Sports Medicine in 1976 was 5–7% for high school wrestlers, half the figure of several years ago. Nevertheless, a study of nine- to twelve-year-old 'experienced' wrestlers in Omaha in 1982 revealed that they had a body fat of 13% as against a 20% reading in a group of non-athletes. Until more specific data is available it may be sensible, in pre-pubertal boys, to stay approximately with the 13% figure. Boys at this age are normally a bit chubbier than they will be in their upper teens and possibly the extra fat is to fuel the adolescent growth spurt. What may be more important is to establish the 'optimum' for your son. At what level does he feel most fit? Also measurements will show where there is scope for gradual weight improvement between seasons by sensible dieting, strict discipline with junk foods and fudge (the noun not the verb!), and regular exercise, such as long distance running. It is the novice wrestler who particularly needs advice, supervision, and encouragement, to keep proper weight records and to develop good habits through the whole year.

Wrestling or gym shoes, incidentally, are not suitable for road work, and if the latter is overdone by a heavy boy all the usual overuse leg strains can develop (see Athletics p. 86).

Crash Reduction

Deliberate dehydration prior to weigh-in is a separate issue to the slow achievement of optimum body weight and composition by balancing dietary intake against energy expenditure. However, all wrestlers do it, some time or other, so here are some more basic rules.

- Forced vomiting or the use of laxatives is crazy.
- Never use diuretic drugs to increase urinary output because such drugs cause excessive loss of the potassium ion as well, and this will cause muscle weakness or, in extreme cases, have an adverse effect on the heart's electrical system.
- Don't try for too much. Detailed weight change studies have only been done in older competitors but a case report from the Institute for Aerobic Research in Dallas, Texas, featured a twenty-one-year-old who, in the day prior to competition, lost 2.73 kg of fluid to weigh in at 48 kg. This 5% loss had no apparent effect on performance but some rehydration was achieved in the allowed time after weigh-in.
- Rapid rehydration is impossible. Don't count on it. At, say 60 kg basic weight, 5% equals 3 kg or 3 litres of fluid. Unless you are a donkey or a camel the stomach will not hold 3 litres at one guzzle; and even if you do get it into the intestine absorption is a slow process, and much of the imbibed fluid will lie in the gut awaiting redistribution back to the muscle compartments. In so doing it will be clashing with the blood circulation demands of competition. High carbohydrate fluids are the best to use for rehydration, although to reemphasise, if muscle glycogen stores (p. 80) have been diminished by a prolonged panic diet, then they cannot be restored quickly by any method and muscle weakness is a certainty.
- To be completely scientific, buy a urine testing hydrometer and do not let urine density rise above 1015 during dehydration tricks.

And now one final warning that the last word has not been written on weight reduction and its consequences. A report to the 1982 Annual Meeting of the American College of Sports Medicine from the Human Performance Laboratory, Blacksburg, Virginia, indicated that repetitive weekly weight reductions of 5.4% in one group of wrestlers left them with a worse level of anaerobic capacity (as shown by the treadmill test) at the end of the season, when compared with a group who averaged only 2.1% weekly reduction. There is also evidence that blood levels of the male sex hormone, testosterone, and one of the pituitary hormones, prolactin, are reduced during the wrestling season if the percentage weight (that is body fat) loss is large, and especially as the level of body fat nears 5%. A low blood testosterone level could even be a signal that the youth is undernourished and should not be in that weight class. It may further be postulated that muscle bulk and strength are being stunted.

Injuries

Pre-adolescent wrestlers, say up to twelve years, are a distinct group. Weight loss, and no doubt it will be attempted, must only ever be minor, and any problem with weight classes should be discussed with the school. Growing children are definitely harmed by persistent weight loss from food restriction and no sport is worth that. Injuries around joints that might involve epiphyses (p. 16) are always a worry but are rarely seen provided, as always in any sport in this special age group, that maturity of speed and aggression are about equal in both contestants. Minor muscle strains, bruises, a bloody nose, a poke in the eye, loosening of deciduous teeth, and aggravation of previous injury, are the injuries most commonly seen. Orthodontic braces should rule out the sport because of the possibility of tongue and lip lacerations, not to mention the risk to costly hardware.

In the teenage years rough and tumble direct blows will cause soft tissue injuries, lacerations, contusions (deep bruises), ear haematomas (blood clots), bleeding noses and the like, or fracture teeth, the nose or a rib. Heavy falls can cause severe contusions, fractures or fracture-dislocations of the fingers, wrist, elbow or ankle. The leverage of classical holds is capable of spraining the knee, shoulder or ankle, and fingers may at any time get caught. Chest pain is a rare worry and almost certainly not 'heart', but rather muscle strain or tear, dislocation of the sterno-clavicular joint (p. 63) in the root of the neck, or separation of the rib from its cartilage near the sternum (breast bone).

Lumbosacral (lower back) ligament strain is always possible but any head or neck symptoms must be taken seriously. A half Nelson, with its rotation and hyperextension forces, can damage the transverse processes of the cervical (neck) vertebrae (p. 28) through which the vertebral artery travels to reach the brain stem. Even transient damage to this artery will cause difficulty in swallowing, dizziness or a stumbling gait. Stiffness of the neck or restricted movement should be checked by X-rays. A proven neck injury would preclude further wrestling or judo because of the risk of recurrent injury. For similar reasons, the International Judo Federation Rules outlaw 'choking' techniques in the under-thirteen age group. Pain or tingling down the arm raises suspicion of stretching of the brachial plexus (the network of nerve trunks gathered in the neck en route between the spinal cord and the upper arm).

Knees, as in every sport, suffer. A minor problem is swelling and inflammation of the pre-patellar bursa (p. 69), probably due to direct injury in the takedown (especially in the lighter divisions), and possibly from infection by organisms on the mat. In the latter case aspiration, culture of the fluid for organisms, antibiotics and rest are essential. Recurrence means that surgery may eventually be needed. Knee ligament strains and meniscal tears deserve special emphasis because the knee, of all spots, has the highest rate of reinjury. Parents must insist that medical advice is followed to the letter and that full muscle power is regained before resumption of training.

A study published in 1982 by Strauss gave the injury rate from four school and college tournaments involving 1049 competitors. The nine- to fourteen-year age group had the least injuries, 3.8%, compared with the overall rate for the remaining competitors of 12%, and even then the figure for the younger group included muscle strains, contusions etc. that the older ones did not bother to report. The injuries received at takedown were equal in number to those on the mat, and in view of the brevity of takedown it proves that it is a high risk moment. One might have expected fatigue to lead to more injuries towards the end of a match but the second period was actually the worst. Of interest too was the finding that the most skilled, those who had had more matches and therefore more previous exposure to injury, in fact had the same average percentage of injuries.

Not exactly an injury but a mishap nevertheless, is spread of infection, and two rare incidents have been reported. In one, a wrestler who ignored herpes found that the virus travelled to a previously injured knee and caused viral arthritis. In a second, hepatitis B spread to others in blood spilled from a laceration. Indeed, sharp exercise when one harbours a virus, even the common cold, is very unwise. With a sports-active circulation the virus can be carried to unusual places and cause serious inflammations, for example of the heart (myocarditis or endocarditis) and brain (encephalitis), to name but two.

REFERENCES:
Garrick J. et al. Medical care and injury surveillance in the high school setting. *Physician and Sportsmed.* 1981; 9:Feb 115.
Lohman T. Body composition methodology in sports medicine. *Physician and Sportsmed.* 1982: 10: October 46.
Sady S. et al. Body composition of nine- to twelve-year-old experienced wrestlers. *Med. and Science in Sports and Exercise.* 1982; 14: 244.
Strauss R. H. Injury of wrestlers in school and college. *J.A.M.A.* 1982; 248: 2016.
Strauss R. H. et al. Weight loss in amateur wrestlers and its effect on serum testosterone levels. *J.A.M.A.* 1985; 254: 3337–3338.
Wroble R. R. et al. Patterns of knee injuries in wrestling: A six-year study. *Am. J. Sports Med.* 1986; 14: 55–66.

PART C

SOMETHING FOR PARENTS

Jogging

> 'To jog or not to jog; that is the question
> Whether 'tis nobler in the mind to suffer
> The pains and groans of outrageous stresses
> Or to take aim against a loss of form
> And by exercising to end it.'

Hamlet, that famous soliloquist, knew what he was talking about, not that his friend Will Shakespeare had a reputation around London as a jogger. A sprinter he, oft in pursuit of his Dark Lady for whatever huff and puff he might come by.

The world is now a giant treadmill with everyone doggedly jogging for dear life. Or are they? There is no proof yet that jogging shoes are a magic talisman to ward off heart attacks. In fact it might seem that the exact opposite can be claimed when fitness fanatics, such as the American Jim Fixx in mid-1984, die on a routine jog; in Jim's case post mortem showed that cholesterol plaques had almost blocked two coronary arteries and there was a clot in the third. But let us examine these brief facts more closely. It is likely that the clot in the functioning artery was fresh and was the final straw that killed him. Was it some sudden extra exertion on the run, a near trip up that had him holding his breath, thus suddenly raising the pressure in his chest, was he not feeling well and thought that the run would blow away the cobwebs, and (very important this) had he been getting angina attacks (chest pain with exercise) but ignoring them in the hope that more exercise would cure them? We can never know. His father had his first coronary heart attack at age forty-five so we may speculate that Jim hoped to ward off such tendency by dedicated exercise. On the other hand, he was still jogging many kilometres a day on, shall we say, one third or less of the total normal coronary artery cross-section, proof indeed of just how much reserve nature has built into the basic design and of how tough the heart muscle is. As a corollary, if we look after the mechanism it should serve us a long time (which brings our debate full circle). Jim Fixx proved one thing conclusively, namely that all the exercise in the world did not prevent *his* atherosclerosis (artery wall disease) from progressing. This reminds me of one of the aphorisms oft-quoted by my teachers from the simpler days before the physiology of the heart and circulation became complicated: 'You are only as old as your arteries.' And what made for good arteries? 'Choose your parents carefully,' was the reply.

There is nothing new to be learned from the regrettable death of Jim Fixx. Sudden death has occurred and been studied in all exertion sports: football (and this includes referees too!), squash, tennis, gymnastics, yachting, and even during a round of golf. The inevitable question is always: did the exertion cause the heart attack or was it going to happen anyway? Death has often occurred just after the exercise or golf round and then been attributed to the after game smoke, the hot shower that caused skin vasodilatation (expansion of blood vessels), or the continued build-up of blood lactic acid, all of which can affect the heart and its electrical conducting system. In such cases there is no doubt that Death chose that particular moment to swing his scythe because of the recent exertion, but with such a precariously balanced heart such a moment could hardly have been far away.

In 1980, in the *American Journal of Cardiology*, B. F. Waller and co-authors from Bethesda, Maryland, reported autopsies done on five white experienced joggers aged between forty and fifty-three years who died suddenly whilst running. All had severe atherosclerotic coronary heart disease but *none* had had clinical evidence of heart disease before beginning to run years before. One runner had felt angina during his jog, which he 'solved' by walking for fifty or so metres when the pain came on, and he alone had had a positive stress test electrocardiogram (measurement of heart action) in his eighth year of running and two years before death. In this man it may be again noted just what one can still achieve even whilst the disease silently progresses, in fact disease processes may be jogging right along with you. One must also deduce that in these cases the jogging prevented nothing—medical records of the five showed that four had high blood cholesterol levels and three had a family history of heart disease. Vladimir Kuts, Olympic middle distance gold medallist, died of coronary artery disease at forty-eight, and Emil Zatopek, famed Olympic treble-distance winner, had a heart attack at sixty-six. Whilst we do not know whether they were still active at that time it is clear that superb youthful fitness does not stop later artery disease. Or, perhaps, severe early stress begins it?

To speculate on these cases is not to ignore the vast literature and accumulated statistics designed to prove that jogging, and other exertion sports for that matter, is safe. In relation to the total number of afficionados it has to be or the human race would soon give it up. What the statistics cannot tell us at the moment is whether jogging prevents, accelerates, or has no influence on the underlying cause of the arterial degeneration that is the real killer. Methodical data gathered on Harvard graduates and British public servants tends to the conclusion that those who exercise regularly have a lesser rate of death from heart disease when compared with non-exercisers but, alas, one is afloat on such an enormous sea of variables in the statistical equations that a final answer may be impossible, even ignoring the fact that the cause of atherosclerosis itself is still heavily debated.

The basic changes in the body induced by regular generous exercise, such as jogging, are clear. The heart has to increase its output considerably, which it can do by either an increased stroke rate or an increased stroke volume. The latter occurs eventually as the heart muscle 'conditions', that is increases its strength; the heart rate need not then be as high as initially and indeed at rest can be quite slow (forty per minute) in superb athletes. Echograms of heart muscle thickness show that as a group, but not necessarily as individuals, endurance athletes do develop thicker, more muscular heart chamber walls. The need for high cardiac output means that one must not jog if feeling unwell or feverish. *Never jog with influenza. Never, ever.* A high percentage of sufferers have been noted to have mild myocarditis (heart muscle inflammation), as shown by transient changes in the electrocardiogram, and exertion could convert this into a lethal condition.

Blood pressure will diminish in fit persons long term, and will show a prolonged drop post exercise in the mildly hypertensive. This may not be due to the act of running but to the fact that other bad health factors such as excess weight, smoking, fat and cholesterol rich diets, and disturbed sleep patterns have been eliminated or modified at the same time.

Sweat is normally secreted at the rate of one litre per hour in acclimatised and fit joggers and it is dangerous to interfere with its evaporation or force its overproduction by wearing sweat suits. Body heat has to be eliminated; if not, heat cramps, heat exhaustion, and the menacing heat stroke can follow. Salt loss is insignificant and need not be replaced by tablets; normal food will suffice.

Blood fat levels slowly alter, seemingly as a direct result of exercise, towards a decent level of the desirable high density lipoprotein (HDL); lipoproteins are globules that are more protein than fat. Tests suggest, unfortunately, that a lay-off of even three days sets in train a reversal, thus proving that to be truly beneficial exercise must be habitual. (Lipoprotein tests as a measure of cholesterol are still being refined.)

Coronary arteries? That important bottom life line? The *hope* is that they will be healthier and of bigger diameter as the heart muscle gets better. Indeed there are some studies to indicate that this can be so. The famous Clarence De Mar, who monopolised the Boston Marathon in the 1920s era, had unusually large coronary arteries. Post mortem examination revealed this when Death somewhat unsportingly tripped him up with a bowel cancer at age seventy. The conundrum remains: was he born with those arteries or did he develop them by constant exercise?

A sense of physical wellbeing is engendered and personality problems such as depression and anxiety are calmed by exercise or possibly any outdoor activity, but especially by jogging. This is in response to endorphins (chemicals) released by the brain. In fact excess production of these deadens the brain itself to pain from structures abused by jogging and contributes to the development of a feeling of euphoria, a jogger's 'high'.

Hormonal responses to jogging are most obvious in women who overdo it; resulting in amenorrhoea (loss of periods) and reversible infertility. This is because the menstrual cyclical mechanism is so delicately balanced and vulnerable to stress. In extreme cases there is the added threat of calcium loss and osteoporosis (brittle bones). Female joggers should include in their log book a record of weight and menstrual flow. Men are in a more steady hormonal state, have no monthly pulses of activity and are not easily disturbed. However, at quite high levels of exercise, at around say 200 km per week, changes will occur, with loss of sperms and reduced testosterone production.

Pregnancy is a special problem and accomplished joggers, tempted to prove they can carry on as if nothing has happened, will be forced by Mother Nature to remember that pregnancy is an overall strain on the system and one that will increase inexorably until something gives. Commonsense dictates that it should be jogging and not the pregnancy. In joggers, in the first three months, the odds on miscarriage by mischance will rise above the usual one in ten. The pregnancy blood volume increases by 45% in seven months and the heart's output must rise with it, extra work that tests the heart's reserve capacity. Any rise in the mother's body temperature, whether from influenza, appendicitis, or heat stroke, is a proven danger to the little foetus. An untrained and unacclimatised pregnant body certainly could never begin to cope with the extra stress.

Joggers burn about 500 kilocalories of energy per hour. For

comparison one uses 60 per hour just keeping the body alive whilst sleeping, approximately 200 strolling along, 300 in gardening, and 400 cycling at 20 kph. A kilocalorie is the same as a calorie, but the term has been updated to stay in semantic line with a kilojoule, another measurement of energy. One kilocalorie equals just over 4 kilojoules. Let us now use two other facts, that 1 gram of metabolised (burnt-up) fat produces 9 kilocalories, and that a 75-kg man with a 20% fat level has 15,000 gms of fat; it can then be calculated that he could jog 2700 km without refuelling, or from New York to Los Angeles. Gentle jogging by itself therefore is not going to make you lose weight unless you start overweight. If you were overweight, and have managed to get back to normal levels, jog and eat carefully to stay there. If you become really hooked on running your next step is competitive marathons, but that is another story in body adaptation.

The Jogger's Ten Commandments

1. Thou shalt consult with thy doctor to establish any obvious risks. Old leg injuries or unfavourable anatomical features may limit the stress your legs can take. The back perforce will have to absorb strain and a dodgy back or suspect disc should be checked by X-ray.
2. Thou shalt have preliminary blood tests for anaemia, cholesterol and lipoprotein levels. Advanced tests such as electrocardiogram, monitored stress test, spirometry (test of the lung), near maximal treadmill test (to measure oxygen intake), etc. are for your doctor to decide upon but anyone really serious about a commitment to good health through jogging ought to seek a high tech roadworthiness certificate, indeed it could give a new dimension to life and better understanding of the body nature has designed.
3. Thou shalt have thy spouse review thy lifestyle. Only such an impartial observer can make a believable stab at what overeating, smoking, alcohol and neglect have already done to her Adonis.
4. Thou shalt honour thy promise to alter. Jogging is not the cure for excess.
5. Thou shalt spend money on good shoes and rush not into the nearest shop to grab the cheapest pair. Feet are vital to long-

term survival. Check the shoes regularly for uneven wear due to anatomical faults in the feet that would benefit from orthotics (inner soles and supports).

6. Thou shalt progress slowly. You are aiming to run for years so build up over many months or strains will end your career before it really starts. Ligaments, tendons, bursae, joint cartilage and muscles, unused for years and years, need to be coaxed, not commanded to perform. The sight of portly perspiring personalities, never athletes in their schooldays, pounding pavements as if their knees had MacPherson struts like their expensive cars is enough to give jogging a bad name. It would be wiser to start with long walks (see below).

7. Thou shalt keep a log book. On one page note the daily distance covered and times, and on the opposite record conditions, discomforts, pulse rate and anything that seems relevant. On later study various patterns will emerge.

8. Thou shalt not covet thy neighbour's performances. In this most individual of pastimes peer pressure is a dangerous spur to overuse injury.

9. Thou shalt be alert to personal danger. Plot your routes carefully to avoid dark lonely stretches (mugging), busy roads and tricky intersections (accidents), roads with high camber or deep culverts (falls), wet slippery conditions, poor visibility due to weather, steep hills towards the end of the course (you do not want them renamed 'coronary hill' in your honour), assorted wildlife, or anything else peculiar to the geography of the area. City air pollution cannot be ignored; noxious carbon monoxide from motor cars has been detected in joggers' blood, inhaled by their heavy breathing, so in your own city avoid peak hour traffic. Additional demands on the body must be allowed for by travelling joggers in sweaty Zaire, shivery Siberia, or elevated Everest. Heat stroke, frostbite, or poor oxygenation at altitude, are factors that must be thought out before carrying on abroad as if one were at home.

10. Thou shalt report to thy doctor every new pain. There is absolutely no way you or your expert friend can decide if it is significant or not for out of little pains do big agonies grow. No matter how fit you feel you must tune into what your body is trying to tell you.

Just to reassure you that a medical consultation is great value for money, consider the following list of possible injuries and conditions that will be jogging your doctor's memory, together with what he or she can do about them, because the last thing a runner wants to be told is: 'Stop it or you will go lame.' He wants to be diagnosed, cured and sent running again, or at worst switched to an alternative activity.

FOOT	Corns and blisters
	Bunions and bursitis
	Plantar fasciitis
	Heel spurs
	Hammer toe
	Morton's neuroma
	Nerve entrapment
	Tenosynovitis of the big toe
	Synovitis of the toe joints
	Sesamoiditis (p. 89)
	Gout
	Stress fractures
	Subtalar arthritis
ANKLE	Subluxation strain
	Achilles bursitis or tendinitis
	Tenosynovitis
	Post tibial tendinitis
	Dislocated peroneal tendons
	Exostoses (bone outgrowths)
	Rheumatoid arthritis
LEG	Tendinitis
	Ruptured Achilles tendon
	Compartment syndrome
	Torn muscle fibres
	Shinsplint (p. 88)
	Ruptured plantaris tendon
	Stress fracture (p. 20)
	Claudication (artery block)
KNEE	(don't ask: just rush to anyone who has swallowed the text book)
THIGH	Hamstring strain
	Trochanteric bursitis
	Buttock tendinitis
	Stress fracture
HIP	Arthritis
	Ilio-psoas muscle strain
BACK	Spondylolysis
	Sacroiliac arthritis
	Disc degeneration

Why not avoid all risk of injury and go in for fastish walking on the flat or exercise machines? Aerobic conditioning at your own pace? Research has proved that brisk steps to get the heart rate up to 70% of maximum, say 120 to 130 beats per minute, and to keep it there for five, ten or fifteen minutes or what you will does raise the aerobic (that is heart and lung) capacity. Furthermore, with walking, the warm up and cool down phases are automatic. For the over-fifty platoon whose level of achievable 'fitness' steadily reduces (that is, they are not capable of reaching or holding the oxygen utilisation level of their youth) brisk walking for forty minutes four days a week expends energy equal to jogging for thirty minutes on three days a week. The only snag is the time factor, but then alternative quicker forms of energy expenditure, such as exercise bikes, treadmills, rowing machines and the like, need money and space. The young forty-year-old, however, will not be satisfied that walking can achieve the level of fitness he is capable of (that is, he will feel his capacity to use oxygen is not being developed to its maximum). Further, the pulse rate when walking may only rise adequately when one goes at a pace at which jogging would be the more natural thing to do.

Statistics collated by the University of Wisconsin-Mount Sinai Medical Centre in Milwaukee, the United States, indicate that beginning joggers are best suited to three workouts per week, of thirty minutes duration. Above that the leg injury rate increases quickly. According to the figures, twice a week activity does not produce weight (that is fat) loss, except when engaged in at a high and unenjoyable intensity, and activity five times a week quashes enthusiasm. So the message is clear: slow, steady and satisfying, leaving forty-eight hours between jogs to allow muscle fibres to recover, is best. Naturally, the older or less fit individual *must* start even more slowly, progress more slowly, increment less often, and take a longer time to achieve maximum capacity. The American Heart Association recommendation is a basic twenty-minute workout three times a week at 70 to 85% of maximal heart rate.

So, off you go now. Make sure your shoes are done up, watch out for cars, stop if you feel you've had enough, hail a taxi if you get a pain in the chest, and be back in thirty minutes.

Whilst you are gone let the family riffle the pages of an equipment catalogue. With so many birthdays to come, they could equip you with a special stereo headset, wrist heart rate watch, gold dog tag with blood group and telephone number, computer shoes with printout mode, high speed pram for the baby, and a pedigreed Doberman minder. Jogging is to be enjoyed, not endured.

Aerobics

Before you begin spare a thought for the instructors, well, more demonstrators really. After your class there is another, and another, and another. They are much more likely than you to suffer overuse injuries (p. 71) and three out of four will get, or aggravate old, injuries. Aerobics as a glamorous exhibition is a mixture of dancing and gyrating to music, gymnastics, and oldfashioned P.T. Every sport is 'aerobic' in the sense that the energy expended is provided by aerobic (that is using oxygen) metabolism of food and the best gauge of anybody's fitness and strength is to measure in litres per minute how much oxygen their body consumes at maximum endeavour. To deliver that oxygen the heart must perform at its peak and the pulse rate reach the maximum possible for that athlete. To benefit from any exercise the heart must reach 70% of its maximum rate. Looking ahead somewhat, if dancing proves to be not for you, turn to brisk walking, cycling, tennis, anything in fact that uses lots of oxygen and you will get equal benefit.

If you have been steadily absorbing knowledge, chapter by chapter, you could almost make your own list of everything to expect by jumping up and thumping down. Try now, but don't land on your heels or the top of your head might fly off. You will have to alight on the ball of the foot and rely on the elastic tension of the arch of the foot, the Achilles tendon, and the flexed knee, to absorb the falling force. These three will first feel the strain of new activity and more so if you are overweight. You can't limber up if you are lumbered down with weight! After one class you will feel extremely aware of oft-mentioned anatomic features such as knee angles and leg alignments, flat feet and curved backs, and appreciate that overuse strain could proceed to real structural damage.

Footwear should be designed to absorb force over the metatarsal heads (toes and ball of the foot). Regrettably, too often it is made to be lightweight and fashionable, the very problem that plagues balletomanes. Jogging shoes, designed with heel pounding in mind, are not quite right for aerobics. The floor is a tricky subject too. It ought to be sprung (p. 140), but you can imagine the cost, not to mention the noise. It is most likely to be made of concrete or wood, which is unyielding.

Mats ought to help but if they are ideally thick or too resilient the foot pronates (sinks and rolls over); to avoid a sprain and keep balance in this situation places almost constant tension around the ankle.

So far, so bad. It is very unlikely that conditions will be adequate or suitable for quality athletic performance or snazzy gyrations. As a joyful artistic group activity and a delight to the eyes of passersby, aerobic classes have strong social appeal. To a bloodhound pup in training they would be an absorbing challenge with the miasma of perfumes, liniments, deodorants, soaps, garments, sweaty soles and perspiring souls that hovers over an active class. As a means of encouraging sedentary types into physical activity they are a boon, but for real aerobic conditioning and balanced muscular toning they are not really a replacement for formal sports, and as a means of losing unwanted fat aerobics are a small help overall but will not affect those special spots you have in mind. (Sorry, but for that you must chat to a plastic surgeon about liposuction.)

Look for a gymnasium that has a beginners' class and is in no rush to push you higher. The first few weeks are the worst; until you reach some semblance of muscle tone and control you cannot possibly enjoy it. You may find that you prefer the true dance exercise routines to those that consist more of callisthenics, so be wary of paying too far in advance. New mothers, so keen to rush to do anything that will tone things up, should first check with their doctor about the state of their pelvic joints and back. Older citizens should look for a class supervised by a physiotherapist who has worked with orthopaedic doctors, rather than a class enthused by an agile, nubile demonstrator.

Previous backache is easily resurrected by heavy landings or too much spine bending. It takes time to reeducate and strengthen the back and abdominal muscles that protect the ligaments against strain. Possible muscle strains follow upon the type of movements and frequency; indeed anyone with old injuries should consult a physiotherapist so that doubtful routines can be discussed and eliminated. Always remind yourself not to emulate, copy, or try to outdo your friend or neighbour. Stop when you have had enough. Your stress plateau for ligament and muscle will differ from his or hers, and your basic and attainable level of cardio-respiratory fitness may not be as high.

Speaking generally acute injury is very unlikely unless you topple over, spraining an ankle, wrenching a muscle, or falling onto the outstretched hand to fracture something. Real overuse foot and leg injury is rare unless you have almost fanatic daily devotion to the cult, or unless you have one of the miscellany of misalignments that plague dogged athletes. In theory, all the things listed for jogging (p. 227) could happen, so that *all* pains must be checked by your doctor even though the most likely cause is muscle strain. Shoulder impingement syndrome (p. 63) is possible as is exercise-induced asthma. In women, there is absolutely no way such exertion could cause ovarian cysts, prolapse, or retroversion (won't cure it either!); all it may do, through subtle symptoms, is draw attention to already existing disease. Non nubile nipples can suffer friction and irritation so make provision for proper support and comfort.

Far more likely is serious strain to the wallet or demise of your credit card if you sign up for things you do not want. Examples abound of classes and gyms closing their doors due to premature bankruptcy; of overpriced snazzy (and unnecessary) gear; and of expensive accident insurance. Après-class smoothies and gourmet offerings are a temptation to avoid. You may need fluid but let it be cold water or mineral water. Burning up about 5 kilocalories per minute, you are shedding fat at the rate of 0.5 gm per minute, or 15 grammes per half hour of continous action. You can put that straight back on by eating the equivalent of a small steak, a meat pie, or a large slice of apple pie, or by drinking six glasses of dry white wine or three pints of best bitter. Whilst your gym would not stock such delicacies you may succumb next day when you take your healthy appetite to lunch. Don't take my word for it. Look up the food tables and check on your favourite snack or tipple before you are tempted to spend more money.

To sum up

Overtraining is a modern danger that slyly sneaks up to inflict stress injuries.

As Dr Lyle J. Micheli, a world-renowned expert from the Children's Hospital Medical Centre in Boston, has said, 'Before organised youth sports we rarely saw overuse injuries in children; now our clinics are filled with them.'

However, there is a reprieve until puberty. That is the dividing line in all sports, especially contact and speed sports. Before puberty, while children grow in size and skill, they will hopefully be able to try out everything, make up teams, fill in, take part, play to modified rules, but above all, to participate whatever the result, until each finds something just right for his or her talents. There are world-class events for under-age experts but injury is nonetheless minimal. Paediatricians often make the observation that children left alone rarely injure themselves; it is only when adults interfere that the picture changes. Exhortations to win and to play harder all too soon distort a child's attitude to the rules and the spirit of the game, and bad habits, learned at an early age, are hard to lose. Worse, when two overaggressive players meet, one is likely to get hurt. The emphasis before puberty has to be on acquisition of skills, adherence to the rules of the game, and strict obedience to the referee or umpire.

After puberty there is an increase in the incidence of injury in all sports. This is inescapable, but must not be made unavoidable through neglect. Proper protective gear is being developed and constantly improved and parents may have to insist on its use, or else! Athletes may have to be handled firmly after injury to make sure that sport is not resumed until recovery is complete and muscle fitness fully restored; in those two matters the word of the doctor must prevail over that of a coach or of that most dangerous expert, 'me mate'. Statistics repeatedly show that the greatest danger to an athlete is re-injury; if that does occur it is time for the parent to step in and ask, 'Why?' Nobody but a parent can be relied upon to do it.

Girls have a special problem that appears in all sports: knee injury. World-wide, girls record a higher percentage of knee injuries than boys. It is partly to do with basic anatomy.

Possessed of wider hips, their knees are just that much more angled, and the patella has more difficulty in keeping its alignment; it needs strong thigh muscles to help it do so and that is just what girls, on average, are more likely to lack. Recreational skiing deserves special attention as a sport where pre-season strengthening exercises are worthwhile; social summer sport is not enough to keep leg muscles strong.

I have tried to provide a solid foundation of basic knowledge that you can add to by experience so that when you have to make decisions vital to your children's welfare you will do so with confidence. There was an era when the best possible exercise for teenagers was held to be the carrying of a load of school text books. The swing of the social pendulum has now focused all endeavour on the body with the hope that a healthy mind will somehow follow. It cannot do so unless parents insist that schoolwork and homework get at least the same attention as sport. Of necessity sport will still dominate the development of those very, very few teenagers with rare talent, self-propelled to strive and to train thirty hours a week in preparation for competition on the world stage; their parents soon learn that they have an indispensable role to play as they follow along with encouragement, practical support and quiet supervision to ensure balanced growth in brain and body, and healthy social integration. It can never be an easy task.

Burnout, that popular but elusive concept, is the fate of many lesser hopefuls and parents are then needed even more to revive and redirect crushed spirits. There is no accurate definition of the word but psychologists currently use burnout as a simple paraphrase for a syndrome of tiredness, irritability, depression, feelings of poor achievement, perhaps a tendency to be accident prone, and vague bodily symptoms.

In a like manner physical fatigue, frustration, feelings of futility and frequent or feared failure, all those things that successful adult sportspersons have overcome, may haunt and hurt the dreams of success to which the young cling. To bandy about the term burnout as if it were a diagnosis is unhelpful. Chronic illness will cause easy fatigue, lack of growth, or loss of strength, and a visit to the doctor is of first priority and may explain all. Careful observation by parents comes next, allied with the advice of a teacher wise in the ways of a variety of teams and athletes. Time-consuming though this is, it is the only way to decide which is preferable, psychological support and persistence, or a switch to other activities. The instinct of a parent is in the end the surest protector and guide.

Attempts to introduce *profiling* into school sport may have to be resisted. It would seem to be a retrograde step for this age group. Sport is ideally a role-play intended to train character for adulthood, and at this age should not be an end in itself. In any case, it is going to be difficult to develop a science for the serious business of detecting deep talent.

Overall, sport is now being indulged in with such intensity and publicity that it may well be time for the pendulum to swing back. Excesses have often had to be curbed and today's headmasters have solid historical backing for the growing view that school sport is waxing only to wane, hopefully whilst still preserving all that is best in it.

Glossary

ACROMIO-CLAVICULAR JOINT   The junction or joint between the acromion and the outer end of the collar bone.
ACROMION PROCESS   An protrusion from the back of the shoulder blade that arches forward over the shoulder joint.
ADDUCTOR   A muscle that adducts, that is, one that moves the thigh inwards to the mid line and crosses the thighs.
ADRENO-CORTICO-TROPHIC   The pituitary gland hormone that stimulates the adrenal gland.
AEROBIC   A metabolic process that uses oxygen.
ALBUMEN (*n.* albuminuria)   A blood protein; it can spill through the kidney into the urine.
AMOEBIC MENINGITIS   Inflammation of the membranes covering the brain due to a parasite instead of an infecting organism (bacteria).
ANABOLISM (*adj.* anabolic)   A metabolic process that builds up new tissue.
ANAEROBIC   Metabolism proceeding without oxygen; lactic acid is produced.
ANNULAR LIGAMENT   A ligament that encircles a bone. The one round the top end of the radius bone keeps it firmly in place.
ANTERO-POSTERIOR   A structure that runs fore and aft.
ANTRUM   The air-filled cavity in the upper jaw, virtually a side chamber of the nose; the roots of the canine teeth often protrude into it.
AORTA   The large artery that emerges from the heart, giving off branches as it runs down the vertebral column to the pelvis where it divides in two.
ARTHROMETER   An instrument that measures the angle of joint movement.
ARTHROSCOPE (*n.* arthroscopy)   A thin, flexible, fibreoptic telescope that can be pushed into a joint to inspect its interior.
ARTICULAR   The adjective of anatomy pertaining to joints.
ATROPHY   A loss or diminution of substance, the best example being a muscle that has become ATROPHIC through disuse.
AUTONOMIC NERVOUS SYSTEM   That portion of the nervous system that works automatically to control organs and blood vessels. The 'solar plexus', a network of cells and fibres, is part of it.
AVULSE   To tear off, as in AVULSION of a ligament or muscle attachment.

BENNETT'S FRACTURE   A special fracture of the thumb metacarpal involving the joint in the ball of the thumb. It needs expert care.
BIMAXILLARY MOUTHGUARD   One that is fitted to the upper jaw on both sides.

BLACK HEEL   A bruised heel, chronically black and blue from old blood.
BRACHIAL   A Latin-derived adjective for 'arm', e.g. brachial artery.
BURSA (*pl.* bursae)   A fluid-filled sac between moving parts or between them and hard structures such as bone.

CALCANEUS   The heel bone. *Also called* calcaneum.
CARDIO-RESPIRATORY   Heart and lungs functioning as a unit.
CARDIO-VASCULAR   Heart and blood vessels.
CAROTID   The large artery of the neck, or an adjective for structures near it.
CAT OR CT SCAN   Short for the technique of 'computerised axial tomography'.
CATABOLISM (*adj.* catabolic)   Metabolism involving the breakdown of tissue.
CEREBELLUM   The lower part of the brain housed in the base of the skull.
CERVICAL   Adjective for 'neck'.
CLAUDICATION   Pain in the leg during exercise due to poor blood supply.
CLAVICLE (*adj.* clavicular)   Collar bone.
COCCYX   The last segment of the spine; the very end is 'the tip of the coccyx'.
COLIFORM   Resembling bacterium coli, an organism in the bowel.
COMPARTMENT SYNDROME   Pain in a muscle group (usually in the leg) caused by the surrounding fascia (fibrous layer) preventing growth or restricting blood supply.
CONDYLE   A round prominence of or projection from a bone.
CONTIGUOUS   Adjoining. Used to refer to an adjoining structure.
CONTUSION   A deep bruise caused by a blow. The skin remains intact.
CORACOID PROCESS   A peg on the shoulder blade just medial to the shoulder joint for the attachment of strong ligaments. (Those binding the coracoid to the clavicle are called CORACO-CLAVICULAR.)
CRUCIATE LIGAMENTS   Two ligaments forming a cross; in the knee they are called either the anterior or the posterior according to the direction each runs from its upper attachment on the femur.

DEFIBRILLATOR   An electrical apparatus for stimulating or starting the heart after cardiac arrest. It administers controlled electric shocks.
DISTAL   Distant from a point of reference such as the centre of the body or the upper attachment of a muscle etc.
DORSIFLEXION   Bending towards the dorsum or back. In the foot this means up, as distinct from down towards the ground.
DURA MATER   (Latin 'hard mother'!) the tough fibrous outer protective layer covering the brain and spinal cord.
DYNAMOMETER   An instrument to measure applied force.

ECHOGRAM   Printout from a machine that can measure, outline and differentiate structures of varying density by the way they reflect sound wave pulses.

EFFUSION Collection of fluid in the tissues or in the body cavities.
ELECTRODIAGNOSIS Analysis of muscle and nerve health by recording their responses to a stimulating electric current.
ELECTROENCEPHALOGRAM (EEG) Recording of the electrical activity of the brain cells.
ENCEPHALOGRAM Special X-ray technique for examination of the brain.
ENDOCARDITIS Inflammation of the heart lining and valves.
ENTRAPMENT When a nerve is bound in fibrous tissue or caught by the edge of a ligament etc. The irritation or compression causes neuritis.
EPHEDRINE Synthetic adrenalin-like drug.
EPICONDYLE Small swelling on a bone for muscle or ligament attachments.
EPIGASTRIC Adjective of epigastrium (the stomach).
EUSTACHIAN TUBE The tube leading from the middle ear (the chamber beyond the ear drum) to the throat, thus allowing equilisation of air pressure between the chamber and the environment via the nose or open mouth.
EXTENSOR A muscle that extends or stretches the limb or vertebral column.

FASCIA Sheet or wide band of fibrous tissue.
FASCICULITIS Inflammation of a bundle of fibres.
FEMUR (*adj.* femoral) Long thigh bone.
FIBRIL Filament of the visible fibre.
FIBROELASTIC Used to describe an anatomical structure which is part unyielding fibre, and part elastic.
FIBULA Thin outer leg bone. Its expanded lower end is the LATERAL MALLEOLUS of the ankle.
FLEXOR Muscle that bends a limb or the trunk.
FREIBERG'S DISEASE Bone necrosis in the navicular bone, the one that forms the prominence on the dorsum (upper side) of the foot.

GASTRO-INTESTINAL Adjective for 'stomach and intestines', as in 'gastro-intestinal tract'.
GLENOID FOSSA A shallow cavity, such as the one on the shoulder blade that forms, with the head of the humerus, the shoulder joint.
GLYCOGEN Carbohydrate suitable for storage in liver and muscles; it is made from blood sugar (D-glucose) and reconvertible to it as needed for energy or to keep the blood sugar level constant.

HAEMATOMA Collection of blood that has clotted after escaping (haemorrhaging) from a broken blood vessel.
HAEMATURIA Blood in the urine.
HAMMER TOE Flexion deformity, i.e. the toe is bent and fixed downwards.
HORSESHOE KIDNEY Fusion of the two kidneys into one mass that is then displaced into the pelvis.
HUMERUS (*adj.* humeral or humero-) Upper arm bone.
HYDROGENATED Combined with hydrogen.

HYDROMETER   A simple instrument that measures the specific gravity of liquids, such as urine.

HYPERTROPHY   Growth in size (often in an unbalanced way) as a response to increased loading. Body building exercises will achieve this in specific muscles and if one kidney is removed the other 'hypertrophies' to compensate.

ILIAC CREST   The prominent rim of the ilium (hip bone) which is the broad flat upper part of the pelvic bone.

ILIO-PSOAS MUSCLE   The strong muscle that runs from the ilium and nearby vertebrae to the lesser tuberosity (upper inner portion) of the femur, and thus contracts to flex the thigh on the trunk, or vice-versa.

IMPINGE (*n.* impingement)   To press onto or be squeezed by. Hence the shoulder IMPINGEMENT SYNDROME where the shoulder muscles impinge on the outer margin of the acromion process of the scapula.

INTRAPERITONEAL   In the peritoneal cavity.

ISCHAEMIC (*n.* ischaemia)   Having a reduced blood supply or being deprived of blood.

ISCHIAL   Adjective for the 'ischium bone', which is the lower portion of the pelvic bone. The ischial tuberosity is the part one can feel deep in the buttock and is the area of attachment of the big hamstring muscles.

LACTIC ACID   The acid produced by anaerobic metabolism of D-glucose; it is a measure of the lack of oxygen supply to muscle, and may be a cause of sore muscles.

LIGAMENT   A tough band of fibre uniting bony points or strengthening joint capsules.

LIGAMENTUM PATELLAE   A fibrous strap joining the lower pole of the knee cap to the tibia.

LORDOSIS   Concave backwards bend of the spine; a 'sway back'.

LUMBOSACRAL   Adjective for 'the lumbar vertebrae and the sacrum'. The LUMBO-SACRAL DISC is a vital junction where the vertebral column (i.e. the trunk) joins and is supported on the pelvis and legs. The sacrum is welded into the pelvic bones to complete the ring around the pelvic cavity.

MACERATE   To soften, as in skin constantly bathed in fluid.

MAGNETIC RESONANCE IMAGING (MRI)   The latest method of getting a picture or outline of a deep structure to aid diagnosis. (X-rays are the oldest method.)

MALLEOLUS   The bone projection on either side of the ankle; there are thus two, medial and lateral.

MALLET FINGER   Hyperflexion deformity of the fingertip.

MARFAN'S SYNDROME   An inherited disorder with widespread defects, two of which are lax joints and congenital weakness of the aorta.

MASTOID *colloq.*   Infection in the mastoid process. This segment of bone comes to a point immediately behind the ear and has a honeycomb-like structure of air cells in communication with the middle ear. Such anatomy allows quick spread of infection from a 'middle ear'.

MAXILLAE The upper jaw bones, one on each side, enclosing the nose, hollowed out by the antrum and forming part of the eye socket.

MEDIAL Used to describe a structure close to the midline, e.g. a ligament on the inner side of a joint.

MENISCUS (*pl.* menisci) Crescent-shaped segment of cartilage inside a joint, in particular the knee which has medial and lateral meniscii.

METACARPALS The bones in the palm stretching from the wrist to the fingers. The five constitute the 'palm'.

METACARPO-PHALANGEAL JOINT The joint between a metacarpal and the first phalanx.

METATARSALS Bones in the sole of the foot similar to metacarpals.

MORTON'S TOE Pain under the ball of the foot with flexion deformity of a toe. There can be other associated features such as a short metatarsal to the big toe, claw toes or neuroma (an irritated nerve).

MUSCULO-SKELETAL Adjective for 'muscles and bones'.

MUSCULO-TENDINOUS Used to describe intertwined muscle and tendon fibres where muscle is inserted into a tendon; the tendon is then attached to bone.

MYOCARDITIS Inflammation of the heart muscle.

NASOPHARYNGEAL Adjective for the area behind the nose and soft palate.

NASOPHARYNGITIS Inflammation of the part of the throat behind the nose and soft palate.

NAVICULAR An important bone in the mid-foot where inversion and eversion occurs. *See also* scaphoid.

NECROSIS Death of a cell or of a whole area of tissue.

NEPHRITIS Inflammation of the kidney.

OEDEMA Accumulation of fluid in the tissues.

OSGOOD-SCHLATTER Two orthopaedic surgeons who first described (and named) the disease where the patellar tendon avulses from its attachment to the tibial epiphysis.

OSTEOCHONDRITIS Inflammation of bone and its overlying cartilage. OSTEOCHONDRITIS DISSECANS is a joint condition where the infected portion cracks or breaks away to become a 'loose body' in the joint.

OTITIS Inflammation of the ear. Hence OTITIS EXTERNA, an inflamed ear or external canal, and OTITIS MEDIA, inflammation of the middle ear.

PALMARFLEXION Bending the wrist forwards.

PARS INTERARTICULARIS The portion of the lumbar vertebrae surrounding the spinal cord that is prone to fracture under stress.

PATELLA (*adj.* patellar) Knee cap.

PATELLO-FEMORAL Adjective for the structures connecting the patella and the femur.

PECTORALIS Denotes the chest or breast. Hence PECTORALIS MAJOR, the large muscle of the front of the chest.

PERITENDINITIS Inflammation of the synovial sheath and tissues around a tendon.

PERITONITIS Inflammation of the PERITONEUM, the membrane that lines the PERITONEAL or abdominal cavity.

PERONEAL   Adjective for structures on the lateral side of the leg.
PERTHES   German surgeon who first described the disease of the hip affecting the epiphysis of the head of the femur.
PHALANX   One of the three small bones of a finger or toe.
PHARYNGITIS   Sore throat; inflammation of the pharynx.
PHARYNX   The hollow tube extending from the back of the nose to the oesophagus or gullet.
PLANTAR   Adjective for the 'sole of the foot'.
PLANTARFLEXION   Bending the foot down, towards the sole.
PLANTARIS   Small muscle in the calf (*colloq.* monkey muscle). Its long thin tendon can suddenly snap.
PLEURA   The membrane lining the inner side of the rib cage and the outer surface of the lungs. Between the two layers is a potential cavity that can fill with air or fluid, compressing the lung.
PONTIAC FEVER   A form of Legionnaires' disease resembling influenza rather than pneumonia, first detected in Pontiac, Michigan.
PROCESS   Prominent outgrowth of bone.
PROLACTIN   Pituitary hormone.
PROLAPSE   To slip out of place.
PUBIC SYMPHYSIS   Fibro-cartilage joining the pelvic bones in front.

QUADRICEPS   Four-headed. Hence QUADRICEPS FEMORIS, the large thigh muscle that lifts the leg; it is a fused mass of four muscle elements acting as one.

RADIUS (*adj.* radial)   The outer of the two forearm bones.
RECTUS FEMORIS   One of the muscles in the quadriceps femoris.
RECURVATUM   Curving backwards.
ROTATOR   A muscle that rotates a limb.
ROTATOR CUFF   The musculo-tendinous arrangement that moves the shoulder joint and is fused with its capsule.

SACROILIAC JOINT   Junction between the sacrum and the ilium of the pelvic bone. It lies under the dimples in the lower back on each side of the mid-line.
SACRUM (*adj.* sacral)   The section of the vertebral column between the lumbar vertebrae and the coccyx. Formed by fusion of five vertebrae into a solid bone, it is the posterior keystone between the pelvic bones.
SCAPHOID   Small important bone in the wrist at the base of the thumb. *Also see* navicular.
SCAPULA   Shoulder blade.
SCHEUERMANN   Danish surgeon who first described the osteochondritis of the thoracic vertebrae that causes adolescent kyphosis.
SCOLIOSIS   Lateral curvature of the spine forming an asymmetric hump.
SEPTUM   Partition between two chambers or cavities.
SESAMOID BONE   Very small bone that forms in a tendon under pressure, e.g. under the ball of the foot. It can fracture or become inflamed (sesamoiditis).
SEVER   American orthopaedic surgeon who first described epiphysitis of the heel bone.

SOLAR PLEXUS Network of nerves and nerve cells directing the function of organs in the abdomen; situated around the aorta below the diaphragm.

SPINAL PROCESS Sharp backward projection from the vertebral arch; it is felt in the midline of the back under the skin. *Also called colloq.* spine.

STERNO-CLAVICULAR JOINT Prominent lump in the neck at the inner end of the clavicle where it joins the sternum.

STERNUM Breast bone.

SUBCUTANEOUS Under the skin as in subcutaneous bursa or subcutaneous injection. *Also called* subdermal.

SUBLUXATION Joint laxity not quite amounting to a dislocation but leaving the joint capsule stretched and weak.

SUBTALAR Beneath the talus bone in the sole of the foot.

SYNOVIA (*adj.* synovial) Lubricating fluid secreted by the membrane lining joints, bursal sacs and tendon sheaths.

SYNOVITIS Inflamed synovial membrane.

TALUS The top ankle bone. It is held firmly in the mortise formed by the two malleoli and rests on the calcaneus that forms the heel.

TARSUS Ankle bones forming a unit between the leg and the metatarsals.

TENDINITIS Inflammation of tendon fibres, either by friction or overuse.

TENDON A tough fibrous cord or strap attaching muscle to bone. At the musculo-tendinous junction the muscle and tendon fibres interlock (and may tear asunder by fraying or degeneration).

TENOSYNOVITIS An extension of tendinitis to involve the synovial sheath as well.

THORAX (*adj.* thoracic) Chest.

TIBIA (*adj.* tibial) The main (and medial) bone of the leg. The shinbone.

TOMOGRAPHY X-rays focused on a specific plane, i.e. to film slices of tissue.

TRABECULA Fibromuscular band, hence TRABECULATED.

TRANSVERSE PROCESS Bone protusion projecting sideways from the vertebral arch for the attachment of ligaments and muscles.

TROCHANTER (*adj.* trochanteric) Bone process on the upper shaft of the femur.

TUBERCLE A round projection on bone.

TUBEROSITY A roughened swelling on bone.

TURNER American physician who described the syndrome of body deformity due to a chromosome abnormality.

ULNA (*adj.* ulnar) Medial forearm bone.

UNDINE Glass vessel with long narrow neck for irrigation of the eye.

VAGUS A long important nerve controlling the heart rate and breathing, and connecting to the solar plexus.

VALSALVA MANOEUVRE Forced exhalation with a closed mouth and nose; the rise in pressure will test whether the Eustachian tubes are blocked.
VASTUS Muscle, with medial and lateral parts, making up the quadriceps.
VISCUS (*pl.* viscera, *adj.* visceral) Organ, especially an intra-abdominal one.

X LIGAMENTS Cruciate ligaments inside the knee joint.

Index

abrasion, 46
acne, 48
acromio-clavicular joint, 62–3
adolescent fibrositis, 91–2
aerobics, 229–31
AIDS, 33
airway, 31–2, 33–4, 35, 45
allergic reaction, 5–6, 11, 86
amenorrhoea, 53, 54, 224
amino acids, 75, 78
amnesia, 25
anaemia, 4
anaphylactic shock, 5–6
angio-neurotic oedema, 12
ankle, 15, 71–3, 87, 94
apophyses, 17
apophysitis, 19
archery, 85
asthma, 11, 165
atherosclerosis, 74, 79
athlete's foot, 48
athletics, 85–95
Australian Rules, 40, 95–6
avulsion, 17, 92

back pain, 10, 30, 94
badminton, 40, 97
ballet, 53, 54, 81, 97–100
barotrauma, 166–7
baseball, 40, 95, 101–4
basketball, 54, 104–8
bee sting, 6, 49
bends see decompression sickness
Bennett's fracture, 105
bites, 49–50
'black eye', 42
black heel, 88, 196
bladder, 38–9
blindness, 41
blisters, 9, 47
blood clotting time, 46
blurred vision, 15
body fat, 53, 55, 213–14
boils, 10–11, 41, 48
bone disorders, 12
bone growth, 16–21
bone loss, 54

boogie boarding, 203
botulism, 5
boxing, 41, 109–12
brain damage, 25, 111–12
bras (sports), 56–7
break dancing, 112
breast injury, 57, 142
breathing difficulties, 12
breath-holding activities, 11–12
bridgework, 45
bruising, 10–11
bulbar poliomyelitis, 5
bursitis, 65, 69

calluses, 47, 48
carbohydrates, 76–7, 80, 81, 82
cardiac arrest, 33
cardiac dysrhythmia, 5
cartilage, 16, 17, 19
CAT scan, 10, 21
cervical rib, 36, 38
cervical vertebrae, 28
cheerleading, 113–14
chest pain, 3–4
cholesterol, 79–80, 82, 222
chondromalacia patellae, 9, 19, 55, 69–70, 90
chronic pain, 10, 14
clavicle, 62–3
closed injuries, 37–9
cold sores, 48–161, 173
collapsed lung, 37
collisions, 4
colour blindness, 40
common cold, 166–7
compartment syndrome, 88
compresses, 87
concussion, 15, 25–7, 41, 109, 111–12, 130, 131, 161–2
congenital syndromes, 5
contact lenses, 41–2, 191
contact sports, 12
cooling, 34, 51
corns, 9, 48
cough reflex, 32
cricket, 38, 40, 115–19
cycling, 120–3
cystic fibrosis, 11

INDEX 245

decompression sickness, 165, 167
detached retina, 41, 43, 110
diabetes, 11
diagnostic signs, 14–15
diaphragm, 37
dieting, 80, 100
digital ischaemia, 103
discs, 22, 28
discus throwing, 94–5
dislocation
   acromio-clavicular joint, 63
   ankle, 72
   double joints, 8
   Down's syndrome, 8
   elbow, 64
   hip, 66–7
   knee cap, 9
   shoulder, 7, 61, 95
diving, 189, 190, 192–3
double joints, 8
double vision, 15
Down's syndrome, 5, 8
drowning, 6, 31, 35, 192–3

ear, 27, 111, 189–90
elbow, 9, 19, 63–5
electric shock, 35
epilepsy, 12, 31, 166
epiphyseal plate, 17, 18, 29
epiphyses, 16–19, 54, 87, 92
epiphysitis, 19
equipment safety, 94
extradural haematoma, 26–7
eye guards, 42–3, 97, 186
eyes, 40–3, 118, 146, 191

falls, 10, 105–6, 156–7
fast foods, 77–8, 79–80
fatigue fracture *see* stress fracture
fats, 75–6, 82
fatty acids, 75–6
feet, 9, 20, 86, 87, 88–91, 92, 107, 197
fencing, 124
fertility, 54
fibreglass, 47
fibrous dysplasia, 12
field events, 40, 94–5
finger stall, 108
fingers, 66, 104–5, 152
first aid
   bends, 167
   drowning, 6, 35, 193–4
   eye injuries, 40, 41
   hypothermia, 179
   jaw fracture, 35

muscle tear, 86–7
neck injury, 162–3
resuscitation, 31–6
skin, 46–51
spinal cord injuries, 22–4
teeth, 44–5
food, 74–82
fractures
   Bennett's, 105
   greenstick, 20
   hairline, 25
   hand, 66
   March, 20, 89
   neck, 22–5, 31–2, 162–3
   ribs, 37
   skull, 10
   stress, 9, 20–1, 54, 87, 90, 92, 93
   wrist, 66
Freiberg's disease, 89
frostnip, 173
'frozen shoulder', 63

Gaelic football, 163
genital protection, 102, 116
girls' problems, 52–8, 71, 90, 92, 93, 106–7, 158, 168, 177–8, 210
glandular fever, 8, 132
glasses, 119
glaucoma, 40
glycogen, 77, 80, 81
goggles, 41
golf, 40, 125–7
golfer's elbow, 125
greenstick fracture, 20
gridiron, 22, 38, 127–136
groin injury, 48
gymnastics, 12, 39, 53, 54, 57, 67, 73, 136–141

hairline fracture, 25
hallux valgus, 58
hammer throw, 94–5
hand, 66
handball, 141
head, 25–7
headache, 26, 27
headgear (boxing), 109–10
hearing defects, 15, 25
heart, bruising, 37
heart disease, 3–4, 221–3, 224
heart inflammation, 7
heart murmur, 4
heart strain, 85–6
heat induced fatigue, 128

heat stroke, 5, 34, 51, 128
Heimlich manoeuvre, 33-4
helmet
  cycling, 121, 123
  gridiron, 22, 124-5, 135, 147
hepatitis B, 32-3
herpes simplex *see* cold sores
high blood pressure, 11-12, 208
hip, 19, 66-7
hockey (field) 43, 142-3
horse riding, 12, 73, 143-5
hurdling, 93
hypothermia, 177, 179

ice hockey, 40, 146-8
ice skating, 148-50
impingement syndrome, 63
infections, 7-8, 41, 32-3, 47, 48, 187-8
infertility, 224
influenza, 7, 223
inguinal hernia, 10
iron, 81

javelin throwing, 94-5
jaw, 35
jogging, 71-2, 221-8
joints, 18, 59-73
jumper's knee, 92, 106
jumping, 73, 92-3

kick boxing, 154
kidneys, 10, 15, 37
kilocalorie, 225
knee, 8, 9, 14, 17-18, 19, 55, 87, 90, 92, 95, 175
knee cap, 9, 19, 69
knee joint, 67-71
knee pads, 133
Kohler's disease, 89
Kundy factor, 179

lacerations, 46-7
lacrosse, 151
leg, 17-18, 86-91
ligament, 93
lightning, 34-5, 126, 142-3
liver, 9, 37
long distance running, 11, 52, 54, 89-91
lumbar curve, 28
lumbar vertebrae, 28
lungs, 11, 37, 38, 118, 165

Mallet deformity, 101, 105, 107
March fracture, 20, 89
Marfan's syndrome, 5

martial arts, 57, 151-4
measles, 7, 8
menarche, 52-4
menstrual cycle, 56, 100
menstruation 52-4, 56, 81, 168
middle distance running, 89
migraine, 166
minerals, 76, 81
Morton's toe, 9, 89
mountain sickness, 172
mouth guard, 45, 96, 110, 135
mouth-to-mouth resuscitation, 32-3
muscle spasm, 14
muscle tear, 86-7, 88
muscle weakness, 8
myocarditis, 7

neck, 10, 12, 22-5, 31-2, 162-3
netball, 155
nose, 27, 111
nutrition *see* food

Orava syndrome, 131-2
organ injury, 9-10, 37-9
Osgood-Schlatter disease, 19, 87
osteochondritis, 19, 67, 89
osteochondritis dissecans, 19, 70, 90
osteogenesis imperfecta, 12

pain, 14-15
pancreas, 38
paraplegia, 10, 22, 85
parasites, 48
patella *see* knee cap
Perthes' disease, 19, 67, 125-6
plantar fasciculitis, 89
pole vaulting, 54, 94
poliomyelitis, 5
pregnancy, 224
pre-sport examination, 3-4, 13
proteins, 75, 78, 79, 81, 82
pulse, 5, 38

quadriplegia, 22

racquetball, 43, 156
recurrent injuries, 13
resuscitation, 31-6, 193-4
ribs, 37, 57
riding hat, 144-5
roller skating, 156-7
rotator cuff, 61-2, 63, 94, 95
rowing, 53, 54, 157-8
rugby, 22, 68, 69, 96, 159-64

sacrum, 28
salt loss, 11, 34, 51, 81–2, 128
Scheuermann's kyphosis, 29, 117, 192
scoliosis, 10, 29–30
scuba diving, 11, 165–9
self defence, 151–4
sesamoiditis, 89
Sever's disease, 89
shinsplint, 88
short sight, 8
shoulder joint, 7, 8, 60–2, 63, 94, 95
skateboarding, 169–70
ski jumping, 172
skier's thumb, 173–4
skiing, 57, 171–81
skimboarding, 203
skin, 46–51
snake bite, 49–50
snow blindness, 173
soccer, 29, 38, 181–4
softball, 184–5
solar plexus, 37–8, 153
spider bite, 50
spina bifida, 10
spinal cord, 22–5
spleen injury, 9, 37, 130, 132
spondylolisthesis, 28
spondylolysis, 10, 28, 138, 207
sprains, 15, 73, 85, 93
sprinting, 11, 57, 73, 86–7
squash, 40, 43, 186–7
stings, 49–50
'stitch', 14
strain, 9, 61, 85–95
stress fracture, 9, 20–1, 54, 87, 90, 92, 93, 94
subdural haematoma, 26
sudden death, 3–6, 222–3
sunburn, 50–1, 117, 173
surfing, 41, 201–3
surgery, 9, 61, 87
suturing, 46–7
swimming, 11, 12, 29, 41, 187–94
synovitis, 59, 67, 69

tampons, 56
Tanner Index, 211
temple, 5
teeth, 44–5
tendinitis, 21, 73
tennis, 40, 43, 53, 194–6
tennis elbow, 97, 195
tenosynovitis, 65, 66, 73, 88
testis, 10, 38

tetanus, 47, 183–4
thumb, 66, 105, 152, 173–4
ticks, 50
tinea, 48, 188
toenails, 48, 90
touch football, 196–7
trampoline, 197–9
traumatic synovitis, 59
triathlon, 91
Turner's syndrome, 5

urticaria, 11, 49

vertebrae, 28–30
vertebral artery, 24, 131
viral infections, 131, 161, 166
vitamins, 76, 81
volleyball, 53, 200
vulval area, 39

walking, 227–8
warts, 48, 188
wasp sting, 49
water polo, 190, 192
water related diseases, 187–9
water sports, 201–5
waterskiing, 204
weight lifting, 206–9
weight reduction, 213–16
weight training 11, 208–10
wheezing, 11, 176
windburn, 173
'winding', 36–7, 38–9
windsurfing, 204–5
wrestling, 211–18, 40
wrist joint, 65–6, 95